MUSIC &
MONARCHY

MUSIC &
MONARCHY

DAVID STARKEY & KATIE GREENING

Based on the series written and
presented by David Starkey

This book is published to accompany the television series entitled *Music and Monarchy*, produced by Oxford Film and Television and first broadcast on BBC Two in 2013.

Series Producer: Peter Sweasey
Executive Producer: Nicolas Kent
Executive Producer for the BBC: Greg Sanderson
BBC Commissioning Editor, Music and Events: Jan Younghusband

OXFORD
FILM AND
TELEVISION

3 5 7 9 10 8 6 4 2

Published in 2013 by BBC Books, an imprint of Ebury Publishing.
A Random House Group Company.

Introduction © Jutland Ltd, 2013
Text © Oxford Film and Television 2013

The Random House Group Limited Reg. No. 954009

Addresses for companies within the Random House Group can be found at
www.randomhouse.co.uk

A CIP catalogue record for this book is available from the British Library.

Hardback ISBN: 978 1 849 90586 2
Trade paperback ISBN: 978 1 849 90681 4

The Random House Group Limited supports The Forest Stewardship Council® (FSC®), the leading international forest-certification organisation. Our books carrying the FSC label are printed on FSC®-certified paper. FSC is the only forest-certification scheme supported by the leading environmental organisations, including Greenpeace. Our paper procurement policy can be found at www.randomhouse.co.uk/environment

MIX
Paper from
responsible sources
FSC® C016897

Commissioning editor: Albert DePetrillo
Project editor: Joe Cottington
Copy editor: Richard Collins
Designer: Seagull Design
Production: Phil Spencer

Printed and bound in England by Clays Ltd, St Ives plc

To buy books by your favourite authors and register for offers visit www.randomhouse.co.uk

CONTENTS

THE SOUND OF GREAT BRITAIN

INTRODUCTION

A WORLD RULED BY MUSIC

Music or Words? Poetry and Drama? Or Anthems, Opera and Oratorio? Which, to personalise and particularise, is the more important
in British history and to the British monarchy: the anniversary of
Shakespeare or the centenary of Handel? The question almost
seems absurd. Nowadays there is no doubt that Shakespeare wins
every time. Shakespeare's cycle of history plays, famously described
by another maker of history, John Churchill, 1st Duke of Marlborough, as 'the only history I ever read', still shapes the popular
understanding of English history and its murderous dynastic rival-
ries; while in their nobler moments the plays (re-)invent the idea
of England herself before going on to adumbrate a larger, mistier
vision of Britain:

> This royal throne of kings, this scepter'd isle,
> This earth of majesty, this sea of Mars,
> This other Eden, demi-Paradise ...
> This happy breed of men, this little world,

This precious stone set in the silver sea ...
This blessed plot, this earth, this realm, this England,
This nurse, this teeming womb of royal kings ...
This land of such dear souls, this dear, dear land.

Who could resist that? George III (1760–1820) for one, who confided to Fanny Burney: 'Was there ever such stuff as a great part of Shakespeare? Only one must not say so!' The eighteenth century more or less agreed with its longest reigning king. The bicentenary of Shakespeare, celebrated five years late in 1769, was a provincial pageant, which, despite the best efforts of the actor-manager David Garrick, made little impact outside the Bard's birthplace of Stratford-upon-Avon and, thanks to torrential rain, was literally a washout even there. On the other hand, the centenary of Handel's birth (celebrated a year early by mistake in 1784) was a grand national event the like of which had never been seen before: not for the greatest general, politician or king, let alone for a mere musician. Fashionable London fought (and queued) for tickets; Westminster Abbey was crammed and ladies were instructed not to wear excessive hoops in their dresses while hats were absolutely forbidden. Even then, demand was unsatisfied and two of the events had to be rerun.

The idea of the centenary celebrations was proposed by a group of noble sponsors and was to consist of a series of commemorative concerts of Handel's music. George III, a Handel devotee since boyhood, eagerly took up the proposal and his patronage was crucial in inflating the scale of the event. He insisted that an extra third day be added to the celebrations, as the two originally planned could not do justice to the quantity and quality of Handel's music. He was responsible for securing the use of Westminster Abbey – unheard of for such an event – and he personally approved the architect James Wyatt's 'Gothick' designs for the necessary temporary galleries and stands.

The result transformed the great nave of the Abbey into what the musicologist Dr Charles Burney, the contemporary historian of the event, called 'a royal musical chapel'. At one end of the nave, in front of the choir screen, Wyatt constructed a handsome elevated state box or 'Royal Pew'. In it he provided 'a throne ... in a beautiful Gothic style' for the king and 'richly decorated and furnished [the box] with crimson satin, fringed with gold'. It was home from home for the royal family from the Chapel Royal proper, where at Hampton Court we can still see a similar first-floor pew with real and painted crimson swags and gold tassels and fringes.

In the Chapel Royal the royal pew faced the altar; in the Abbey the state box confronted, at the opposite end of the nave, a towering, many-tiered structure on which the huge choir and orchestra of several hundred were artfully arrayed, like figures on a Gothic wedding cake. The stage culminated in a temporary organ, in its own lavishly carved and ornamented Gothic case, which, reaching far up towards the vaulted roof and merging with the tracery of the west window, 'wonderfully corresponded', Burney enthused, 'to the style of architecture of the venerable and beautiful structure' of the Abbey itself.

Before the festival proper began, the royal family, headed by the king, visited Handel's tomb nearby in the south transept to pay their respects; then they processed to their box and listened, rapt, as Handel's *Messiah* was performed. The towering stage facing them became a sort of altar; and Handel's music, written to the glory of God, became instead part of the composer's own cult.

The reversals are astonishing: the Abbey, the principal shrine to England and her kings, had been transformed into a 'a royal musical chapel' where even music itself was inverted. Music had once honoured kings; now the king led the nation in honouring – worshipping scarcely seems too strong a word – Handel and his music.

A world ruled by music indeed!

cℬ

So this is not a book *about* music. It is a history of England written *in* music, in which both the history and the music are reappraised to their mutual benefit. But we begin, not in the sacred spaces of Westminster Abbey or the Chapel Royal – however often we will return there – but on the battlefield. Henry V's victory over the flower of French chivalry at Agincourt is – thanks not least to Shakespeare – one of the great battles of the world. But perhaps the most surprising thing about it to modern eyes is how the king made his immediate preparations for the conflict on which he had staked everything: reputation, kingdom, perhaps even life itself. He did not hold a council of war or interrogate spies; instead he heard mass. And not a field mass, hurriedly muttered at a makeshift altar, but one beautifully and elaborate sung by the full complement of his Chapel Royal, vested in their precious copes, and with the altar hung with rich fabrics and groaning with gold: candlesticks, images, reliquaries, the crucifix itself.

For Henry, as Shakespeare again makes clear, thought he was fighting a holy war, a veritable crusade in which right as well – it transpired – as might were on his side. Or, rather, might was on his side because God and Right were: '*Dieu et Mon Droit*' in the words of the royal motto. Most surprisingly of all, it is possible that some of the music sung by his Chapel choir at Agincourt was by the king himself. Settings of two parts of the movements of the mass, attributed to 'le roy Henry', appear in the Old Hall Manuscript – the contemporary choirbook that originated in the circle of the royal family and later passed into the hands of the Chapel Royal itself – and are almost certainly his work. And what is not in question is that Henry was also a liturgical reformer, expanding and elaborating the already lengthy devotions of the Chapel Royal with anthems devoted to St George, the patron saint of England, and the Blessed Virgin, as protectoress of Henry's person and kingdom.

This introduces one of our major, and perhaps rather disturbing, themes: the close relationship of music, monarchy and war. 'The English, a manly, *military* race, were instantly captivated by the grave, bold and nervous style of Handel, which is congenial to their manner and sentiments,' wrote Charles Burney as he tried to explain how it came about that the German Handel 'may be said to have formed our national taste'. The creative role of war was at least as strong in the music of the fourteenth and fifteenth centuries as in that of the eighteenth. Henry V's mass compositions were written at the height of the Hundred Years War, when the king's astonishing run of victories on land and at sea made it look as though England really was going to conquer France.

And not only conquer France. For the Hundred Years War was not just an unprecedentedly long and bloody conflict; it was also a huge national effort which remade England as well. It transformed the constitution and made parliament a power in the land. It changed religion, made God English, and beautified the face of England with magnificent churches whose architecture itself was uniquely English. It made English, for the first time since the Norman Conquest, the language of literature and the elite. And, above all, from our point of view, it invented English music, gave it a timbre and sonority recognizable today, and set it to conquer Europe.

The Hundred Years War was begun by Edward III in 1337. Edward claimed the throne of France and quartered the lilies of France with the lions of England in his coat of arms. Five years later, in 1342, Edward founded an order of warrior knights – the Order of the Garter – to honour and encourage his brother-in-arms in the struggle with France. He established a chapel for the Order in his favourite palace of Windsor Castle and dedicated it to the Virgin and St George. The effects were profound and long lasting. St George became the patron saint of England, and his red cross on a white background became the national flag. Windsor joined Westminster as one of the two cultic centres of the English monarchy, eventually giving its name to the dynasty itself. And St George's Chapel became the model for a new kind of religious foundation, with a new scale of musical establishment.

These new foundations were called colleges. All over the country – at Warwick, Arundel in Sussex, Tattershall in Lincolnshire, Ewelme in Oxfordshire, Cobham in Kent, Fotheringhay in Northamptonshire, and many others where barely a trace remains – junior members of the royal family and other great nobles, who were themselves knights of the Garter, set up colleges in imitation of Windsor. They endowed them heavily with land and gave them fine churches and residential quarters. There they built their tombs and there the priests and choristers of the college would sing for their founders' prosperity in life and pray for their souls in death.

The most famous and most influential were established by Henry V's own son. Henry VI, scarred by his long minority, showed himself indifferent, if not actually hostile, to his father's military legacy and quickly lost all – and more – than he had gained. But he did inherit Henry V's piety and his devotion to the Virgin. This was reflected in the twin foundations that he regarded as the masterwork of his reign: 'The King's College of Our Lady of Eton besides Windsor' and King's College, Cambridge, which is likewise dedicated to the Virgin and bears her white roses in its coat of arms. We think of them as primarily educational foundations – the 'most famous school in the world' and one of Cambridge University's most prestigious colleges. But they were founded as colleges in the fifteenth-century sense of the word, not ours, to pray and to sing for the souls of Henry VI and his family. The Eton Choirbook is one of the most important surviving guides to the choral repertory of late fifteenth-century England, while the choir of King's College, Cambridge, remains at the heart of the Anglican musical tradition. The daily evensong is an opportunity to hear some of the most beautiful works in the repertory performed by the College choir, which consists of adult choral scholars, who are also students of the College, and boy choristers, who are trained at the nearby King's College School. The annual Christmas Eve Service of Nine Lessons and Carols (which is actually a Victorian invention) is a British national institution, broadcast by the BBC since 1928 to millions around the world.

King's College, with its incomparable musical tradition, is nowadays a rare survival. In the fifteenth century it was one of many and, with its buildings incomplete and its founder's extravagant endowment truncated, by no means the most distinguished. That accolade instead belonged to the Chapel Royal. The Chapel had no endowment and no fixed home, since it followed the king in all his wanderings. But its staff of dean, chaplains, Gentlemen of the Chapel Royal and boy choristers followed the collegiate model and sang the collegiate repertory of complex, magnificent, sonorous polyphony in the elaborate daily devotions of the king and court. And, since it was backed by the king's more or less bottomless purse, it sang it better than anywhere else – recruiting the best composers and singers, both boy and adult, from other colleges, as well as training many internally.

The result of this countrywide network of colleges – between which promising choirboys were poached ruthlessly and adult performers moved freely – was that late medieval England supported a flourishing musical life. It was the pride of English kings and the envy of European monarchs. English composers like John Dunstable enjoyed the highest reputation abroad, where their works were copied and performed widely. English music, with its particular harmonies and sonorities, known as the '*contenance angloise*', set the fashion for the rest of Europe, and English choirs were marvelled at for their technical skills and virtuosity at either end of the scale: for their magnificent bases, on the one hand, and their boy trebles on the other, who sang fiendishly difficult polyphony at sight and improvised descant to plainsong with equal facility.

It was a moment to savour, for the reputation of English music, basking in the warm sunlight of royal and noble patronage, would never be so high again.

This world of flourishing colleges and choirs, with their rich endowments, royal and noble patrons, and unending round of prayer and sacred song, provides the unexpected climax to Sir John Fortescue's *The Governance of England*. Fortescue's treatise is a response to the malaise of English politics that followed the collapse, under Henry VI, of the great royal and national enterprise of war against France. Kings would only be free to govern, Fortescue argued, and their subjects only be free to enjoy their own property, if taxation, which parliament voted resentfully and too little, too late, were replaced by a re-foundation or re-endowment of the crown with a landed capital sufficient to generate an adequate income for the king 'to live of his own' without resorting to taxation.

If this royal endowment were to happen, Fortescue was convinced, all England would be united in gratitude to his new patron, Edward IV. Fortescue ends by illustrating the point with a sustained simile: the re-endowment of the crown would be like a national re-foundation; England would become like a college, singing anthems of praise to King Edward as its (re-)founder. As a final touch of authenticity, Fortescue even provides a parody text for the anthem:

> *For this shall be a college, in which shall sing and pray for ever more all the men of England, spiritual and temporal. And all their song shall be such among other anthems: 'I bless be our Lord God, for that he hath sent King Edward IV to reign upon us. He hath done more for us, than ever did king of England or might have done before him … We shall now more enjoy our own good, and live under justice, which we have not done of long time, God knoweth. Wherefore of his alms it is that we have all that is in our own.'*

In other words, 'God bless the king for abolishing taxes!' Such is the tribute that one of the first masterpieces of the dismal science of political economy pays to the noble art of music, and to the colleges of fifteenth-century England where music had made its home. Unfortunately – and so much for political prophecy – when the re-endowment of the crown *was* put into effect half a century later in the 1530s, the colleges – and music itself – would be among its principal victims.

The agent of this change – and the rather surprising one – was Edward IV's grandson, Henry VIII. Henry bore a strong resemblance to his Yorkist grandfather: in looks, height and intelligence; in his gargantuan appetites and eventual girth; in his unforced charm and devastating, unpredictable spasms of savage cruelty. But, above all, from our point of view, Henry is justly famous as the supremely musical king, under whom the late medieval flourishing of English music reached its apogee, before, in one of those characteristic, terrifying reversals, he threatened it with wholesale destruction.

Henry was a trained musician, highly skilled in both theory and practice. He had been taught to play both string and wind instruments and had a fine voice. He was a composer, too, and able to turn out fiendishly complex polyphony, like five-part masses. He had an outstanding collection of musical instruments, with its own curator who also taught music to Henry's children. The choir of his Chapel Royal was the envy of Europe. But it was occasionally bested at home by the even more splendid establishment of his cardinal-minister, Thomas Wolsey. King and cardinal fought over promising boy trebles, who became stars in their own right.

This was the world of royal piety and musical patronage as it had flourished under his predecessor and youthful role model, Henry V. The great collegiate foundations of the fifteenth century were completed as well, as both King's College Chapel and the Henry VII Chapel at Westminster were finished in Henry VIII's first decade. The two buildings, with their perfect proportions, filigree stonework and the engineering perfection of their fan vaults, are the supreme examples of the last great flowering of Gothic architecture in England. Their style is known as 'Perpendicular' and it is peculiarly English. So, too, was the music for which they were designed: the magnificent polyphony of late medieval England, which also reached its apogee under Henry. Above all, as under Henry's Lancastrian and Yorkist forebears, the buildings, the style and the music were *royal*.

So it is as a *musician* that Henry VIII is represented in the psalter, heavily annotated in his own hand, which was written and illuminated for him in the early 1540s by the French calligrapher Jean Mallard. The illumination for Psalm 53, 'The fool hath said in his heart, There is no God', shows Henry seated, playing reflectively on his harp, while his Fool listens, uncomprehendingly, to its higher harmonies. This is Henry as a new King David, the supposed author of the psalms, leading his people in the true, melodious worship of God. God, as He is addressed in the psalms, was the 'Chief Musician'. He maintained the universe in harmony through the music of the spheres. Consequently, music was the only learned art and the only one taught in the universities of Oxford and Cambridge. It was also the only art that could be practised by a gentleman – or a king.

Above all, God was to be worshipped with music:

Sing we merrily unto God our strength: make a cheerful noise unto the God of Jacob. Take the psalm, bring hither the tabret; the merry harp with the lute. Blow up the trumpet in the new-moon: even in the time appointed, and upon our solemn feast-day. (Psalm 81:1–3)

The illumination in Henry VIII's psalter for this psalm once again domesticates the scene by showing a group of Henry's court musicians in the kind of exotic fancy dress they donned for masques and revels. Three of them are playing in consort: the drummer, with his tabour, and the harpist focus their eyes on the player on the stringed psaltary; in the background, a lone trumpeter with bulging cheeks blows blasts on his instrument. Above, lit by a ghostly light in a clearing in the clouds of the night sky, God the Father, bearded and wearing a triple crown as he was customarily depicted at this time, looks down approvingly. Henry held to this traditional view of the centrality of music in the worship of God to the end of his days, marking approvingly passages like Psalm 98: 5–6:

Praise the Lord upon the harp: sing to the harp with a psalm of thanksgiving. With trumpets also, and shawms: O show yourselves joyful before the Lord the King.

Worship *was* music: the matter was closed, for Henry at least.

But by the end of his reign, Henry came near to demolishing the magnificent structure of royal and sacred music he had built up. And, curiously, he did it through music. Alongside the sacred music of his Chapel, there was the profane music of his chamber. Here Henry excelled as well. He wrote both the words and music of the great, popular hit of the first decades of the sixteenth century, 'Pastime with Good Company'. And he turned out love songs by the yard. In the fullness of time, he would make love to Anne Boleyn through music and win her, too.

But in order to have Anne he had to break with Rome. Would the great English musical traditional of his Church and Chapel go as well? This brings us to our second principal theme: the relationship of religion and music. In the old faith, especially as practised by English kings, music was inseparable from religion: mass was rarely *said*, it was *sung*, with every variety of skill and elaboration and instrumental accompaniment. But for the new faith the Word was there to be *spoken*: clearly, simply, directly. Words were to be understood and anything that got in the way of understanding, like music, or a foreign language, or ritual, was wrong. It did not matter if it moved the emotions or plucked the heart strings. Such were the wiles of the Devil, to be swept aside by the pure, redeeming Word of God.

The result was a new royal religious enterprise. The old had been the creation and development of the great English polyphonic tradition in which England and her kings petitioned the Virgin for victory in war and the fruits of peace. The new was the great exercise of translation into English of the Bible and the liturgy. Both were royal enterprises and dependent on the royal will – though of course the actual work was done by others. The Great Bible, the first official translation into English of both the Old and New Testaments, was published under Henry VIII's patronage in 1539. The task of translating the liturgy took longer. It began under Henry VIII with the translation of the Litany but it was not complete until the reign of his young son Edward VI when the English Book of Common Prayer was published in 1549 and heavily revised in 1551.

The key figure in both these enterprises was Thomas Cranmer, archbishop of Canterbury. He had provided the theological arguments which legitimated Henry's divorce from Catherine of Aragon and his remarriage to Anne Boleyn, and Henry – in so far as he was capable of it – owed him a profound debt of gratitude. But in the matter of translation, Cranmer often went dangerously ahead of his king. And, in the matter of music, they disagreed utterly. Henry remained convinced of the appropriateness, even the necessity, of elaborate music in the true worship of God. Cranmer came to reject it. And he did so, significantly, as a consequence of his first attempt at liturgical reform with his translation of the Litany in 1543. The Litany – the petition for God's mercies – was closely associated with religious processions and processional singing. Cranmer disapproved of processions; instead, he wanted the congregation to focus on the meaning of the words they uttered. As these words were now to be in English, rather than Latin, this was possible. But only if the music did not get in the way. This led Cranmer to the revolutionary proposal that music should become a mere handmaid to language and that as a matter of principle, there should be one note per syllable. Out would go the luxurious thickets of sound of professionally sung polyphony; in would come congregational singing in simple unison. In the former, the words were lost; in the latter they shone forth.

Cranmer's opportunity to put all this into practice came with Henry's death and the removal of his idiosyncratic control of religious policy. As a necessary step to his divorce and remarriage, Henry had assumed the Supreme Headship of the English Church and embarked on a programme of wholesale, but erratic, religious reform. Its first target was the 600 English monasteries which, ranging from impoverished rural nunneries to opulent cathedral-like Benedictine abbeys, were one of the most striking features of the medieval landscape. In a mere four years, from 1536 to 1540, all were dissolved: their lands confiscated; their treasures seized; their monks and nuns pensioned off; most of their buildings demolished and the very lead stripped off their roofs and sold.

The initial impact on the English musical tradition was substantial and the potential impact much graver. The sung offices of the religious themselves – the monks and nuns –were essentially amateur and of widely varying quality. But the greater Benedictine abbeys were a different matter. They had lady chapels (dedicated to the Virgin Mary) with professional choirs of singing men and boys, and services open to the general public. Here the standards were of the highest and fully comparable to those achieved by the royal colleges and the Chapel Royal itself. As the career of Thomas Tallis shows, there had also been easy professional mobility between posts in the monastic, collegiate or royal choirs. With the Dissolution, one of these categories of musical employment vanished. But the others remained. For how long, however?

The principal motive for the Dissolution had been fiscal. Henry VIII's extravagance in peace and war had long since exhausted the treasures left him by his careful father. Parliament, as usual, was reluctant to grant taxation. To bridge the gap, the king's new minister, Thomas Cromwell, took a leaf out of Fortescue's *Governance of England* and persuaded Henry to re-endow the crown with the former wealth of the monasteries. This was mere expediency. But Cromwell, Cranmer, and even Henry himself, were also concerned with the principles at stake. The vast endowments of the monasteries were justified by the Catholic doctrine of Purgatory. Purgatory was conceived of as an intermediate state between Heaven and Hell. The passage of the souls of the dead through Purgatory – providing they had not been irretrievably wicked in life – could be aided by the prayers and offerings of the living. These invoked the merits of Christ, His Mother and the saints, which were entrusted to the Church and dispensed by it – for a price. And the price, to cut a long story short, was the endowments of the monasteries, which paid for prayers, masses and a perpetual cycle of invocation and intercession – and for the professional musicians who sung it.

But where was Purgatory in the Bible? The new approaches to Christianity, called the New Learning by contemporaries and 'Evangelical' by historians, made the Bible – especially the Bible in English – the measure of all things. And Purgatory was to be found nowhere in the Bible. Nor were prayers, intercessions and sung masses for the dead. Instead, salvation depended wholly on the Christian's relationship with God and his fellow men in *this* world, not the next.

At a stroke, the Dissolution was transformed from a fiscal expedient into a necessary step of religious reform. But how far would reform go? The great religious changes in England had begun for the narrowest and most self-interested of motives: Henry's urgent desire for divorce and remarriage. But they coincided with the great European-wide movement of religious reform known as the Reformation. Henry's relationship with the Reformation was an uncertain one. He had been one of Luther's earliest and most prominent opponents, winning his papal title of Defender of the Faith for his anti-Lutheran tract, *Assertio septem sacramentorum*, and the two were never reconciled. Cranmer's theology, on the other hand, moved more and more into the mainstream of European reformed thought, even going beyond Luther towards the more thoroughgoing Zwingli and the other Swiss reformers.

While Henry lived, Cranmer kept all this more or less concealed. But with Henry's death, his position was transformed. Under the old king, who prided himself on forging a lonely middle way between the extremes of the Old and New Learning, Cranmer had been one counsellor among many. With the accession of Henry's nine-year-old son, Edward VI, a regency government was set up in which Cranmer was one of the two principal voices: the king's maternal uncle, Edward Seymour, Duke of Somerset, exercised supreme power in matters of state, while Cranmer determined the pace and extent of religious change.

Now, and only now, is it proper to talk of a Protestant Reformation in England. And only now were the full effects felt on music. The destruction of choral institutions continued apace as the royal colleges, which Henry had protected to the last out of a mixture of dynastic piety and musical pride, followed the monasteries into oblivion. Oxford and Cambridge, and King's College itself, hung by a thread. But worse was to come with the introduction of the English Prayer Books. The whole of the Latin liturgy, and perforce the music that had been written for it, were now illegal. Choirs were disbanded, organs dismantled and torn out, and choirbooks and other musical manuscripts burned or recycled as scrap. Not even St George's Chapel or the Chapel Royal were spared, and the entire legacy of English polyphony – one of the great achievements of Western civilisation – was on the point of disappearing entirely.

And if Edward had lived, it would have done so. It was spared only by Edward's premature death at the age of 15 and the succession of his Catholic half-sister Mary. Mary restored the music along with the other beliefs and practices of the pre-Reformation church. But her reign, too, only lasted for five years and, as she was childless, she was succeeded, according to the terms of her father's will, by her half-sister Elizabeth.

Elizabeth, as Anne Boleyn's daughter, as well as by personal conviction, was indelibly Protestant. But it was a Protestantism that was as idiosyncratic as her father's amalgam of beliefs. For Elizabeth valued ceremony and adored music. If she had had her way, her preferences would have been forced on the whole of the restored Protestant Church of England. But, in this respect at least, her authority stopped at the palace gates. Within them she reigned supreme and her Chapel Royal displayed a decorous and ceremonious pattern of worship that her father would have recognised. The Communion table was placed at the east end and draped and ornamented like an altar with candlesticks and (to begin with at least) a crucifix. A choir of men and boys, just as numerous as Henry's own and wearing lavish copes on occasions of ceremony, sang a new repertory of sacred music. Like the liturgy, it was largely in English but in its elaboration and musical demands it was a direct continuation of the pre-Reformation tradition. Some of the musicians of the Chapel Royal even continued to compose in the old way, and the most eminent of them were Catholics to boot.

All this has led historians and musicologists to talk of the reign of Elizabeth as 'a golden age of English church music'. But it was a golden age that was circumscribed within the Chapel Royal and extended scarcely beyond its walls. By the end of Elizabeth's reign, however, there are signs of a significant change in the aesthetic tastes of the elite. Nobles and gentlemen were becoming weary of the stripped-down aesthetic of Protestantism, with its whitewashed churches and clear-glass windows. If the early days of the Grand Tour had taken them to Italy, they especially yearned for paintings other than portraits, stained glass, rich music, colour and the other joys of the senses. In other words, I suppose, they were catching up with their queen.

But the real effects were felt after Elizabeth's death with the succession of the Stuarts. Charles I, who succeeded his father, James I and VI in 1625, was in the vanguard of the new aestheticism and accumulated Europe's finest collection of Old Master paintings. Like his Tudor predecessors, he was intensely musical; he played the viol well and had a particular fondness for the difficult, esoteric music of the fantasias composed for him by his court musician and leading light of the Chapel Royal, Orlando Gibbons. But, unlike Elizabeth, he was determined to impose his tastes on others , especially in the matter of religion.

He found a willing co-adjutor in William Laud, who became archbishop of Canterbury in 1633. Laud was doctrinally suspect to mainstream Protestant opinion (maligned by the court with the abusive sobriquet 'Puritan'). But the real bone of contention was what Laud called 'the beauty of holiness'. In practice, this amounted to an insistence – enforced by royal decree – that all churches should follow the practice of the Chapel Royal and have communion tables placed altar-wise at the east end, draped and railed and officiated at by clergy in vestments to the sound of elaborate music accompanied by the organ. All this, since almost all such ecclesiastical ornaments had been destroyed during the course of the Reformation, was expensive – which was one source of objection. The other, and much more powerful one, was that Laud's programme of the 'beauty of holiness' amounted to a reversal of the Reformation and a return to Catholicism.

Church music and musicians, as at the time of the Reformation, now found themselves in the front line of religious controversy. The advance of Laudianism can be measured by the installation of church organs, most of them built by the Dallam family of organ builders. And its retreat – when resentment at the policies of Charles and Laud led to civil war – by the corresponding dismantling and destruction of the newly installed organs by the triumphant Puritan armies. The civil war was an organ war and its outcome entailed as thorough a destruction of church music, in its emerging Anglican guise, as anything perpetrated in the Reformation.

These events also represent a schism within English Protestantism and the Church of England itself, between what later became known as low church and high church. The former derived from Puritanism and enjoined simplicity in worship, the supremacy of preaching, and the pulpit as the true and only means of communicating the Word of God. The latter descended from Laudianism; it adhered to the programme of 'the beauty of holiness' and saw the sacraments and the altar as the heart of worship. And there was no doubt which side music and monarchy were on: they were high church, and Charles I, by his execution, was their martyr.

The Restoration was thus as much a triumph for music as for the monarchy. Indeed, music thrived as never before. One of Charles

II's first acts was to begin the reconstruction of the Chapel Royal. The tradition of boy trebles had disappeared in the Civil War. Now it was reconstituted as new recruits were obtained, if need be by impressment. Charles also established a new instrumental ensemble: the Twenty-Four Violins. Their primary purpose was to act as the dance band of the court, playing the kind of tuneful, heavily accented music that Charles, as was his wont, could beat time to, or, when the mood took him – which was often – dance to with style and agility. In time, the Twenty-Four Violins would serve as the nucleus of the baroque orchestra and, combined with the choral resources of the Chapel Royal, provide the forces for that most English of forms, the orchestral anthem.

But the Chapel Royal was above all a human resource. It offered an unrivalled musical training from boyhood; it exposed a chorister to the best music; it made constant demands on his energy and performing skills and, if he continued beyond puberty and became a singing man, it offered the best creative opportunities, too. He could learn composition alongside the best practitioners of the day and, in a world dominated by the constant royal demand for novelty, he could be confident that his work would see the light of day – and continue to do so if it pleased the king.

The product of all this was Henry Purcell. He is the greatest musical genius born on British soil and he was Chapel Royal through and through: boy, youth and all-too-short manhood. There are many epitaphs for composers, usually dying young and untimely deaths, on the lines of: ' ——— is dead, and music dies'. In the case of Purcell, the difference is that it was true.

This assertion is not romanticism; it is hard, political fact. For Purcell's early-flowering maturity coincided with another great upheaval in Britain's turbulent royal history. In 1685 Charles II died without legitimate issue and was succeeded by his brother, James II. James had been an early convert to Roman Catholicism and, despite the repeated political crises that it caused, had remained faithful to his adoptive faith. It is a measure of Charles II's good luck and political skill that, for all his brother's obduracy, he was able to pass on the throne and ensure James's trouble-free accession. James even felt free to celebrate the fact with the most elaborate and best-recorded coronation to date. It featured music by Purcell of unparalleled quality and written for unprecedentedly large forces. But it was there to fill the gap left by James's refusal to participate in the Protestant communion that was the spiritual and musical heart of the coronation service.

It was only the first of many provocative acts by the king that succeeded in throwing away, in three short years, all the political advantages he had inherited from his brother. It is a measure of his absolute failure that Princesses Mary and Anne, his own children by his first marriage, who had been brought up as Protestants, turned against him with the rest. Mary's husband, William II, Prince of Orange and Statholder of The Netherlands, was invited to protect the liberties and religion of England. He invaded with a substantial army and a ready-primed printing press. Propaganda, the revolutionary song 'Lilliburlero' and James's own crippling indecisiveness in the crisis handed the day to William. James's army commanders deserted him and James, after one bungled attempt at flight, was permitted to leave the country. After furious debate, William and Mary were jointly offered the throne and were crowned at Westminster Abbey in April 1689.

Purcell also wrote music for this service. But it is briefer and more modest in scale. For this was a coronation that was to be dominated by *words*: by the heavily revised coronation oath sworn by the king and queen that committed them irretrievably to observe both the Protestant religion and parliamentary legislation; by the English Bible presented to the royal couple; and by the coronation sermon that rejoiced in the fact that England had chosen a benign middle way between the extremes of monarchical absolutism, as in Louis XIV's France, and republican chaos, as in the English Commonwealth. The sermon was even given a hearty round of applause. The sense of a political, rather than a sacred, event was heightened by the fact that the members of the House of Commons were present en masse for the first time at a coronation and were given prime seats in a grandstand in the north transept directly overlooking the coronation theatre itself.

The last time there had been anything like it was the equally radical coronation of Edward VI. Cranmer, against his better judgement since he thought they were popish absurdities, had gone through with most of the old ceremonies. But he had rendered them nugatory by delivering an extraordinary address which explained why they were of no effect: the coronation oath could not bind the king because he was answerable only to God; nor could the coronation oils hallow him since he was already God's anointed.

The reason for the parallel is that both King Edward VI and King William II were that rarity among English monarchs: thorough-going, conscientiously convinced Protestants. And the fate of music was to be the same in both reigns. Even before the coronation, William and Mary had already begun to cut the Chapel Royal down to size. They had forbidden the use of any instrument in the Chapel apart from the organ. This killed at a stroke the string anthem which had elicited much of Purcell's best music. They had reduced the number of Gentlemen singers of the Chapel Royal by over a third. And William continued to display an indifference that bordered on hostility.

Purcell, bereft of royal patronage, transferred his energies to the theatre and, when he died in 1695 at the tragically early age of 36, had no successor. And he had no successor because the Chapel Royal, also bereft of royal patronage, withered on the vine. The institution continued, of course, with its Gentlemen, choirboys, organists, composers and the daily round of services, but, without royal interest and connoisseurship, the life went out of it. And this time it did not return. Edward VI had eventually been succeeded by Elizabeth whose enthusiastic commitment had saved English church music from the holocaust of the Reformation. William, who was childless and had been predeceased by Mary, was succeeded by his sister-in-law Anne. Anne liked to affect the Elizabethan manner and even chose the same motto: *Semper eadem* ('Always the same'). But she was no Elizabeth and the Chapel Royal was to know no second revival. It died a creative death with the Glorious Revolution, and English music, it is no exaggeration to say, died with it.

Purcell's death had another grievous consequence. In his later works for the theatre, like the music drama *The Indian Queen*, Purcell had come near to finding the Holy Grail of a through-sung English opera. Charles II had tried to mount a court opera. But the post-Restoration monarchy's resources were inadequate to meet the costs involved. In the booming economy of 1690s London, cost was no object to the commercial stage. It was genius that was in short supply. With Purcell's death, it disappeared entirely, taking with it the possibility of an English opera. The London stage was left open instead to the triumph of Italian opera, with its foreign composers and foreign star singers performing to an English audience in a foreign language.

The result was a paradox and an absurdity. Perhaps the greatest achievement of the English Reformation was to enable the English to have their religion – whether it was said, read or sung – in their own language. With the triumph of Italian opera, the London stage saw a kind of secular Counter-Reformation. The ironies were all the richer as the Glorious Revolution had seen the final political victory of Protestantism, while the reign of Anne saw a series of unprecedented military victories that turned England from a French satellite into the dominant European power in a single generation and opened the way to world power status thereafter.

And yet, England was without its own music and listened to its opera in a language it could not understand, save through the cheaply printed bilingual word books that served as Augustan-Age surtitles. All this was seized upon by Richard Steele in the first, and perhaps the most effective attack, on the Italian takeover. 'Britons, ' he exhorted his fellow countrymen:

From foreign insult save this English stage.
No more th'Italian squalling tribe admit,
In tongues unknown; 'tis popery in wit.
The songs (their selves confess) from Rome they bring,
And 'tis high mass, for aught you know, they sing.
Husbands take care, the danger may come nigher,
The women say their eunuch is a friar.

Instead, he pleaded, let England match her new-found military power by corresponding cultural achievement:

Let Anna's soil be know for all its charms;
As famed for liberal sciences as arms:
Let those derision meet who would advance
Manners or speech, from Italy or France.
Let them learn you, who would your favour find,
And English be the language of mankind.

But, as far as an English music and an English opera were concerned, Steele pleaded in vain.

The supreme irony had yet to come in that the successful theatrical setting of English was to be left to a German. Handel had come to England to exploit the opportunities offered by the infant Italian opera and it was as a prolific opera composer that he enjoyed his initial London triumphs. But, almost from the beginning, he had shown a parallel commitment to learning English and to setting English texts in English musical forms, like the court birthday odes he composed for the queen in the last years of her reign. In his setting of 'Eternal source of light divine' for the birthday ode of 1713, he wrote sublime music *despite* the high-flown vapidities of Richard Elfort's text. What would he do with words that matched the power of his musical invention? We find out when he is invited, at George II's insistence, to compose the anthems for the coronation of 1727.

The anthem texts were derived, as was customary, from the two great Reformation sources: the King James Bible of 1611 and, for the psalms, Matthew Coverdale's translation as it had appeared in the Book of Common Prayer. Handel, again at George II's insistence, seems to have been given unusual freedom about the exact words he set and he showed himself a sensitive and effective editor. He cut out some passages – often long ones – and he added others. And, in both his additions and deletions, he was driven by the same urge: to find drama in the phrases and royalty itself in the words. The result is seen most clearly in his addition of the verse 'Glory and worship hast thou laid upon him' to the anthem 'The King shall rejoice in Thy strength, O Lord!'. Most of the anthem is elaborately contrapuntal. But Handel sets the inserted verse quite differently. The choir sings in massive unison, and trumpets and timpani exalt around the key words 'Glory' and 'Worship'. English had found its musical voice at last and had been given it by a German!

Here there is another, and final, paradox. The texts of the English Bible and the Book of Common Prayer had been written by men who were bitterly hostile on principle to the use of elaborate music in worship. But these unmusical men had written wonderful prose, whose words, phrases and narrative drive cry out for *music* –

and music of corresponding majesty and dramatic power. Handel heard the cry and was able to provide the music: first in the coronation anthems and later in the English oratorios. The oratorios develop the same musical language and use similar biblical and Prayer Book texts. Some of the oratorios, like *Saul*, have a dramatic narrative; others, like *Messiah*, do not. But too much has been made of the difference. The real drama is in the words as such, whose bold strength came as a relief after the insipidities of Italian opera libretti and, at its best, elicited a different order of musical inspiration.

The path to Handel's royally endorsed apotheosis as the English national composer was clear.

⚬∞⚬

But the sleight of hand could only go so far. Handel was a national composer without a national musical tradition. And, until the musical infrastructure which had been destroyed twice over, by the iconoclasm of the Reformation and the principled Protestant philistinism of the Glorious Revolution, was rebuilt, it would remain without one. To fill the skills gap, Georgian London imported foreign musical talent on a prodigious scale and at every level: not only eminent foreign composers and lavishly paid virtuoso singers, but quite humble folk as well, like the German orchestral players who provided almost all the performers in the private royal bands of George III and the Prince Regent.

It was kings who had demolished. And only kings, or at least Victoria's eldest son, the Prince of Wales, could provide the necessary patronage for the foundation of the Royal College of Music in 1882.

The Royal College picked up where the Restoration Chapel Royal had left off. It provided intensive training in both performance and composition and it demanded productivity in both. And it was the crown that reaped the benefit. When Edward VII, as he called himself as king, succeeded his mother Victoria in 1901, Britain exchanged a monarch who had loathed ceremony and public performance for one who loved them both. And Edward, as his princely patronage of the Royal College showed, loved music as well. He was loved in turn by musicians like Edward Elgar, who saw himself as a troubadour or musical knight-errant for his royal master. The result was that Edward's coronation in 1902 was the most musically distinguished in almost two centuries. It featured compositions like Parry's 'I Was Glad' that were able to stand comparison with even Handel's coronation anthems; it also included composers from earlier centuries, including Handel's 'Zadok the Priest', in a conscious attempt to embody the gamut of a rediscovered and revivified English musical tradition. And where the coronation of 1902 led, those of 1911, 1937 and 1953 followed. It was a case of practice makes perfect, as each capped the other in terms of ceremonial perfection and musical quality.

Which brings us, I suppose, to a sort of end. As a boy of eight, I watched Elizabeth II's coronation service on television. It was the first time I had watched television, and the first time I had heard the music. I have never forgotten either experience. And now, as the sixtieth anniversary of the coronation approaches, I see this project as a tribute to the queen's younger self – and a nod to the curious, excited little boy I once was.

◌∞◌

As I hope will be clear from this overview, the researching and writing of this project has been an intellectual delight which has forced me to see historical problems, familiar to me as a political historian, in a quite unexpected light. It has also been an anecdotal pleasure: music speaks to monarchs and elicits some surprising replies! Who would have thought that the warrior-king and brutal strategist Henry V was also an accomplished church composer and liturgical reformer? That Henry VIII spent his last years worrying about the legitimacy of church music along with the state of his immortal soul? That Charles II, vulgarian that he was, insisted on the unforgivable sin of beating time to music? (Or perhaps in his case it isn't so surprising after all.) That one of the most frequent entries in the journal of the young Queen Victoria is a complaint about how dreadful the singing of the Chapel Royal at St James's was and how impossible it was to do anything about it? 'The Bishop of London ought really to be spoken to about it', she had said to her fatherly, old prime minister, Lord Melbourne. Melbourne had replied, 'They're such obstinate dogs, those bishops; I believe if you was to say it was very good he would be more likely to change it!'

Musicians speak to monarchs as well, and often boldly. William Cornysh the Younger, composer and master of the boys of Henry VIII's Chapel Royal, was on joking terms with his formidable sovereign. Courtiers, like Cornysh, were entitled to 'bouge of court', a daily allowance of wine and bread. Once, during the progress time when horse provender ran low, Cornysh spoke for his fellow courtiers by playing on the idea of 'bouge of court' and petitioning the king for its equine equivalent: could he have, he asked with a flourish, 'a bottle of hay and an horse-loaf!'. Perhaps it is as well that Handel did not have a Henry VIII to contend with. But he argued vigorously with George II about the orchestration of the *Music for the Royal Fireworks*: the king wanted it to be scored for warlike instruments – brass, wind and timpani – only; Handel, with an eye on profiting from future indoor performances, insisted on violins as well. And Handel seems to have won. Handel had earlier taken on the archbishop of Canterbury over the text of the coronation anthems. 'I know my Bible very well', he is supposed to have said, 'and shall choose for myself.' Which he did, to the immense benefit, as we have seen, of both the words and the music.

But the greatest pleasures of all, of course, have been musical. I have been privileged to hear some of the finest music in the canon, sung and played by some of the best performers, and for me – incredibly – as an audience of one. And I have heard them in the buildings where the music was first heard and for whose interiors it was composed. It was Goethe who said 'architecture is frozen music'. The words are extraordinarily vivid. But the idea takes on richer meaning still when the music unfreezes, as it were, and lives, and you can listen, as I have done, to masterpieces of fifteenth-century English polyphony performed by the chapel choir in King's College, Cambridge: the original building, the original performing forces, the original music, each illuminating and enriching the other. The music, as the word 'polyphony' means, is a series of separate lines, each distinct yet each intertwining with the rest in a wall of complex sound – just as above the ribs of the fan vaulting join themselves into gossamer patterns whose apparent lightness defies the solidity and weight of the stones that compose them.

Or when you hear a viol consort, in the like of which Charles I played, performing a fantasia by Charles's court composer Orlando Gibbons in one of the State Apartments at Wilton House that were designed and decorated for Charles's lord chamberlain and intended to house the king himself in surroundings whose splendour mimicked his own palaces – palaces which have gone while Wilton remains.

And, most frequently and most movingly of all, when I have sat and listened and sometimes wept tears (I trust invisible ones) in the Abbey. Westminster Abbey was designed specifically by Henry III and his architects to accommodate the coronation service and the best coronation music returns the compliment. Handel's 'Zadok the Priest' exploits the extraordinary acoustics of the building and the way that sound, loud or soft, travels undistorted and undiminished along the length of the vault. Parry's 'I Was Glad' even reflects the building's dimensions and the distribution of spaces within it. Its first section covers the king's entrance into the Abbey and his procession up the nave; then, as he passes through the choir screen, the traditional shouts of the boys of Westminster School *Vivat Rex* (God Save the King) are incorporated into the music. A quieter, more reflective section follows as the royal procession moves through the choir, before the full majestic forces of choir, organ and brass-rich, late Romantic orchestra return for the king's ascent to the coronation theatre or stage.

Making a television series is always a collaborative enterprise; in addition, on this project, I've been invited to step outside my academic comfort zone. For that I owe a debt to Janice Hadlow and Jan Younghusband at the BBC, and also to Nicolas Kent and his colleagues at Oxford Film and Television. Happily, I've been able to call upon the musicological expertise of our series consultants, Dr David Skinner, Peter Holman and Professor Jeremy Dibble, to whom I pass on my profound thanks. And for the first time I've collaborated on a book with a co-writer; after the Tudor section I've passed on the conductor's baton, as it were. Katie Greening has been working on the project since our earliest production meetings, and has greatly expanded the scripts I wrote for the screen. She's also been able to include much of the in depth research which we simply couldn't squeeze in to four hours of television.

The result of all our labours has been to recreate a centuries-long royal pageant in music – and through the magic of television, and the pages of this book, you can listen and look and be there with us.

David Starkey, January 2013

GOD
AND KING

KINGS
AND CHOIRS

Our story begins with King Henry: the man who was our greatest king and finest general; who made the name of England feared; who reshaped the English Church for his own purposes; who employed an unprecedented number of musicians; who was even a composer himself.

I mean, of course, King Henry V.

Our King went forth to Normandy
With grace and might of chivalry
Ther God for hym wroought mervelusly
Wherefore Englonde may call and cry ...

This is a popular song written 600 years ago. It is a musical account of Henry V's overwhelming defeat of the French at Agincourt in 1415, when Henry's much smaller army overcame a far bigger one. It is the moment at which the English came nearest to achieving the centuries-old ambition of conquering France. And it quickly became the stuff of legend, as in this song:

He set sail, forsooth to say,
To Harflu town with royal array;
That town he won and made afraid
That France shall rue till domesday!

The song is known as the Agincourt Carol. Nowadays we think of carols as only for Christmas. But then they were used to celebrate any joyful event: mostly the sacred, like the birth of the Christ-child; but sometimes the apparently secular, like this great military victory.

Then went hym forth, owre king comely,
In Agincourt feld he faught manly;
Throw grace of God most marvelusly,
He had both feld and victory
Deo Gratias Anglia redde pro Victoria
(Give thanks to God England for victory).

The Agincourt Carol follows the typical carol form – familiar to us today from 'Hark the Herald Angels Sing', with its chorus of '*Gloria in Excelsis*'– of having the verses in English and the refrain in Latin.

To our ears the English verses, with their uninhibited glorying in battle and bloodshed, and the refrain – with the solemn liturgical phrase '*Deo Gratias*' (thanks be to God) – belong to different worlds. But to Henry V and his people they were one and the same, and their combination of military ambition and the church militant is the foundation of royal music in England.

At dawn on that cold, wet St Crispin's Day, before Henry went into battle, he heard mass. And despite being on a battlefield in France, the mass would have been an elaborate – and beautifully sung – service. Because alongside his knights, archers and horses, his siege train of cannons, his munitions and weapons, and endless quantities of food and drink, Henry had brought the staff of his Chapel Royal.

These were the most important military supplies of all: dozens of priests, choirboys and singing men, along with all their equipment of rich vestments, massive altar plate of gold, relics, choirbooks and sacred banners.

Henry's cannons might batter down the walls of Harfleur; his Chapel Royal was there to bombard the gates of heaven with praise, so that God looked kindly on his enterprise and gave him the victory.

For this, Henry believed, was a crusade, a holy war – to be fought with the sacred weapons of prayer, and song, and music.

The Chapel Royal performed the daily devotions of the king and his court. Despite its name, the Chapel Royal was not a specific place or building – though there were chapels in all the major royal residences; it was a personal, highly mobile body of priest, singers and composers who accompanied the king on his relentless travels and officiated at whichever palace, manor house, castle – or indeed battlefield – the king happened to be. The Chapel had existed in some form or other since the time of William the Conqueror. But as a specialised body of liturgical musicians the Chapel Royal first took shape during the reign of another great conquering king,

Edward I (1272–1307). Edward's grandson Edward III (1327–77), who launched the Hundred Years War against France, increased its numbers still further. But it was Henry V, mindful of his dignity as both King of England and King-Designate of France, who expanded the Chapel to the unprecedented size of 32 'Gentlemen' (adult singers, a mixture of clerks and chaplains) and 16 Children (boy choristers). The members of the choir, however, would rarely sing together at any one time: during this era, liturgical music was sung mostly by soloists, or two to a part.

At the same time, the liturgy of the Chapel became steadily more elaborate. By Henry's reign, services were held at least four times a day: matins (begun after midnight, often around 3 a.m.) lauds (at daybreak), vespers (at twilight) and compline (before retiring to bed). Henry attended three, and sometimes all, of these services along with the majority of the royal household.

With a total of 40 or 50 singers belonging to this elite 'Gentleman's club' for music – some three times the size of the largest cathedral choirs – the Chapel Royal was by far the biggest musical establishment in England. Under Henry V it also became the best, and not only in England but in Europe as well.

Henry's standing in Europe had been transformed by his great victory at Agincourt. The following year, in 1416, the Emperor Sigismund came to England for a summit conference. As German or Holy Roman Emperor, Sigismund was the premier ruler in Europe – alone being addressed as 'Majesty', and alone wearing the arched or imperial crown. Sigismund's original purpose was to try to make peace between England and France; he ended up by signing a treaty of alliance with Henry at Canterbury.

It was a diplomatic coup to rival the military victory of Agincourt; and, just as at Agincourt, the Chapel Royal and its music were to the fore.

On 21 August, news arrived of another crushing English victory – a naval one this time at the Battle of the Seine. Henry and his new ally, Sigismund, came to the great cathedral at Canterbury, the heart of English Christianity, to offer up thanks to God by hearing a service sung by the choirs of the cathedral and Chapel Royal.

It is still possible to stand where the king and emperor stood 600 years ago, and to hear the same kind of music – some would even argue, the actual pieces – they heard. As the choir sings, it is one of those moments when the centuries dissolve and a window opens on the past. For the Emperor Sigismund, on the other hand, it would have been a glimpse into the future: despite all his Europe-wide travels, the emperor would never have heard anything like it – or as good.

The English victory at the Battle of the Seine – which preserved the toehold the English had established by Agincourt and laid the foundations for Henry's ensuing successful invasion of France – took place on 15 August 1416: the Feast of the Assumption of the Blessed Virgin Mary. For Henry, this was proof positive of divine intervention in English affairs and that his prayers and music worked.

So, like the hard-headed strategist that he was, he played to his strengths and multiplied the already elaborate daily devotions of the

Chapel Royal. He added three antiphons – or sung anthems – to the morning high mass of his Chapel and no fewer than six antiphons to its evening service. His reformed liturgy included new psalms that thanked God for the great victories as well as 'memorials' to the saints with whom Henry particularly wanted to be associated: the Virgin Mary, of course, along with St George, who Henry was keen to promote as patron saint of Britain.

Never before had there been such profusion of praise and thanksgiving, never such a demand for music.

⌒∞⌒

The Old Hall Manuscript, now housed in the British Library, was most likely the direct result of the demand for music. Compiled in the years when Henry was conquering Europe, from around 1415 to 1421, it is the earliest English choirbook with settings, generally by named composers, of each of the different parts of the mass (Gloria, Credo, Sanctus, Agnus Dei) together with the additional antiphons and motets that Henry had added to the daily services of his Chapel. The manuscript seems to have been produced for Henry's brother Thomas, Duke of Clarence. Thomas, only a year younger than the king, was his chief lieutenant in the war against France. He also, as this manuscript shows, kept a similarly magnificent Chapel. When Thomas was killed fighting the French in 1421, the book passed into the hands of the Chapel Royal itself, four of whose musicians, such as John Cooke, duly added works of their own.

But the most surprising composer was Le Roi Henri, that is, King Henry V[1] himself, who composed a Gloria and a Sanctus. Henry led his armies from the front, because that was how he inspired men to lead victories. He was equally hands-on as a composer and liturgist, because that was how he believed you got God's favour, which was the most important victory of all.

This combination of demand and supply created a rapid expansion in English musical creativity – and made possible the achievements of the first great English composer whose name has come down to us: John Dunstable. Indeed, in term of his continental reputation, Dunstable is probably *the* greatest English composer, whose music would go on to conquer Europe even more effectively than Henry's armies.

❧

The music of the medieval liturgy was a combination of plainsong – single-line, unaccompanied chant – and polyphony, the elaborate multi-line, choral music that was designed to bring the listener closer to God. Plainsong carried the main text of the service; polyphony was reserved for the most intense moments of religious experience. It used the power of sound to illuminate and beautify religious texts, and it created a transcendental atmosphere that could not be achieved with words alone. Moreover, polyphony was a highly specialist art, requiring educated and skilled composers and musicians to write and perform it. This meant, in turn, that since only the wealthiest patrons could afford it, polyphony was a sign of high status as a sort of religious observance de luxe.

Henry V understood this both as a consumer and composer of music. He was also in the fortunate position of having, in John

Dunstable, one of the greatest polyphony composers of all time under his patronage.

We know neither the time nor the place of Dunstable's birth, but he enjoyed a long and fruitful career, much of it spent on the periphery of the royal service. He is believed to have composed music for Henry's Chapel Royal (indeed, bearing in mind his eminence, it would be rather surprising if he had not). But his known patrons are other members of the royal family: Dunstable worked for Henry's third brother John, Duke of Bedford and Regent of France; for his stepmother, the Queen Dowager Joan; and, finally, for Henry's youngest brother, Humfrey, Duke of Gloucester, the great bibliophile and founder of the University Library at Oxford. Humfrey's academic interests chimed well with Dunstable's own, since he was a practising astronomer as well, and the author of several influential treatises on astronomy and mathematics. Such scientific skills overlapped naturally with music since the complex polyphony Dunstable composed was itself virtually a branch of mathematics, with its intricate, interlocking patterns of repeating rhythms and melodies.

But the most striking thing about Dunstable was his reputation outside England. He travelled to the Continent, possibly as part of the Duke of Bedford's musical retinue, and probably stayed and worked there for extended visits. Most of his surviving music is to be found in European manuscripts, with one of the most important collections being compiled as far away as Ferrara in Italy. And he was widely praised by Continental practitioners and theorists as a great, indeed revolutionary, composer and the founder of a sweet new English style known as the '*contenance angloise*'.

The characteristic of the new style, which heralded a new musical age, was a distinctive mellifluousness. It used full, rich harmonies based on the third and the sixth of the chord, a bright major tonality and smooth part-writing that included the 'preparation' and 'resolution' of harmonic dissonances. As the fame of English music and Dunstable in particular spread, the *'contenance angloise'* was emulated by great continental composers such as Guillaume du Fay and set a European new fashion. The result was revolutionary for Western music, marking a shift from the more primitive-sounding open harmonies (as heard in the Agincourt Carol) into a style of polyphonic writing that would dominate throughout the Renaissance.

It was almost certainly music in this new style that Henry arranged to be performed before Emperor Sigismund at Canterbury cathedral. One of the works sung might have been Dunstable's own setting of the motet *Preco Preheminencie*. The motet, which honours St John the Baptist, was one of those Henry added to the devotions of the Chapel Royal. Dunstable seems to have taken it as an opportunity to highlight the contrast between his own writing and that of earlier composers: compare the bright major tonality and mellifluous part-writing of *Preco Preheminencie* with, say, the motet *Eya dulcis/Vale placens* by the once-popular French composer Johannes Tapissier.[2] The latter sounds harmonically confused and structurally disunified against the fluent elegance of the former.

Sigismund, we can imagine, would have been as impressed – and surprised – by this fashionable new style of music as he was by Henry's military victories.

More recent scholarship suggests somewhat different circumstances for Dunstable's composition of *Preco Preheminencie*. The
words of the motet, which are, of course, in Latin, include these lines:

> *At first, the suffering homeland*
> *was hard pressed;*
> *verily, the royal court*
> *receives the ones restored.*

This points to a triumphant homecoming after battle. And one was
at hand: the return of Henry's brother, the Duke of Bedford, who
had led the English fleet to victory at the Battle of the Seine.[3]

Dunstable's motet was clearly a hit a court. Its inclusion in Henry's
liturgical reforms as one of the daily memorials to be performed in
the Chapel Royal would thus have been the opportunity to hear a
well-loved piece over and over again. But it was much more. It was a
daily reminder of England's most recent victory in battle – and of the
part played in that victory by the God of Battles, whose name was
invoked by the awe-inducing powers of Dunstable's music.

⬥

Dunstable's music had been borne across the Channel by Henry's
victories and the prestige of England's name; after this he was under
his own steam and his success depended only on the quality of
his music. It was enough. Dunstable's influence on the Continent
spread beyond the reach of even English armies; it also proved to
be longer lasting.

Henry V died in 1422, aged just 35, and was succeeded by his infant son, Henry VI. Few kings have had a finer inheritance than the boy; none has been less worthy of it. He was crowned King of England at the age of six months, and King of France nine years later in a magnificent ceremony in Paris. His double coronation was unique and he was the only king to have worn the crown of both kingdoms. Within three decades he had lost them both as well: France through disastrous military defeat and England through bloody civil war.

There was an exception to this comprehensive record of failure, however: in his commitment to music and the religious destiny of England, Henry VI was his father's true heir. And here, ironically, the permanence of his legacy exceeds his father's. Nothing remains of Henry V's great victories save their names. But the colleges, chapels and choirs founded by his son still delight us with their music today.

He maintained the Chapel Royal in such splendour that it was admired and imitated as far away as Portugal. He also founded twin institutions which have preserved both the ethos and the music of the Chapel Royal right up to the present: Eton College, Windsor, and King's College, Cambridge, over both of which his statue still presides.

Eton has been called the most famous school in the world. But first and foremost it is a *college*: that is to say a community and, by origins, a religious one. Throughout the Middle Ages, the Church had been at the heart of musical life: most musicians worked in some kind of religious establishment, in particular the hundreds of monasteries scattered across the country. But by the fifteenth century there was an upsurge in new religious institutions called 'colleges'. Monasteries were closed communities that, in theory at least, turned their backs on the world. But colleges were 'secular' and were intended to be involved in it.

They were communities nonetheless. Their members lived together in accommodation round a courtyard, ate together in a hall and worshipped together in a chapel. In the late Middle Ages, as these were communities of priests, it was the collective worship of the chapel and its music that was the most important. As well, the colleges had a variety of functions, not just religious, but also educational and charitable, and they were often associated with great castles and houses or noble, wealthy families. It became fashionable for such families to found and endow these institutions, which were seen as invaluable opportunities to advertise their dynastic status, power and piety. Moreover, it was regarded as a wise investment in religious terms: to employ a chapel of priests to pray for your soul was a sure guarantee of gaining favour with God, and avoiding hell or purgatory after death.

Leading the new fashion was the English monarchy. Henry V and his brothers had maintained magnificent chapels as well as splendid choirs which had sung great music. But they had been too busy fighting to have the leisure to found institutions. For Henry VI, on the other hand, personal piety was central to his idea of kingship. He wanted to be remembered, not for his military victories, but for the two great monuments he built in the name of God and his kingdom.

There was another crucial point of continuity with his father: both Eton and King's were dedicated to the Virgin Mary, whom

both father and son regarded as the peculiar patroness and inter-
cessor for England. The formal title of Eton is: 'The King's College
of Our Lady of Eton besides Windsor'. Its coat of arms features the
White Lily, one of the symbols of the Virgin; the coat of arms of
King's features the White Rose, which was another. Both foundation charters depict Henry VI kneeling before Her, with parliament
joining in worship behind. Eton College's beautifully illuminated
charter – which has pride of place in the college archives in Eton's
Old Library – also shows choirs of angels, who blow on trumpets
and, as the charter puts it, 'sing praises to the glory of God'. Henry's
intention was that his foundation would do the same: with the 4
clerks or singing men and 6 choirboys – soon increased to 10 and 16
respectively – echoing the heavenly choirs here on earth.

And where the king's colleges led, others followed. The result
was that this new fashion for founding colleges turned out to be
the best thing that ever happened to English music. Since they
had more money than other religious organisations, colleges were
free to invest heavily in music. And as they were not restricted to
using men who had taken holy orders, they could draw on a much
wider pool of musical talent. Colleges began to employ 'lay clerks'
– full-time, professional singers – and choirs expanded in size and
quality. Once there had been one voice per part; now there were
many. The choral sound became richer and more complex, and
the possibilities for composers to exploit that sound far greater.
And there was strength in numbers, too: hundreds of colleges, all
employing and supporting musicians, were established along the
length and breadth of England during the fifteenth century. It was

musical employment on an unheard-of scale. Talented performers moved easily from one college to another and this new network became a breeding ground for musical creativity. An outpouring of new and complex English polyphonic music followed, laying the foundations for the development of English music over the next two centuries – and far beyond.

Even today we can still see the evidence of the musical infrastructure set up by the kings, bishops and nobles of the fifteenth century: in the colleges of Oxford and Cambridge with their world-famous choirs; in the choir schools such as Eton, King's and Westminster, which still continue to train boys in music; and in the cathedral foundations, many of which are still centres of musical excellence.

But the most important monument of the musical flowering of the fifteenth century is the Eton Choirbook. When it was created it would have been nothing special. True, it was opulent, as befitted a royal foundation, but it was only one of many hundreds of such books, since every college chapel in the country had its own music store with similar collections of its most regularly performed repertory. But the Reformation had led to a holocaust of musical manuscripts, leaving the Eton Choirbook as one of the sole surviving collections of medieval and Tudor polyphony.

As its name suggests, this particular choirbook, preserved through a chance miracle of history, was designed for use at Henry VI's foundation of Eton College. Written in about 1500, it is richly illuminated and enormous – large enough, indeed, for 20 choirboys to sing from with ease. It contains about 50 complete works from 24 different composers; these composers can be categorised into three different groups – early, middle and late – according to the period of the fifteenth century in which they were working. The number of musical parts in later works increased dramatically, reflecting the gradual rise in complexity of English polyphony as its popularity spread and the investment in it rose.

John Dunstable is the most famous – and by far the earliest – composer featured in the first group. John Browne, who rivals Dunstable in terms of talent and reputation, belongs to the middle group, and his importance is demonstrated by the fact that he has more works than any other composer in the Eton Choirbook, including the extraordinary eight-part *O Maria Salvatoris Mater* that was given pride of place as the opening composition in the manuscript. Although Browne is believed to have worked for an aristocratic family's private chapel (most likely the Earl of Oxford's), he also had royal connections, as is shown by his six-part setting of *Stabat iuxta Christi crucem* (Near the cross of Christ stood Mary). This was probably composed for Henry VII's queen, Elizabeth of York, to console her for her own torment following the untimely death of her eldest son, Arthur, Prince of Wales in 1502. The music makes use of a 'cantus firmus': that is, a pre-existing melody that forms the basis for a new composition, which was a characteristic feature of English polyphony at this period. In this case the melody used also has royal associations as it is taken from the carol 'From Stormy Wyndis', which prays for God's protection of 'Arthur oure prynce'. This cantus, coupled with a text that speaks of Mary's mourning for her son Jesus ('Mother of the King of glory/There she saw Him cruelly crowned/Saw the spear his side that wounded/Watched as death overcame her Son'), results in a subtle, complex and poignant memorial to the young prince.

The composer Robert Wylkynson, based at Eton College, belongs to the final and latest group of musicians in the Choirbook. He is responsible for the enormous nine-voice choral work *Salve Regina* (probably written to rival Browne's), as well as the astonishing *Jesus Autem Transiens*, a piece of staggering ambition that uses 12 voices to represent each of the 12 apostles, as well as an extra one to signify Jesus passing through them all. All these pieces were perfectly designed for the cavernous, high-ceilinged college chapels and cathedrals they would have been heard in: lengthy, rich, unbroken walls of sound to fill overflowing lavish, expensive, ornate structures.

The Perpendicular Gothic style was pioneered by royal architects William Ramsey and John Sponlee in the mid-fourteenth century and went on to influence many of the greatest royal buildings of the next 200 years: St George's Chapel, Windsor, the Henry VII Chapel at Westminster Abbey and, above all, Henry VI's two great foundations of Eton and King's College.

The fate of the two buildings was to be very different. Henry VI intended Eton College Chapel to become one of the biggest, richest and holiest churches in England: as long as Lincoln cathedral, as wide as York Minster, his very own Westminster Abbey. But constant changes of plan, which led him to demolish parts already built and start again, meant that only a fragment of the vast scheme was completed when he lost power in 1461. And a fragment it remained: roughly roofed and finished, and with its intended splendours dying with the king who had imagined them.

King's College was Henry VI's twin foundation at Cambridge. It was intended to continue the education which his scholars had begun at Eton – and to maintain a similar cycle of music and prayer. It also suffered from the same problems of the king's overweening ambition and failing resources. At the time of Henry VI's fall, only the foundations of the chapel were complete and only the walls at the east end rose to something like their full height. But the great vault had not even been begun. At first work ceased entirely under Henry VI's supplanter, Edward IV, the first king of the House of York, whose religious patronage focused on the Yorkist family college at Fotheringhay in Northamptonshire and St George's Chapel, Windsor, where Edward is buried. But eventually building resumed and continued rather more purposefully under Richard III, Edward's usurping brother.

In 1485 the House of York fell in turn, when Richard III was defeated and killed by Henry Tudor, Earl of Richmond, at the Battle of Bosworth. Richmond, who ruled as Henry VII, owed his parents' marriage to Henry VI, was named after him and honoured him as his uncle of the half-blood. Alongside these multiple personal obligations, Henry VII also shared Henry VI's religiosity (though without anything of his impracticality) and, towards the end of his reign, his interest in collegiate foundations. This last was much encouraged by his mother, Lady Margaret Beaufort, who was herself the founder of two Cambridge colleges.

The result was that, on a visit to Cambridge in 1507, Henry VII gave King's College £5000 to complete the chapel 'as our uncle intended it'. A further £5000 was supplied by Henry VII's executors after his death, specifically to build the vault. The great work was finished by 1515 and it remained only for Henry VIII to add the magnificent stained-glass windows and carved wooden screen.

Thus completed and scarcely altered since, King's College Chapel stands as the most perfect example, inside and out, of the last flowering of Perpendicular architecture. It is also the perfect place to hear the later works of the Eton Choirbook. What is it that makes King's so perfect a setting for such rich polyphony? In other words, what do the music and the architecture have in common? It is a sense of proportion. A perfect balance between extremes of simplicity and elaboration. And the achievement of almost impossible effects with seemingly effortless technical skill. In the architecture it is the fan vaulting. It looks almost gossamer-light. In fact it is held in place by its very weight, which locks the voussoirs – shaped stones – into place. In the music it is the multitude of different lines that weave together just like the ribs in the vault: each separate, each interlocking with the other into a solid structure of miraculous sound.

Above all, both the music and the architecture are uniquely, archetypically English. And they are almost as exclusively royal – because only kings could afford them.

After the death of Prince Arthur, so eloquently mourned in John Browne's motet, the heir was Henry VII and Elizabeth of York's second son, Henry. Henry was a talented boy: intelligent, athletic and with a dazzling personality. He was also intensely musical and was carefully trained as well, with separate teachers for string and wind instruments. He learned to play the lute, the keyboard, the recorder and the harp (he appears with one as King David in an illumination in his own psalter). He could sing 'from book at sight' and was reported to have a fine voice.[4] He even studied composition.

This meant that the music King's College Chapel was built for was in his blood. He grew up hearing it performed in his father's Chapel Royal. As king himself he patronised its best performers and composers. He even, like his namesake and role model Henry V, composed such music himself.

But there is a difference. Henry V, the story goes, got his bad behaviour out of the way as a young man. Henry VIII's character, on the other hand, darkened and deteriorated as he grew older, and, as it did so, threatened to bring down everything that King's College Chapel stood for: choir, church, music, the lot.

The clue is in the choir screen, the finishing touch that Henry VIII added to the chapel in the 1530s. Amidst the dense filigree of Renaissance ornament, there are repeated interlaced initials, tied with a lover's knot: 'H' and 'A': Henry and Anne Boleyn – his mistress, second wife and the most controversial woman to have sat on the throne of England.

THE YOUNG
HENRY VIII

The year 1509 was an *annus mirabilis* for Henry VIII. The young Henry acceded to the throne on St George's Eve (22 April); he remained in purdah until his father's funeral on 9 May; then, in quick succession, he was married on 11 June, crowned on the 24th and celebrated his eighteenth birthday on the 28th. Not coincidentally, his coronation day, when he was crowned jointly with his new wife, Catherine of Aragon, was Midsummer Day.

The dominion of the Winter King was over; the reign of the Summer Prince had begun and the trumpets blew and the drums rolled to prove it. We do not know the precise liturgical music performed at the coronation, but there are possibilities: one is a partially surviving mass called 'God Save King Harry' by Thomas Ashwell; another is a setting of *Lauda vivi Alpha et O*, by Robert Fayrfax, which contains in its coda a prayer to Henry VIII. But, whatever was performed, we can be sure that it was lavish and impressive. Henry appreciated, as much as his ancestor Henry V, the importance of enhancing royal ceremony by music, and his own musical standards were at least as exacting.

And not only ceremony. Henry wrote poems and composed songs; he sang and danced; he took part in revels and masquerades; he hunted and wrestled and shot; he jousted and tourneyed with swords and rode at the ring; he made love and war. And he did it all to music – much of it of his own composition.

The so-called Henry VIII's Songbook is an extraordinary surviving source of the king's own music. It is a large collection containing over a hundred secular pieces and it gets its name from the fact that Henry, with 33 pieces ascribed to 'The Kynge H. viij', is by far the most frequently named composer in the book. The manuscript is well written and illuminated on parchment, and must be a product of Henry's own inner circle. Quite why it was created is unclear,

Henry VIII's Songbook, which contains 33 of the Tudor king's own compositions. Among them is the catchy folk song 'Pastime with Good Company', which became a national hit in its day.

however. Perhaps it was meant as an anthology of typical secular songs of the period. Or it could have been an educational music book to teach royal and courtier children how to compose – using Henry's own musical progress to do it.

This would account for the fact that the manuscript includes music by Henry from the whole gamut of his composing career: from first steps to musical maturity. Several of the early pieces by the king – such as the four-voice text setting of 'Gentil Prince de Renom' – are faltering and full of mistakes. But this is hardly surprising since the pieces may have been composed when Henry was as young as 11 – and it is no basis on which to judge Henry's compositional skills. Some of the later works, on the other hand, are extremely competent pieces by a young man of marked musical ability. One such is 'Taunder Nakan', a cheerful three-part instrumental work in which the three lines interweave cleverly and the long, elaborate phrases make complete musical sense despite the somewhat over-flamboyant top line. This is a composer in control of his musical material. Of similar quality is the defiant choral song 'Though Some Saith', in which Henry, employing sweet, melancholy melody and pleasing harmonies, defends himself to his critics who accuse of him of being ruled by his youth:

> *Though some saith that youth ruleth me*
> *I trust in age for to tarry*
> *God and my right and my duty*
> *From them shall I never vary*
> *Though some saith that youth ruleth me.*

Most famous of all, and Henry's masterpiece, is 'Pastime with Good Company'. With its raucous words and catchy melody, this song was so popular that it broke out of the court milieu to become a national hit, sung like a folk ballad in houses, taverns and on the street. It was so well known that words from it were used as the text of a sermon by a trendy Tudor vicar. It even became popular abroad.

Pastime with good company
I love and shall until I die
grudge who lust but none deny
so God be pleased thus live will I
for my pastance
hunt sing and dance
my heart is set
all goodly sport
for my comfort
who shall me let?

At first sight it seems very straightforward – all about youth having its fling etc., which is why, no doubt, it was so popular. But, once again, there is an odd quality of defiance about it. This stems from the fact that Henry *had* just been stopped from relaunching Henry V's war on France, which he had come to the throne determined to continue. Instead, his council forced him into a humiliating climbdown. Henry reacted by going into a sort of internal exile, and spending the second summer of his reign – in 1510 – enjoying himself and writing music. And it is then that most of the mature songs in the Henry VIII Manuscript would have been composed.

One song is missing, however, from the songbook. And for good reason: despite popular myth, Henry did *not* write 'Greensleeves'. Instead, the tune is based on an Italian chord progression that only reached England after the king's death.

☙

Nor did Henry limit himself to writing secular works. There is an account in Hall's *Chronicle* that, in that same summer Henry wrote 'Pastime with Good Company', he 'did set .ii goodly masses, every of them five partes, whiche were song oftentimes in hys chapel, afterwards in diverse other places'. Perhaps he was hoping to emulate the Sanctus and Gloria set by Henry V, who, as a legendary warrior and pious Christian, represented the young Henry's ideal of kingship. Unfortunately these masses are now lost (there would have been strong political motivation to suppress Latin text settings by the king during and after the Reformation) but the very fact that he wrote them demonstrates the young king's exceptional energy, and also perhaps that he was a composer of rather greater and more serious ability than is shown in the songbook. Generally, young Henry's compositional ability seems reflective of the precocious talent noticed by all those who encountered him – the Dutch scholar and humanist Erasmus found it hard to believe that a letter he received in 1507 was actually by Henry, such was the quality of the Latin composition – and of a competitive young man who made a point of excelling at everything he did.

Here, then, is something new again: it is words and music as royal autobiography. This makes the songbook a principal – and, by political historians – a much underused source for understanding the character of the young king. Henry, of course, was by no means the only member of his court to compose words and music. But for a man of his unique status, for whom self-image was everything, thus to expose himself artistically in front of his peers and elders and court denotes either bravery or arrogance, or some combination of the two – as inscrutable and as notable in its way as the breathtaking self-confidence the king demonstrated in his political actions in his later years.

But, finally, the main point is more simple: the king clearly loved music – to perform and to listen to, as well as to compose – perhaps more than any other monarch before or since. There are numerous contemporary accounts that confirm this. In July 1517, for example, he listened for four hours on end to the playing of the Venetian organist Dionisio Memo, whom Henry employed as a favoured performer at his court. That same year he also made the court listen 'to a lad who played upon the lute, better than ever was heard, to the amazement of his Majesty, who never wearies of him'.

The result was that, with Henry's accession, musical activity at court took on a new lease of life. But more was involved than personal passion. Henry's ambition was to have the grandest and most magnificent court in Europe: a court to cow his enemies and impress his rivals; to give visiting diplomats something to write home about – literally; to convey to his subjects and everyone else that the English monarchy was glorious once again.

Music was all part of the plan. Funded by a large inheritance left him by his father, Henry set about creating the most vibrant musical establishment the country had ever seen. He employed an unprecedented number of musicians – nearly a hundred by the end of his reign – which was two or three times the number serving any other institution in England. And he employed none but the best. The result was that royal life was like a grand tapestry unrolling to a perpetual soundtrack of music, much of it merely incidental, but some that was intended to be listened to, to varying degrees. Fanfares of trumpets and drums heralded the arrival of the king and queen and distinguished visitors; horns blew signals in the royal hunt, and trumpet blasts punctuated jousts and tournaments; music for voices and instruments accompanied meals; string music beat out the time for dancing and lutes, and soft voices accompanied royal love-making and enticed the king to repose.

And that was just the music of the secular life of the court. Here was a clear distinction of status and favour between the musicians who played 'haut' (loud) instruments – trumpets, drums, as well as raucous wind instruments such as shawms and sackbuts – and those who played 'bas' (soft) instruments – lutes, flutes and keyboards. The former blasted out fanfares in the tiltyard and for royal processions, functioning just like a modern military band. Their music was simple and stirring; sometimes they even performed on horseback and often in outdoor spaces (court painter Hans Holbein's *Musicians on a Balcony* depicts this kind of ensemble). The latter were reserved for more intimate occasions and informal concerts.

This division by type of instrument also corresponded more or less to the strict rules of court access which musicians, like everyone else, had to abide by. The Privy Chamber was the most intimate living and working area of the monarch, into which only those particularly favoured by the king were allowed. All others – that is, the vast majority of persons at court – were restricted to the more public Presence Chamber and the Guard Chamber, the latter of which was open to courtiers of all ranks.

Henry possessed a private body of personally selected musicians in the Privy Chamber. These musicians, mostly lute and keyboard players, some of whom doubled up as singers as well, were highly skilled and highly paid virtuoso soloists, who performed for Henry's personal pleasure in his private quarters. They also taught the royal children and one of them, the composer and lutenist Philip van Wilder, acted as curator of the king's impressive collection of musical instruments and director of his private music. We can speculate on the sort of music they would have performed: secular songs like those found in the Henry VIII Songbook (for example, the cheerful and cheekily erotic song 'Blow Thy Horn, Hunter' by William Cornysh, of whom more shortly) as well as instrumental music, like the beautiful French chansons (for lute and keyboard) by van Wilder.

For sacred music, the rules were reversed, and it was the performers of the public spaces of the Chapel Royal who mattered. The Chapel Royal – now consisting of 12 Children and 32 Gentlemen (the men would have probably sung in rotation, not all at once) – provided the king with a daily round of elaborately sung choral services, just as it had done for Henry V a century earlier.

The Chapel Royal was known to be the finest choir in England and one of the finest in Europe, a fact of which Henry was justifiably proud and exploited shamelessly. Sagudino, secretary to the Venetian ambassador, tells how, in May 1515, Henry 'wooed' diplomats by inviting them to the Chapel to hear mass:

> *His Majesty invited the Ambassador and all their retinue to hear Mass and dine with him; so we went to church, and after a very grand procession had been made, high mass was chanted ... and it was sung by his Majesty's choristers, whose voices were really rather divine than human; they did not chant, but sang like angels ... and as for the counter-bass voices, I don't think they have their equals in the world.*[5]

Such exposure meant that the Chapel Royal was under pressure to maintain the very highest standards of performance.

Then, as now, attention focused principally on the boys of the choir, who regularly stole the show with their angelic demeanour and precocious talents. Such does not come naturally and considerable effort went into providing for their education, wellbeing and discipline. They were looked after by the 'Master of the Children' of the Chapel Royal, who was responsible not only for their selection and musical education, but also for mundane matters like their board and lodging. From 1509 the post was held by William Cornysh the Younger. Between 1509 and 1517, several royal choristers boarded with Cornysh, and from June 1517 onwards all 12 of them did. It must have been quite a job: the choristers were all aged between

7 and 14 years old (depending on when their voices broke), and out of their cassocks were a normal bunch of rowdy little boys. But they were extraordinary singers, and highly sought after by their patrons.

They even became a source of friction between Henry and his principal minister, the Cardinal-Chancellor, Thomas Wolsey. Wolsey had built a magnificent palace at Hampton Court, where he kept a court – and chapel – every bit as lavish as Henry's own. Indeed, rumour had it that the cardinal's choir was better than the king's. Matters seem to have come to a head at the turn of 1517–18 when the Twelve Days of Christmas gave abundant opportunities for the rival choirs to show off their skills. Henry was mortified that Wolsey's choir was the clear winner, trouncing his own, especially when it came to sight-reading a new composition. To redress the balance somewhat Wolsey, ever the courtier, deemed it politic to offer the king a boy called Robin,[6] who was one of the stars of his own choir. The king leapt at the offer and kept badgering until the boy arrived safely at court. There he lived up to his promise, both as a singer of composed polyphony and in his ability to improvise descant to plainsong. Cornysh, whose nose must have been out of joint, had to acknowledge the boy's skills and congratulate Richard Pigott, the Master of the Children of Wolsey's choir, 'for the teaching of him'. Wolsey, when the circumstances were right, played the same game himself and poached 'one Clement of my chapel, which singeth a base part', from William Warham, archbishop of Canterbury.

The Chapel Royal was also a useful pool of performers for secular entertainments at court. Its members took part in pageants, 'disguisings' and other revels, of which Cornysh, extending his

administrative and creative role, acted as actor-manager and dramatist. He was well suited to the task. Like many choirmasters, Cornysh
had a flamboyant personality and a colourful character: he was a wit,
who dared to joke with the king; a romantic who wrote numerous
love songs – and perhaps even a bit of a scoundrel, too. In 1504 he
was sent to the notorious Fleet prison off what is now Farringdon
Street in London; his offence is unknown, but while inside he wrote
a poem which protests at his wrongful accusation[7] and is rich in
imagery derived from his musical experience.

But his closest relationships were with his choirboys who were
often the stars of his productions. The boys could do serious drama,
as in a pageant which included 'comely mermaids, one of them a man
mermaide, the other a woman ... and in ever of the said mermaids a
Childe of the Chapell singing right sweetly and with quaint harmony'.
But they were even better – and certainly enjoyed themselves much
more – in comedy, as in the Shrove Tuesday revel of 1522 when eight
of the boys (of Wolsey's chapel, as it happened), blacked up and in
drag, led the resistance to Henry and his lords when they stormed a
pasteboard castle. First the lads threw rosewater and sweet cakes at
the besiegers; then, as things hotted up, they resorted to bows and
balls before three of them hurled part of their valuable disguises as
well. Cornysh himself, playing the speaking part of Ardent Desire
and arrayed in robes of crimson satin embroidered with burning
flames, marshalled the assault on the castle and presumably tried
(not very successfully) to stop the boys going too far.

Cornysh also played his part in the most lavish entertainment of
them all: the Field of Cloth of Gold in 1520. This meeting between

Henry VIII and Francis I, King of France, was engineered by Cardinal Wolsey and was intended as a turning point in the poisonous history of Anglo-French relations. Instead, it became an immediate byword for the futility and senseless extravagance that has dogged summit conferences from that day to this.

The idea of a permanent, as opposed to a merely tactical, peace with France represented a reversal of everything that Henry had stood for hitherto. He had come to the throne determined to renew the Hundred Years War with France and to carry it to triumphant conclusion. His jousts were intended to train a new warrior elite of companions-in-arms for this great enterprise. As well as being a love match, his marriage to Catherine of Aragon was intended to cement an alliance with Spain against France. At first all went well, and in 1513 Henry commanded in person the largest and best-equipped English army to invade France since the days of Henry V. He defeated the French at the so-called Battle of the Spurs; captured the major city of Tournai; wrecked French ambitions in Italy and turned European power politics upside down.

Not since the time of Agincourt had the reputation of English arms stood so high in Europe. And, as at Agincourt, the English celebrated with music. One song in the Henry VIII Manuscript, the anonymous work 'England, Be Glad!', is a product of these early, heady days of the war of 1513:

England, be glad! pluck up thy lusty heart!
Help now thy king, thy king, and take his part!

Against the Frenchmen in the field to fight
In the quarrel of the Church and in the right
With spears and shields on goodly horses light,
Bows and arrows to put them all to flight.

But the optimism could not last. A new King of France, Francis I, as ambitious as Henry and even younger, succeeded the decrepit Louis XII and the superiority of French resources began to tell. Wolsey, with his usual panache, now presented the case for peace as effectively as he had once driven forward the war. Above all, he made peace palatable by pandering to Henry's appetite for magnificence: the Field of Cloth of Gold, as he envisaged it, would wrap the doubtful business of peace-making in a splendid display of competitive feasting, jousting and entertainments. Rivalry with France would still be there. But – rather as in the modern Olympic Games – national enmities would be shifted from the battlefield to peaceful, if intense, competition in spectacle, the tiltyard – and the choir.

Music played a key role in this exercise in the politics of splendour. All the Gentlemen and boys of the choir were shipped across the Channel, along with 'a very beautiful silver organ, with gold ornaments', and other instruments that were used for secular entertaining. It was a pretty good deal for the Gentlemen, who were paid handsomely to attend, and were given the extra perk of unlimited free wine during the course of the trip. The ceremonies reached a climax on Midsummer Eve, 23 June, when the chapels of the English and French monarchs combined forces to sing the final mass. Wolsey himself was the celebrant and the two choirs took it in turns to sing the service:

About noon the English legate commenced the high mass De Trini-
tate. The first introit was sung by the English chanters, the second
by the French. They had arranged that when the French organist
played the French chanters should sing and vice versa.

The alternation continued, with the French singing the Kyrie and the English the Gloria and so on through the ordinary of the mass. Mostly the choirs were accompanied by their respective organs. But for the Credo, sung by the French, sackbuts and fifes lent an added flourish. The service concluded with several motets, which offered further opportunity for choral pyrotechnics.

The alternation of choirs, like the careful reciprocity of all the ceremonial at the Field of Cloth of Gold, was intended to emphasise the parity between the English and French. But, with the eyes of all Europe on the event, the mass also offered the perfect opportunity for a competitive display in which the two choirs, both enjoying a high international reputation, showed off their performance skills – and the abilities of their respective composers. As it happened, two of the most prominent composers of each nation were present: Jean Mouton and Robert Fayrfax. At 56 years old, Fayrfax was a Chapel Royal veteran, having been a Gentleman for over 20 years, and he was almost certainly personally known to Henry. Both Mouton and Fayrfax had composed showpieces that would have been ideal for the occasion and perhaps we can imagine the French concluding by singing Mouton's dazzling *Nesciens mater Virgo virum*, a complex canon in eight parts and the English, Robert Fayrfax's five-voice Magnificat *Regale*. This particular Magnificat setting is certainly elaborate enough to befit the splendour of the occasion, alternating plainchant sections with complex polyphony, showing off to perfection Fayrfax's facility for counterpoint writing.

Secular musicians, or 'minstrels', also accompanied Henry on his trip across the Channel, and music was a significant part of the nightly revels put on by both the French and English courts. We know that William Cornysh was responsible, as he was now back home, for devising the pageants performed during banquets on Sunday nights (as well as maintenance of the ten young choristers who attended the occasion). These pageants most likely combined speech, song, dancing and scenic effects. Some of the music included was probably written by Cornysh himself: for example, his wonderfully melodramatic song 'Adieu My Hertes Lust', where the narrator is tearfully bidding farewell to his lover. No doubt Henry VIII, who was a dab hand at love songs himself, approved.

The Field of Cloth of Gold failed in its immediate political mission and England and France were at each other's throats again in a matter of months. But the event was a success in cultural terms. We know that this meeting, and others like it, encouraged exchange and inspiration for composers on both sides of the Channel and there are numerous examples of forms, structures and even melodies shared between English and French composers. In France, Claude Gervaise wrote 'Pavane D'Angleterre', a polished dance setting of the well-known English ballad 'Heaven and Earth', which he had perhaps

picked up during a rowdy night of ballad-playing at the Field of
Cloth of Gold. In England, several new European dances appeared
at court; one fashionable form in particular, called the 'pavan', would
become one of the staples of the courtly dance genre.

In general, English musicians throughout the 1520s were
becoming increasingly cosmopolitan, as a result not only of journeys by the court aboard, but also of an increased Continental
presence at Henry VIII's court. Throughout his reign, Henry
employed more foreign musicians than any previous monarch,
from the aforementioned Dutch lutenist Philip van Wilder to the
Jewish-Italian families of instrumentalists like the Lupos and the
Bassanos, who fled Italy to escape the Inquisition and remained in
royal employ for decades to come. By 1526, 20 out of 28 court musicians[8] – that is, over two-thirds – were foreigners. Henry himself
keenly collected compositions by foreign masters, as his own songbook demonstrates. One work, 'En Vray Amoure', is a reworking by
the king himself of a vigorous French chanson by the internation-
ally renowned composer Loyset Compère.[9]

Such Continental influences were responsible for broadening
the creative outlook of musicians who worked at the English court:
it encouraged them to experiment with unusual forms and styles,
and even to write for new instruments, such as the viol (which first
arrived in England around this time[10]). And it was through court
that such novel musical fashions were disseminated into the wider
musical community, as aristocratic households across the country
emulated the king by setting up personal musical establishments.

Within a few years of the Field of Cloth of Gold, Henry's prodigious extravagance in both war and peace was beginning to tell. The fortune Henry had inherited from his father was long spent and the patience of his subjects for further taxation was wearing thin. In such circumstances retrenchment was inevitable. As usual, Wolsey stepped in. Henry spent a symbolically modest Christmas at his childhood home of Eltham; then, in January 1526, the cardinal published the reforming Eltham Ordinances, which imposed cutbacks on all departments of the royal household.

The Chapel Royal was not spared. The full complement of 32 Gentlemen and 12 Children was to officiate only when the king was staying in his principal residences; at all other times, and 'specially in riding journeys and progresses', the Chapel was to be reduced to a skeleton staff of six men and six boys. The elaborate round of Chapel Royal services was to be correspondingly trimmed: on weekdays, Wolsey (himself a prince of the Church) declared, a mass of Our Lady in the morning would suffice, while on Sundays and holidays the choir should also sing the mass of the day and an anthem in the afternoon.

The contrast with the devotional opulence and intensity of Henry's former role model of Henry V is striking. Otherwise, the effect of the Eltham Ordinances on the Chapel Royal has been much exaggerated. The Chapel Royal still remained peripatetic. Whenever the king wished to make a show, the whole complement of the Chapel still accompanied him on journeys – whether in England, as on the grand royal progress to York in 1541, or abroad, as in his second summit conference with Francis I in 1532. The real change effected by the Eltham Ordinances was a different one. A clear hierarchy of royal residences now began to emerge, with a marked distinction between a handful of the larger palaces and the rest. The former became 'standing houses' and were kept more or less fully furnished; the latter were treated as mere hunting boxes or stopovers.

And it was, of course, for the standing houses that Henry created the magnificent Chapel Royal interiors which have come down to us: at Hampton Court, with its blue and gold vault, gorgeously carved with pendant angels blowing trumpets; or at St James's, with the ultra-fashionable pattern of its barrel-vaulted ceiling copied from a design by the Italian architect Sebastiano Serlio.

Nevertheless, the Chapel Royal *was* a bellwether. The partial curtailment of its ceremonies and establishment – like the Eltham Ordinances themselves – was a symptom of a broader malaise in the mid-years of Henry's reign. For Henry had failed, whether he admitted it or not, and failed by the standards he had set himself. He had failed to conquer France; failed to maintain his court as a second Camelot; his marriage had even failed the most fundamental test of all and failed to produce a male heir.

But at least Henry was in love again.

HENRY VIII: ANNE BOLEYN AND REFORM

Anne Boleyn – though she was the sister of one of Henry's former mistresses – was unlike any woman Henry had met before. She had spent a large part of her youth across the Channel as maid of honour to Queen Claude of France, and her demeanour, manners, tastes and even her preferred language were all unmistakably French. She was witty, intelligent and sharp-tongued, as well as being graceful and an excellent dancer. She was not beautiful exactly – at least by contemporary canons of beauty. But she was alluring, smouldering even, with fine dark eyes. She was also well-educated; interested in poetry and literature; receptive to ideas of religious reform – and, naturally, well versed in music. She played the lute, harp and rebec[11] and could sing well.

In short, Anne was the ideal object of the game of courtly love of which the young Henry, in his role as Prince Charming, had been a past master. Henry was ageing somewhat now but it was almost certainly while playing this game that they met. Henry had probably first noticed Anne in the Shrove Tuesday revel in 1522, when she played one of the female Virtues who, with the enthusiastic assistance of the boys of Wolsey's Chapel as the female Vices, had resisted the attack of Henry and his court favourites on their hearts. Sometime later – when exactly is unclear – Henry started to bombard Anne with long, elaborate letters written in French in the high courtly style:

> *I and my heart put ourselves in your hands, begging you to recommend us to your good grace and not to let absence lessen your affection, for it were great pity to increase their pain.*

Henry, troubadour-like, probably wooed Anne in song as well. Indeed, the surviving love songs written by the king use texts with just the same high-flown, courtly language as his early love letters to Anne.

> *O My Heart, and o my heart;*
> *My heart it is so sore*
> *Since I must needs from my love depart*
> *And know no cause wherefore.*

But this song in particular, set to a yearning, melancholy melody, seems to hint at something deeper – even to have been conjured from the very depths of Henry's soul.

And that is what happened. Henry's love for Anne, beginning as a game, became an all-consuming passion that would brook no opposition. Only Latin would do now to express its seriousness: it was *aut illic, aut nullibi* – 'either there [marriage] or nowhere', as Henry wrote to Anne in early January 1527.

But, of course, there *was* opposition: from Henry's wife, Catherine of Aragon; from her nephew, the Holy Roman Emperor Charles V; from the Pope, whose predecessor had permitted Henry to marry his brother's widow, as Catherine then was; from Henry's family, his friends and his people. It was Henry (and Anne) against the world: *aut illic, aut nullibi*.

First to go was Wolsey, destroyed for his failure to get Rome onside. Then, one by one, by fair means and foul, the remaining obstacles were overcome until Henry and Anne had what they wanted. She was married, bigamously, in January 1533, acknowledged as queen at Easter and crowned on Whitsunday.

Anne's coronation was celebrated lavishly, beginning with a grand river pageant from Greenwich the day before. The procession was headed by a boat with a fire-breathing dragon and 'terrible monstrous wild men' making hideous noises; next came the lord mayor's barge transporting 'shawms, sackbuts, and divers other instruments' and finally the barges – dozens of them – of the London livery companies, 'every company having melody in his barge by himself'. Thomas Cranmer, the newly appointed archbishop of Canterbury, who had at last granted Henry his divorce, was particularly struck by the music: 'all the ways playing, making great melody, which, as is reported was as comely done as never was like in any time nigh to our remembrance', he wrote to a friend. The music continued on land, when a 'choir of singing men and children', which 'sang new ballads made in praise of her grace', sere-naded Anne from the roof of St Martin's.

Anne had indeed got what she wanted: she was sailing in Cath-erine's barge and would shortly wear her crown and sleep in her bed. But not for long. Just three years later, Anne was dead, and her downfall was linked inseparably to the fate of one of the king's musi-cians. Anne was charged with adultery, incest and sexual perversion in a trumped-up indictment that linked her carnally to five differ-ent men, including her own brother. But her real crimes were less exotic. She had failed to adjust from the dominant role of mistress to the submissive role of wife – and, above all, she had failed to give Henry a son. The humblest of the men accused as one of her accomplices was Mark Smeaton, a handsome musician who played the lute, virginals, viol and organ. He had also played the game of courtly love. And with fatal consequences.

At the Royal College of Music in London is an illuminated music manuscript that probably belonged to Anne Boleyn. It contains 39 religious motets and 3 secular chansons, all of which seem carefully chosen for their topical relevance to her brief reign. The majority of the works are in praise of the Virgin Mary or prayers to female saints in which the name 'Anne' figures strongly; two further pieces by the French court composer Jean Mouton, who had been in attendance at the Field of Cloth of Gold, place strong emphasis on childbearing. This was a theme of huge concern to Anne, who was under constant pressure to produce a male heir for Henry. (Her one surviving child was a daughter, Elizabeth.) There are visual links, too: one illumination in the manuscript shows a female head with a long, characterful face and prominent chin that is almost a caricature of Anne's known appearance; other illuminations illustrate the falcon, Anne's badge or emblem, and the pomegranate emblem of Anne's rival, Catherine of Aragon; there are even representations of a falcon, wings extended, pecking furiously at a pomegranate!

It is highly likely that Mark Smeaton compiled this manuscript for Anne himself[12] – it is not of great quality, suggesting that it was created by someone of modest rank, but with court connections and an acquaintance with Anne's tastes in music. Perhaps Smeaton was aware that Anne's star at court was waning and wanted to provide some solace; or perhaps Anne requested it herself, wanting to find in music an expression for her mounting troubles.

It might also contain the clue to her fall, since, among the improving sacred works, the three French chansons strike a raffish note. 'I will give you joy, my love, and lead you where your hope lies', one voice promises romantically. 'I would be really sad at your death!' the other voice answers in impudent mockery. This is music. But the tone is strikingly similar to the smart repartee of the real-life exchanges of Anne and her supposed lovers which supplied the sole (and very inadequate evidence) of her alleged affairs. As a performer, Smeaton would be expected to sing the songs – and with feeling; but, as a mere musician, he could not take part in the parallel game of courtly love in which life imitated art.

The distinction seems to have been obvious to everybody apart from Smeaton himself. For he was a pushy performer. 'You, Mark,' another member of Anne's circle remonstrated, 'maker of poor songs, by reciting them to me more than is right, make them worse … Anything overdone is unwelcome; it is an old saying that even honey, if taken too much, becomes bitter.' He was pushy socially, too, anxious to distance himself from his humble origins and eager to grasp at the money-making opportunities offered by his new status as royal darling. Here the Latin wordplay between his name, *Marcus* and *macer* (thin) opened the way to a cruel jibe at his lithe dancer's body. 'Curb your hunger for riches, check your thirst for gain', he was warned, 'or you will be asked, Mark, why are you still so thin?'

In short, Mark, on the back of his looks and musical talents, had risen too far, too fast: from the cottage where his father worked as a carpenter and his mother spun, to the pampered heart of the Tudor court, where he was the delight and plaything of Henry and Anne. Not surprisingly he was confused. The confusion came to a head on that fatal Saturday, 29 April 1536. Anne went into her Presence Chamber or Throne Room where she found Mark standing in one of the great bay windows. He was pensive, probably extravagantly so, in the manner of a lovesick swain. It was an attitude he had struck often enough when performing a haunting love song. Then he had been applauded. Now the circumstances were different: he was no longer singing and had crossed over the forbidden boundary from performance to real life.

Anne's reaction was different, too: then she had petted him; now she was provoked into administering a stinging rebuke. 'Why are you so sad?' she asked. 'It was no matter,' he replied. And then, still in character, he sighed. Anne's patience snapped. 'You may not look to have me speak to you as I should do to a nobleman,' she said, 'because you be an inferior person.' 'No, no, Madam,' he answered, 'a look sufficed me, and thus fare you well.'

But in the Tudor court, windows, like walls, had ears. Henry was desperately anxious to be rid of Anne and his new minister, Thomas Cromwell, had been charged to find the means. Poor, vain Smeaton's silly posturings provided the perfect grist to this cruel mill. Within 24 hours Smeaton had been arrested, interrogated and tortured into confessing adultery with the queen. He was the only one of her supposed lovers to admit to anything. But it was enough and the queen and the five men charged with her were condemned and executed.

And all because of a musician who spoke out of turn!

'Mrs A. Bolleyne nowe thus: o o o ∅', someone wrote in Smeaton's music book for Anne. The musical phrase – reminiscent of 'the fate motif' in Beethoven's Fifth Symphony – says it all: three short years of marriage and then the sudden, terrible finality of downfall and death. And, it seemed also, oblivion. Anne's body was taken the few yards from the scaffold on Tower Green to the Chapel of St Peter ad Vincula and hastily buried in a bow-stave chest. Within 24 hours Henry was betrothed to Jane Seymour and ten days later they were married. It did not matter that Jane had stepped to the throne through blood. Both her predecessors were dead and, by any reckoning, Jane was Henry's lawful wife. Similarly, when she gave birth to Henry's longed-for son, Edward, on 12 October 1537 that child, too, was indisputably legitimate and, as it was male, indisputably the heir.

Twelve days later Jane died of puerperal fever. But for Henry she would always be his one true wife next to whom he would be buried at Windsor. He gave her a more immediate memorial as well in the great dynastic mural Hans Holbein was ordered to paint on the walls of the Privy Chamber in Henry's new palace of Whitehall. Two generations of the Tudor royal family are arranged on carpeted steps around a large, altar-like monument in the centre. Henry – legs astride and arms akimbo – and Jane, painted posthumously,

This engraving gives an impression of what Hans Holbein's famous mural at Whitehall Palace looked like; the original was of course destroyed when the palace burned down in 1698. The painting depicts Henry VIII (left) next to his parents (centre) Henry VII and Elizabeth of York, along with the King's third wife, Jane Seymour (right).

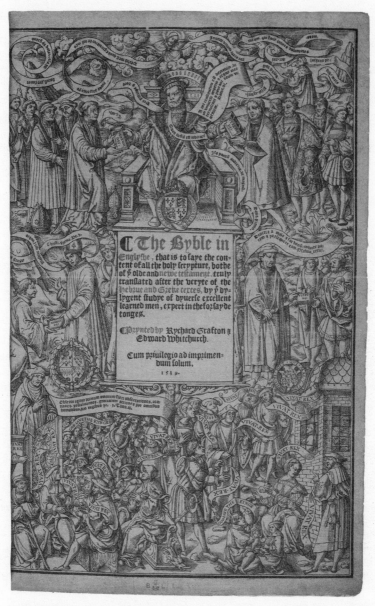

Hans Holbein, Henry VIII's favourite royal painter, is believed to have designed this extraordinary title page to the Great Bible, which was published in 1539. The Great Bible was the first authorised bible to be printed in English and made available to congregants throughout Henry VIII's newly-reformed Church of England.

appear in the foreground; behind and above are Henry's parents, Henry VII and Elizabeth of York. The central monumental panel is inscribed with Latin verses, which are, in effect, a joint epitaph for the first two Tudor kings.

Both Henry and his father are great, the verses declare. But which was the greater? Henry VII, they answer, was great because he brought to an end the Wars of the Roses and gave peace to a distracted country. But Henry VIII was still greater, they claim.

The son, born indeed for greater things, from the altar
Removed the unworthy, and put worthy men in their place.
To [his] unerring virtue the presumption of Popes has yielded
And while Henry VIII wielded the sceptre in his hand
Religion has been restored, and during his reign
The doctrines of God have begun to be honoured.

It is Jane who appears in the painting. But, ironically, it is Anne Boleyn who is really commemorated by these bombastic verses. It was to marry Anne that Henry had had to break with the Pope and declare himself Supreme Head of the Church. And it was Anne who had introduced Henry to the ideas of religious reform – and to the books that carried the ideas of reform like a virus.

Here it is the composition of the mural that is striking. At first sight it is – with the huge slab of Latin text at its centre – puzzling. But a moment's reflection shows it to be modelled on the illustrated title page of a book. With the invention of printing less than 50 years old, the early sixteenth century was the great age of the book. And of one book in particular: the Bible. Holbein, or a close follower, also designed the title page for the Great Bible of 1539. In so doing he created an image of Henry VIII's kingship worthy to stand alongside the Whitehall Mural itself.

At the top, borne up on clouds, is Christ. As the Redeemer, He brings the Bible, inscribed as *Verbum Dei*, the 'Word of God', to mankind. But He hands the actual book over only to Henry VIII, who, gigantic, enthroned and bonneted even in the presence of the Lord, dominates the composition. Henry, in turn, gives the Bible to his Bishops, headed by Archbishop Cranmer, who has set aside his mitre, on his right, and to his lay Privy Councillors, headed by a bareheaded Cromwell, on his left. Cranmer and Cromwell, in turn, pass on the Bible to clergy and laity respectively, while below are the fruits of its distribution. On one side, a preacher in a high pulpit expounds the Word of God to an intently attentive congregation; on the other, a gaol incarcerates those who reject or abuse the Good Book. And all – even, rather implausibly, the prisoners – cry in gratitude, *Vivat Rex*, 'God Save the King'.

Here we see the Supremacy in action as Henry intended it. As the 'Supreme Head of the Church of England in Earth only under Christ' (to give him his full title), Henry was – as he is presented here on the title page – the sole mediator between God and the English. As such, it was up to him to decide the speed and extent of reform and, in particular, whether, when and how far the Bible in English should be made available to his subjects. It is an extraordinary vision: blasphemous, megalomaniac, monstrously and capriciously cruel in its application and yet magnificent in its way. Even more remarkably, such was the force of Henry's personality, the vision was, and remained, the reality until the hour of Henry's death.

Then the floodgates opened.

ᴄ∞ᴐ

But the writing had been on the wall long before then – even when the writing was in still in Latin rather than in English. The idea of *sola Scriptura* ('by Scripture alone') had been given its first and most influential exposition in Latin by the great Dutch scholar Erasmus. Lured to England by promises (unfulfilled as it turned out) of the young Henry's lavish patronage of scholars, Erasmus had spent the first half-dozen or so years of Henry's reign labouring within the libraries of Cambridge where he had prepared his revolutionary new translation of the New Testament from the original Greek into Latin, and his even more revolutionary *Commentaries* on the biblical text. Taken together, these presented the case that the Gospels as the Word of God – and not tradition, or canon law, or papal authority – were the true and only guide to morality and religion.

And even to music. Indeed, for Erasmus the great tradition of English polyphonic music, which we see as one of the glories of the late medieval English Church, represented in microcosm everything that was wrong with it. We can dissent from the judgement, but we have to admit that Erasmus knew what he was talking about. He was a familiar face at court where he would have heard the Chapel Royal in full voice; he had visited Canterbury and was on the friendliest terms with the then archbishop, William Warham, while, as a resident of Queens' College, Cambridge, he had lived next door to the great Chapel of King's College, which was then rapidly approaching completion.

Unfortunately, such familiarity bred contempt: Erasmus hated the lot. He set out his objections at length in his *Commentary* on I Corinthians 14. In this chapter on the conduct of worship, St Paul emphasises that the first and basic criterion of any utterance in church, however ecstatic, is that it should be *understood*. 'I thank my God, I speak with tongues more than ye all,' St Paul writes: 'Yet in the church I had rather speak five words with my understanding, that by my voice I might teach others also, than ten thousand words in an unknown tongue.'

To drive home his point, St Paul observes that even musical sounds, if they are to serve their purpose, must be unambiguous. 'For if the trumpet give an uncertain sound,' he demands, 'who shall prepare himself to the battle?'

This discussion of music and meaning gives Erasmus the perfect opportunity to launch his diatribe. He begins by attacking the prevalence of polyphony, with its sacrifice of the clarity of the words to the complexity of the music:

> *In some countries the whole day is now spent in endless singing, yet one worthwhile sermon exciting true piety is hardly heard in six months, ... not to mention the kind of music that has been brought into divine worship, in which not a single word can be understood. Nor is there a free moment for the singers to contemplate what they are singing.*

By its very elaboration, he continues, this music encourages the wrong approach to church services. Instead of humbling themselves in worship, people come to enjoy the music:

> *We have brought into the sacred edifices a certain elaborate and theatrical music … Straight trumpets, curved trumpets, pipes and sambucas resound everywhere, and vie with human voices … People flock to church as to a theatre for aural delights.*

The means, in Erasmus's view, are as bad as the end since, to maintain this quality of music, a tribe of professional musicians – 'the dregs of humanity … as a great many are drunken revelers' – have to be employed on 'large salaries', together with 'crowds of children who spend every summer in practicing such warblings, meanwhile studying nothing of value'. The cost is substantial and wholly unjustified since it diverts the resources of the Church from its proper function of charitable relief.

Which brings him to his English experience. The worst and most extreme examples of all these practices, Erasmus states feelingly, are to be found in the musical tradition of the English Church:

> *These activities are so pleasing to monks, especially the English, that they perform nothing else … They think God is pleased with ornamental neighings and agile throats. In this custom also in Benedictine Colleges in Britain young boys, adolescents and professional singers are supported, who sing the morning service to the Virgin mother with a very melodious interweaving of voices and organs.*

He concludes with a contemptuous sideswipe at descant and impro-visation, the glory of the boy chorister's art:

> *Those who are more doltish than really learned in music are not content on feast days unless they can use a certain distorted kind of music called descant. This neither gives forth the pre-existing melody nor observes the harmonies of the art. In addition, when temperate music [that is, plainsong] is used in church ... so that the meaning of the words may come more easily to listener, it also seems a fine thing to some if one or other part, intermingled with the rest, [is ornamented and] produces a tremendous tonal clamour, so that not a single word is understood.*

Oh dear! Through the distorting glass of Erasmus's diatribe, we can glimpse the whole world of late medieval English church music we have described so far: the Chapel Royal and the colleges of the Lancastrian and Tudor kings, with their lavishly funded choirs of men and boys; the professional singers and choirmasters they employed, like William Cornysh, who were, indeed, the records show, prone to hit the bottle; the composers, like Dunstable and Fayrfax, with their development of steadily richer and more complex sonorities; the choirboys, like Robin, traded for their skill in descant, and the patrons like Wolsey and Henry VIII himself, who acted as financiers-cum-impresarios to the ecclesiastical concerts performed by their virtuoso choirs. All are arraigned by Erasmus before the judgement seat of *sola Scriptura*, all are found wanting and all are condemned.

But what is really striking is how quickly the condemnation took effect. Erasmus had written his diatribe in 1516. Only 20 years later, in 1536 the Dissolution of the Monasteries began in England. Monasteries were another target of Erasmus's wrath. With their elaborate rules and rituals, their relics, shrines and pseudo-miracle-working images; their encouragement of pilgrimages; their failure to engage with the real lives of ordinary Christian men and women – yes, and their elaborate musical establishments – the monasteries embodied everything that Erasmus thought worst about 'traditional' religion. From Henry's point of view, there were more mundane motives at work as well. The monasteries were rich and the Dissolution poured that wealth into the royal coffers, as their land and buildings, the gold, silver and jewels of their altar and ornaments, even the very lead from their roofs were confiscated by the crown in an unprecedented orgy of sacrilege.

The impact on church music was severe. The monasteries – along with the collegiate churches – were the institutions where English music was born and developed; where polyphony was invented; where musicians were educated; where sacred music was composed and performed on a daily basis. They were institutions that musicians depended on, not just for the nurturing of their creative impulses, but for their education, livelihoods, and for their bed and board. By 1540 it was over as the last of the 500-odd English monasteries followed the rest into oblivion. Erasmus, who had died in 1536, was not there to see it. But those great Benedictine foundations, whose Lady Chapels with their professional choirs and elaborate daily devotions in honour of the Virgin, had so offended him, were dead, too.

The Old Hall Manuscript, one of the earliest collections of English part music in existence, which contains a Gloria (shown here) and a Sanctus by a composer mysteriously named 'Roy Henry'. The most likely identity of Roy Henry is King Henry V himself.

The extraordinary Perpendicular Gothic architecture of King's College Chapel. The history of the college lives up to its royal name: founded in 1446 by Henry VI, and continued by Richard III, Henry VII and Henry VIII, its musical reputation was as highly regarded in Tudor England as it is today.

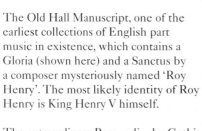

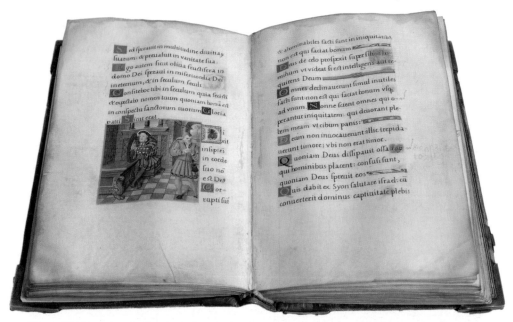

Henry VIII's psalter (collection of psalms), which the king would have used personally for his private devotions. This page depicts Henry playing the harp, flattering him by aligning him to the biblical King David who played the same instrument. Henry may not have actually played the harp, but he certainly played the lute, organ and virginals.

This anonymous painting of the Field of Cloth of Gold belongs to the Royal Collection and was probably painted for Henry VIII himself, presumably to commemorate the sheer magnificence of the meeting between the English king and his French rival, Francis I.

Hans Holbein's *Musicians on a Balcony*: this drawing by Henry VIII's favourite court painter depicts one of the 'outdoor' ensembles that would have performed daily duties at court. The five musicians pictured play a trumpet, a sackbut (an early form of trombone) and three recorders.

Members of the viol ensemble Fretwork sit in the magnificent room at Wilton House designed by architect Inigo Jones, who was also responsible for the set design of many royal masques.

The extraordinary blue and gold ceiling of Hampton Court Palace's Chapel Royal, built for Henry VIII in the 1530s. The gilded design remains today exactly as Henry and his choir would have seen it, and contains 60 winged angels and 32 repetitions of Henry's motto, *Dieu et Mon Droit* (God and My Right).

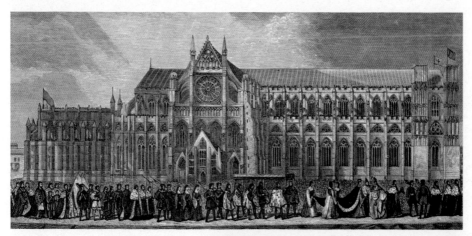

An illustration of Westminster Abbey as Tudor England would have seen it, long before the two distinctive towers were built in 1745. The Abbey has been the home of the coronation since 1066, and has witnessed nearly a thousand years of magnificent coronation music.

Anne Boleyn's Song Book: a collection of 39 Latin motets and three French chansons, possibly compiled for Anne herself by a court musician named Mark Smeaton (who would later go on to be tortured and executed on charges of committing adultery with the queen).

Thomas Tallis: one of the greatest Tudor composers, whose life (c.1505–1585) spanned the reigns of four successive monarchs, and who was employed at court from c.1544 until his death.

St Nicholas's Church in Oddington, Gloucestershire, one of the many hundreds of English religious establishments whose medieval Catholic murals were whitewashed during the Protestant Reformation.

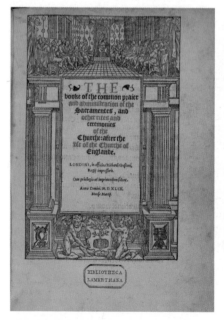

This first-edition version of the 1549 Book of Common Prayer represents the pivotal act of the English Reformation: the banning of Latin service text in favour of this simpler, shortened English-language version of the liturgy.

This exquisite miniature of Elizabeth I playing the lute was painted by Elizabeth's favourite court painter, Nicholas Hilliard. She also played the virginals, and enjoyed singing and dancing.

Inigo Jones's Banqueting House, with its spectacular ceiling by Peter Paul Rubens, which proclaims – through a central image of James I being crowned by the heavens – the Divine Right of the Stuart dynasty.

Oliver Cromwell, the king in all but name, who ruled England as 'Lord Protector' from 1553 until his death in 1558. Despite his puritanical outlook, he was a music-lover who kept a small band of private musicians at his court.

Charles II, pictured here on horseback in a grand eve-of-coronation procession from the Tower of London to Westminster in 1661. He was the first king to rule England after 11 long years of the Interregnum, and the monarch who would rebuild the Royal Music after its near-destruction during the Civil Wars.

Purcell: perhaps the greatest English composer of all time, whose education, young life and early career were completely dependent on the royal musical establishment.

The ruins of Holyrood Abbey in Edinburgh: destroyed by an anti-Catholic mob in 1688 amid uprisings against the deeply unpopular Catholic king, James II.

We can trace the vicissitudes that followed through the life of Thomas Tallis, one of our finest composers. His extraordinarily long life (c.1505–85) spanned the reigns of four successive monarchs of wildly differing religious beliefs and the entire Reformation period of which he was the greatest survivor. As such, he did not merely witness, but experienced first hand the great shifts and changes – political, cultural and religious – prompted by Henry's Supremacy and the ensuing Reformation and Counter-Reformation. The changes affected his personal and professional life; they also shaped and reshaped the very style and form of the notes he wrote. With a lesser man, this would have produced mere time-serving and confusion. Instead, Tallis's music reflects the changes of his lifetime with extraordinary skill and versatility, making works written at the beginning of his career utterly distinct from those produced later. It is almost as if they had been written by a different man, although one of equal genius.

Tallis was probably a Kentish man and his first known employment was at the Benedictine Priory of Dover, where he was organist during the early 1530s. There he produced, in so far as we can date it, his early music, which continues the great English devotional tradition of composers like Dunstable and Fayrfax. The masterpiece of this period is his five-part 'votive antiphon' *Salve Intemerata*, a setting of a highly traditional Latin text intended for the daily Office. *Salve Intemerata* is an extraordinary work, probably written when Tallis was only in his mid-twenties: highly imitative, ornate and incredibly long, almost rambling in style, with a detailed text addressed to the Virgin Mary. It would, much later, provide the basis for his mass of the same name. The antiphon was possibly the longest single movement in the entire Tudor repertory – with a duration of anywhere between 17 and 25 minutes, depending on the tempo – and was utterly beautiful, with long, luxurious lines and a kind of holy languor.

But, beautiful though it was, the piece was also self-consciously archaic, with its use of five parts in the manner of early antiphons in the Eton Choirbook dating from the 1480s, and its strict application of the medieval 'phrygian mode' for its harmonies. This was emphatically music of the past, already deeply frowned upon by avant-garde thinkers like Erasmus when it was written and soon to be forbidden altogether.

It was at this point that the Reformation began to catch up with Tallis. He probably remained at Dover Priory till it was dissolved in 1535. He was next found working briefly in London before moving to the rich Augustinian monastery of Waltham Cross in 1538. This, too, surrendered to the crown in 1540, the last monastic foundation in England to do so, and, as one of its lay employees, Tallis was paid off with a gratuity. But though the monasteries had gone, for now at least cathedrals, parish and collegiate churches were largely unaffected, or were re-founded as secular institutions that continued to employ musicians in large numbers. With the easy professional mobility that characterised so many singing men of the late Middle Ages – the 35-year-old Tallis promptly took advantage of the fact and moved to Canterbury cathedral, where, as a native of Kent, he presumably had contacts who assisted him in finding the job.

Canterbury, like almost half of the cathedrals in England, had previously housed a monastery of Benedictine monks. But when this monastery was dissolved, the cathedral was re-founded as a secular cathedral. There was hot debate about the nature of the new foundation, but the traditionalists won and it was equipped with a large professional choir, made up of 10 boys and 12 men. Tallis's name heads the list of singing men and he sang and composed for this choir for the next two years.

They were tumultuous ones. Canterbury was the scene of fierce religious controversy that mirrored the national struggle. On one side was Thomas Cranmer, now the archbishop and one of the king's most trusted counsellors, who was a leading advocate of religious reform; on the other were several influential members of the cathedral chapter, who were staunchly traditionalist and eventually attempted to prosecute their archbishop for heresy.

Similar disputes divided the choir at another great royal foundation, St George's Chapel, Windsor. Here the conservative majority were pitted against one of the singing men, Robert Testwood, who, unusually for a member of his profession, was an early convert to the cause of reform. The dispute turned into a musical duel between Testwood and a visiting Gentlemen of the Chapel Royal, Robert Philips, during the singing of Robert Fayrfax's highly complex *Lauda vivi Alpha et O*. Philips had chosen the piece both to show off his voice and to irritate Testwood with its concluding invocations to the Virgin Mary, which were anathema to Reformers. But Testwood gave as good as he got:

When he heard Robert Philips begin to fetch his flourish with O redemptrix et salvatrix! *('O redeemer and saviour!') Testwood was as quick, on the other side, to answer him again with* non redemptrix, nec salvatrix! *('Neither redeemer nor saviour!') and so, striving there with* O *and* Non *who should have the mastery, they made an end of the verse.*

Perhaps it was to escape a similarly poisonous atmosphere at Canterbury that Tallis moved on again by 1543. Or perhaps it was mere ambition. For this time Tallis's new appointment was as a gentleman of the Chapel Royal. It was the summit of his profession and he remained for 40 years. Tallis's move to court coincided with a new gyration in the tortuous politics of Henry's reign. In July 1543 the king married for the sixth and last time. He pronounced his vows 'with a smiling countenance' but his new and deeply music-loving wife, Catherine Parr, took her marriage with profound seriousness as a divinely ordained mission to further the cause of the Reformation. To this end, she cooperated effectively with Archbishop Cranmer in extending the religious use of English. This had been profoundly controversial since the late fourteenth century when John Wycliff and the Lollards had made the Bible in English the standard-bearer of the last great wave of heresy in England. Erasmus's insistence that the Word of God must be intelligible to every Christian had begun the process of change. Anne Boleyn had been a notable advocate of the Bible in both her languages of English and French. But it was Cranmer and Thomas Cromwell who had carried the project for an official translation of the Bible into English to a triumphant conclusion with the publication of the Great Bible in 1539.

Cromwell had been executed the following year after his disastrous misjudgement in sponsoring Henry's marriage to Anne of Cleves, but now Cranmer and his new ally Catherine Parr took the first steps in the use of English in the liturgy. The occasion was Henry's renewal of war against France. Catherine wrote and published suitable English prayers; Cranmer promulgated an English translation of the litany for use in prayers and religious procession of intercession in the national wartime emergency. In his covering letter to the king, Cranmer considered the question of an appropriate music for the new English text. Once again, Erasmus was his guide: 'Let us sing vocally,' Erasmus had ended his 1516 *Commentary* on I Corinthians 14, 'but let us sing as Christians; let us sing sparingly, but let us sing more in our hearts.' It was this 'sparing' singing that Cranmer advocated now. 'In mine opinion,' he wrote to Henry, 'the song that shall be made thereunto would not be full of notes, but, as near as may be, for every syllable a note; so that it may be sung distinctly and devoutly ...'[13]

'For every syllable a note' became the new mantra and set a new fashion in music for clarity and simplicity. Tallis's Mass for Four Voices is a perfect example of the change. The text of the Holy of Holies of the mass remains in Latin, as it would until Henry was safely dead; but the music is radically pared down, both in number of voices and in texture, as the setting adheres largely to the rule of one syllable to one note. This makes the text much more audible and comprehensible than the long, florid antiphons of Tallis's youth. But, despite the restraints imposed, the composer still manages to create a wide range of colour and texture within this simple form –

and there is still the occasional decorative flourish, as if he can't quite kick the habit of elaboration. Tallis's versatility under constraints – a quality that would become his trademark – is evident in this simple yet beautiful little work.

But these kinds of experiments aside, the role of the Chapel Royal continued essentially unchanged, and in all its old magnificence, in the last years of Henry VIII. It did so because of the king himself and his view that music remained at the heart of monarchy. We can see this clearly from Henry VIII's own psalter, or book of psalms, specially written and illuminated for him in the 1540s, and annotated in the king's own unmistakable handwriting. The psalter is a profoundly personal book that reflects the ageing Henry's vision of himself, and of his kingship – and both focus on music, which figures largely in the lavish illuminations. The illumination for Psalm 14, 'The fool saith in his heart, there is no God', shows Henry playing on the harp like the Old Testament King David, the supposed author of the psalms, while Will Somers, Henry's fool, looks uncomprehendingly on. Even more striking is the illumination for Psalm 81, where a group of court musicians, playing pipe and tabor, harp, psaltery and trumpet, 'make a joyful noise unto the God of Jacob':

Take the psalm, bring hither the tabret; the merry harp with the lute.
Blow up the trumpet in the new-moon: even in the time appointed,
and upon our solemn feast-day. (Psalm 81: 1–3)

Henry was, of course, familiar with the intense debate on what music – if any – should be employed in Christian religious services.

But for him, as his Latin annotations in this manuscript show, the psalms settled the matter firmly in the traditional sense: music was a good, even a necessary, part of worship. In the margin of Psalm 49: 4, 'I will open my dark saying upon the harp', he writes 'NB: with praise upon the psaltery'; by Psalm 66: 1–2 ,'Make a joyful noise unto God, all ye lands: Sing forth the honour of his name; make his praise glorious', he notes 'NB: of the praises to be given to God'; while by Psalm 98: 5–6, 'Praise the Lord upon the harp: sing to the harp with a psalm of thanksgiving. With trumpets also, and shawms: O show yourselves joyful before the Lord the King', he writes simply 'of worship'. Worship *was* music: the matter was closed, for Henry at least.

But what would happen if another Supreme Head of the Church of England succeeded him who did not share Henry's love of elaborate sacred music? Who instead agreed with Erasmus and Cranmer and saw it as a popish corruption that should be rooted out?

England and its musicians would soon find out.

EXTREMES

The king who succeeded Henry VIII was a nine-year-old boy: Edward, Henry's son, and the product of his third marriage to the late queen Jane Seymour. Only three weeks after his father's death the orphaned child was crowned Edward VI at Westminster Abbey in a ceremony led by Thomas Cranmer, the ringleader of the Church's new radical reforms. His presiding role in the service was a taste of things to come: now, with the moderate Henry dead, and Edward under the influence of his uncle the Duke of Somerset, also a devout Protestant, the way was open for religious change to proceed at full tilt.

Ritual and imagery were banned across the country; stained glass was shattered, crucifixes and paintings of saints were torn down and whitewashed. Churches dotted throughout the English countryside still show evidence of this whitewashing: at St Nicholas' church in Oddington, Gloucestershire, exquisite medieval murals show eerily through the translucent white paint. Six months after Edward came to the throne, a royal visitation was sent by his entourage to ensure that popish rituals had been abolished in all the major cathedrals – from Winchester, to Canterbury, to York, to

Windsor. No more than two candles were to be lit at mass; bells were rung at the start of the service and at no other time. Monkish habits were to be suppressed and musicians were no longer even allowed to have their hair tonsured.[14]

The injunctions laid down by the royal visitors at specific cathedrals show just how radically things were changing. At Lincoln cathedral, the visitors decreed that:

> *[The choir] shall from henceforth sing or say no anthems of our Lady or other saints, but only of our Lord, and them not in Latin; but choosing the best and most sounding to Christian religion they shall turn the same into English, setting thereunto a plain and distinct note for every syllable one: they shall sing them and none other ...*[15]

But the rules were slightly different everywhere: at Canterbury, the visitors instructed that mass could only be sung by the choir; at York the mass was forbidden to be sung more than once a day; at Winchester it was decreed that chapters from the Old and New Testaments should be read to the choir before mass and evensong. Liturgical change was fragmented and haphazard, and many people resented the changes to a religious tradition that had previously developed, uninterrupted, for nearly a thousand years.

Along with the outlawed icons and processions went the charitable institutions, such as hospitals, schools, town guilds and chantries, abolished as part of the 1547 Chantries Act. This meant the closure of the collegiate churches – such as those founded by Henry VI – which housed large, professional musical establishments employed to sing masses for the soul of the deceased donor. The donors believed that good works on Earth would gain them favour in the afterlife, but Protestants believed that the soul would be saved by faith alone, so the chantries were seen as part of the 'old religion'. Many collegiate churches and similar institutions were closed down – Beverley, Ripon, Fotheringhay, Hemingbrough, Maidstone, Rotherham, Staindrop, Tattershall, Wallingford and many others – all of them once churches with generous provision for music. Smaller establishments went too, such as the collegiate church in the tiny Suffolk village of Stoke, which had had a choir of 18 men and boys – and their dean, Matthew Parker, who would one day become archbishop of Canterbury.[16] Such places were the last strongholds of traditional Latin polyphony, and the careers of many professional musicians ended abruptly. Organs were sold or dismantled; countless precious stores of music were lost or destroyed. Almost every institution had its own musical archive, with centuries' worth of medieval manuscripts: today, a few choirbooks and a handful of fragments are all we have left of the old polyphonic tradition, and even less of the plainchant that came before it.

One of the few outlets left for musical training and education was the Chapel Royal. As the sovereign's personal establishment, it remained out of danger from the hands of reformers; but it was forced to conform to the new standards of liturgical music, and was even used as a testing ground for new reforms and services which were then implemented elsewhere. In May 1547, only three months after the coronation, the Chapel Royal first sung an experimental English form of the evening service (the compline); in November, the mass ordinary was sung in English at Westminster Abbey, and by the following year English translations of sections of the mass ordinary were available in print.[17] Thomas Tallis and his peers were charged with creating a new liturgy in the language of the people.

Tallis rose to the occasion, producing some of the greatest works in his repertoire. His four-part anthem 'If Ye Love Me' is written for men's voices only, reflecting the lack of boy choristers, since they were no longer emerging from abbeys and collegiate institutions that had once trained them. It is an elegant and restrained setting of a text reflective of Protestant doctrine: there is no mention of the Virgin Mary here; instead the text depicts Jesus calling to his disciples for obedience:

> *If ye love me,*
> *keep my commandments,*
> *and I will pray the Father,*
> *and he shall give you another comforter,*
> *that he may 'bide with you forever,*
> *e'en the spirit of truth.*

'Remember Not', another four-part anthem, is also simple and direct in style, with a text that praises God and urges Him to forgive the sins of those on Earth who give thanks to Him. Like 'If Ye Love Me', it is a mostly homophonic setting, written without decoration or elaboration, with one 'syllable a note'. These compositions are no longer abstract sounds full of melisma[18] and decoration, but direct instructions to the congregation concerning the word of God.

On 21 January 1549, the first Act of Uniformity was passed by parliament, stating that within four months 'the Book of Common Prayer' should replace all existing Latin service books. This English service book, drawn up by Cranmer himself, was central to the Protestant ethos to restore the word of God to its rightful place at the heart of public worship. It was not only in English, but also shorter and more simplified than the Latin service, a streamlined Divine Office of two daily services of matins and evensong. For those who had grown up with the Latin service and held its ritual close to their hearts, taking away such ritual – the candles and rosaries, the relics and icons, the pilgrimages and prayers – was damning their souls to hellfire. Not surprisingly, the popular reaction to the Book was riot and uprising: in Exeter that year, rebels gathered and demanded from Edward's government the restoration of several elaborate religious ceremonies.

The rebels were easily defeated, but Edward found a more dangerous opponent in his half-sister, Mary Tudor. For Mary, the daughter of Catherine of Aragon, the Royal Supremacy had always been a personal affront as well as religious heresy. Faced with the radical reforms of her brother's regime, she became a staunch defender of the Catholic faith; she continued to openly hear the Latin mass, and – as siblings are wont to – argued fiercely with her brother. As he grew older, Edward was now starting to form his own very particular and zealous opinions. He had been tutored by Protestants, and it was with them that his allegiances lay: at the age of 12, he wrote an essay that included a description of the Pope as 'the true son of the devil, a bad man, an Antichrist'. He became determined, like his elders and councillors, to reform England into a fully Protestant, godly nation.

The second edition of the Book of Common Prayer, revised again by Cranmer's own hand and even more radical than the first, was the high-water mark of Edward's reign, and it barely mentions music. References were few, and dismissive: it was regarded as a hindrance, not a help, to devotion. Only five years previously, the great tradition of English music had been central to Henry VIII's vision of his kingship and his church. Now, under his son, it hung by a thread. The choirs and organs had gone, and even the memory of the music risked disappearing entirely, as thousands of choirbooks were burned or sold for scrap, leaving only a hundred or two leaves as the relics of the entire body of medieval music. The Reformation was at its peak, but music as a cultural and political force was on the brink of destruction. Indeed, if it had continued for a year or two longer, the entire religious tradition of music in England would probably have been annihilated.

But fate played a hand. In the winter of 1552, Edward began to cough blood; the young prince was suffering from tuberculosis, a result of weakened immunity after catching the measles. In March 1553 the Venetian envoy reported that, although still quite handsome, Edward was clearly deteriorating, and on the evening of 6 July, he died, aged only 15.

Mary was determined to become queen, at any cost: as she saw it, the future of the Catholic faith in England was in her hands. But her half-brother Edward, as he lay on his deathbed, had drawn up, in his schoolboy hand, an extraordinary document headed 'My

Device for the Succession'. It excluded Mary and Henry's daughter by Anne Boleyn, Elizabeth, from the succession on the grounds that they were both bastards, and instead placed his cousins, the Grey family, in line to the throne. On 10 July 1553, four days after Edward's death, Lady Jane Grey was taken to the Tower of London to be proclaimed queen – but she would never leave its walls again. Lady Jane's supporters had made one fundamental mistake: they had failed to arrest Mary, who – according to Henry VIII's will – was the legitimate heir to the throne. Mary and her supporters made a claim for the throne, and Queen Jane was deposed after less than two weeks. When Mary's ascendancy was announced on the streets of central London, there were scenes of triumphant exultation and music was heard from every quarter: bells rang in celebration, people sang in the streets and at St Paul's Cathedral the organ boomed out – for the first time in years – with the sounds of a joyful Te Deum.[19] Among the general population, 'sincere' Protestants were as yet few and far between and the prospect of returning to the old ways was welcomed by the majority.

On claiming the throne, Mary's first task was to reverse the reforms undertaken by her brother and father over the preceding decades. To begin with, the reconversion was hesitant: people were 'encouraged', not forced, to return to the old faith. But gradually the pace of reform quickened: the early Acts of Uniformity were overturned; the queen authorised the return of former Church property that had been displaced during the Dissolution of the Monasteries; and 'all such divine services ... as were most commonly used in the realm of England in the last year of the reign of our late sovereign

Lord King Henry the Eighth'[20] were reinstated. Ideally, Mary would have wanted religion to revert to how it had been two decades earlier, as if her brother's reign had never happened. Necessarily, though, this was a different form of Catholicism from what had gone before – the extent of Edward's zealous reforms meant that it was still dramatically simplified. In music, although some monasteries and collegiate institutions were re-founded, the wholesale reallocation of land that followed the Dissolution made it impossible to restore many. The damage had been done.

Nevertheless, organs were restored to many parish churches. Tellingly, a large number of Latin service books that ought to have been surrendered to Edward VI's commissioners were now brought out of hiding, as if their owners had not believed that the Protestant phase would last.[21] Although no Latin liturgical books with music had been printed in England since 1520, at least 13 appeared between 1554 and 1557.[22] For a period of five years, the old Latin order was restored, allowing a whole generation of composers – whose stylistic development had been utterly changed by the reforms – to revert to the old ways of ornate polyphony. Composers at the Chapel Royal led the way, urged on by the queen herself: such was Mary's emotional commitment to the religious world of her childhood.

Thomas Tallis led the way, reinventing Latin composition for the new era – with works like 'Videte Miraculum' and 'O Nata Lux' – as well as returning to enormous, luxuriant polyphonic works in the old-fashioned, Henrician style, such as his votive antiphon *Gaude Gloriosa*. This magnificent piece, written for six parts and with a devotional text that pays homage to the Virgin (as well as, perhaps, the queen herself), is the greatest unbroken span of florid polyphony produced by any Tudor composer; over 15 minutes long, full of sumptuous textures and sonorities, it is a truly triumphant return to the old Catholic form. The listener is left in no doubt of the pleasure Tallis derived in writing a work of such scale and complexity. It is tempting to speculate on Tallis's allegiances to Mary and the Catholic faith as a result, though it is more likely that *Gaude Gloriosa* simply demonstrates Tallis's supreme skill and adaptability to whatever challenges were placed before him.

Composer John Sheppard was also evidently a key musician in Mary's new musical programme. He was a native-born Englishman who had previously worked at Magdalen College, Oxford, and joined the Chapel Royal in the early 1550s, but was clearly writing music before then for the Catholic rite (although much of it has been lost). Most of Sheppard's extant work is from the Marian period, and is testament to the splendour of Latin church music throughout Mary's reign. Of the five Latin mass settings he wrote, the Cantate Mass is the most elaborate, an exceptionally ornate yet sonorous work written for six voices, almost certainly composed for Mary's own Chapel. The four movements – Sanctus, Agnus Dei, Gloria and Credo – all exhibit Sheppard's consummate skill at writing complex yet coherent vocal lines, and the overall effect is one of great drama, in particular through the use of 'antiphony', i.e. playing off different groups of voices against one another. Such music would have transported the listener back two decades to the time of the old faith.

The composers for this period didn't revert completely to the old ways, just as the religion they were writing for didn't either.

Music composed during this period – not just by Tallis and Sheppard, but composers such as William Mundy, Robert Parsons and Robert Whyte – is extremely ornate, written for many parts and deploying Latin texts, but also betrays a significant influence from the Continent in the use of imitation, textural contrast and clear declamation. It is very possible that such influences were the result of the presence in England of the Spanish Chapel Royal, a group of singers and composers who had travelled from the Continent with the future Prince Consort, Philip of Spain.

While her cautious religious reforms of the nation were underway, Mary was under pressure to marry and produce an heir: otherwise the throne would immediately revert to her Protestant half-sister, Elizabeth. Mary wasted no time in selecting a husband – Philip of Spain, the son of her cousin Charles V, the Holy Roman Emperor. Philip was only 26 years old – 11 years her junior – and they were married at Winchester cathedral in July 1554. A royal wedding mass was performed by three choirs united for the occasion: the Chapel Royal, the choir of Winchester cathedral and the Spanish Chapel Royal, or 'Capilla Flamenca'. All was looking good for Mary, not least her husband, whose appearance she apparently approved of: he was small and slender with a sandy complexion.[23] (Philip, it appears, was not quite so enamoured of Mary, describing her as dressing badly and having no eyebrows.) But things got even better for the queen later that year: in November, England underwent a formal reconciliation with Rome, and papal supremacy over the nation was restored. Best of all, Mary believed she was pregnant.

In April of the following year, Mary withdrew to Hampton Court for the birth of her child. An entourage was prepared to receive the baby – there was even a cradle ready for the royal infant – and in the London streets bishops sang litanies in celebration.[24] Good Catholics rejoiced at the forthcoming birth, but also at the realisation that the serious business of enforcing Catholicism had finally begun. The first burnings had taken place in February of that year, and over the next three years more than 300 men and women died in agony at the stake. Hundreds of pro-Catholic street ballads were written around this time: this one, probably conceived in April just as Mary retired to Hampton Court, proclaims 'Now England is Happy' in its title:

> *Nowe Englande is happie, and happie in dede,*
> *That god of his goodnes doth prospir [her seed];*
> *Therfore, let us praie, it was neuer more nede,*
> *God prosper her highnes, god send her good sped.*

> *Howe manie good people were longe in dispaire*
> *That this letel england shold lacke a right heire ;*
> *But nowe the swet marigold[25] springeth soo fayre*
> *That England triumpheth without anie care.*[26]

The ballad's words take on a sinister tone, given the persecutions that were taking place around this time: the use of the words 'good people' in particular is pointed. As Catholics sung songs of rejoicing in the streets, thousands of those considered 'bad people' fled in exile to Europe. One of them was a Protestant cleric named John Foxe, who decided to write a history of the persecution. Detailing the trials, eyewitness accounts and writings of the martyrs themselves, the book became known as *Foxe's Book of Martyrs*. It became, after the Bible, the second most widely read book in English, and damned the queen's reputation for ever as 'Bloody Mary'.

But Mary's hopes of a fully Catholic nation were evaporating, as it became clear that her pregnancy was a phantom. Her belly had deflated, her breasts stopped producing milk. By summer she was a public laughing stock, and her power began to dwindle. Parliament wriggled from her grip; her husband, Philip, abandoned her. Despite this she grimly persisted with the persecution of Protestants, among them Thomas Cranmer, who died triumphantly denouncing the Pope as the Antichrist and in so doing becoming the most influential public martyr of the Protestant cause. It was another nail in the coffin of Mary's faltering reign, and Mary herself died only two years later, 42 and childless. It had, in fact, been an oddly fruitless period in power. Despite the queen's impressive ability to impose her religious will on the nation, the legacy of her father, Henry, and brother, Edward, lived on, and Protestantism had proved itself to be resistant and enduring in the face of adversity. For music, too, Mary's reign had been a five-year aberration: the beautiful but dying gasp of a medieval tradition that was now well and truly over.

Under Queen Elizabeth, it was all about to change again.

ELIZABETH I

The Great Service by William Byrd is one of the finest sacred works written during the reign of Elizabeth I, and can still be heard in church services today. It is a work of extraordinary scope and scale, written for up to ten voices and in seven elaborate sections. The listener is bewitched by the complexity and density of the textures and harmonies, and the overall coherence of so many voices: the juxtaposition of high voices against low, polyphony against homophony, and solo against full choir. So elaborate is *The Great Service* that it is hard to believe it comes from the reign of a Protestant monarch. The work itself was probably intended specifically for performance at the Chapel Royal: no other institution would have had the resources to perform it. On closer listening, it becomes only more intriguing; the text accompanying the decoration and long, melismatic lines is in English, and the movements are all part of the scaled-down Anglican service of matins, evensong and Communion. It is a piece unlike anything heard before: a curious hybrid of old and new, and all the more captivating and beautiful for it. Where did it come from, and how did it become part of the Church of England's repertory? In other European countries where Protestantism took hold, most ornament and elaboration in services was phased out. How did we avoid the sparse, dull Protestant services characteristic of countries like Sweden?

The answer is largely due to the tastes and personality of Elizabeth I herself. Like her father, Elizabeth had a moderate approach to religion, and was wary of extremes on both sides. She lived through the tumult of Edward's reforms and Mary's reversals, and had seen the destruction that both sides wrought; she believed that the only way to ensure peace and stability was with compromise. And she loved music; it had been central to her childhood. She played the spinet,[27] and her own magnificently decorated instrument survives in the Victoria and Albert Museum, bearing the royal coat of arms and a falcon holding a sceptre, the emblem of her mother, Anne Boleyn. She may also have played the lute, and there is beautiful miniature by her favourite court painter, Nicholas Hilliard, of the queen holding that instrument. Although Elizabeth was probably not a highly skilled performer (one courtier wrote – tellingly, after Elizabeth's death – that 'in matters of recreation, as singing, dancing and playing upon instruments, she was not ignorant nor excellent'[28]), it was obviously an important part of her everyday life, not least in religious services. Elizabeth grew up with all musical trappings of the Catholic faith. It is not surprising that, in her vision of a new religion, music was to play a vital role. In implementing that vision Elizabeth would become the defender of the musical faith.

Elizabeth came to the throne in November 1558, and her first task was to establish a new religious settlement. Small changes were made immediately to her Chapel Royal, notably the substitution of Cranmer's English litany for the Latin procession, which within a month had been authorised by royal proclamation for use throughout the country. Beyond this, however, the Latin services remained, surprisingly, much as they had under Mary.[29] In 1559, Elizabeth's Act of Uniformity was passed, which authorised the use of a new Elizabethan Prayer Book. This book was in essence Cranmer's Book from 1552 – which pleased the Protestant radicals – but Elizabeth insisted on one major change: The so-called Ornaments Rubric empowered the queen to retain traditional ceremonies, such as making the sign of the cross at baptism or requiring the clergy to wear traditional vestments like the surplice and the cope. Such decorative 'popish' features were offensive to extreme Protestants, but Elizabeth believed that religion, like monarchy, needed ritual. The ceremonial qualities invested so heavily in by her ancestors were powerful, and to include them in her vision for the Church of England would invest royalty with that same power. Such ceremony should include music, which possessed – as she remembered from the incense-filled chapel services furnished with rich polyphony in her youth – its own peculiar power and impressiveness.

In the summer of that year, Elizabeth laid down a series of Injunctions, one of which made clear her views on music in worship. There should be, she proclaimed:

> *a modest distinct songue, so used in all partes of the common prayers*
> *in the Church, that the same may be as playnely understanded, as yf*

it were read without syngyng, and yet nevertheless, for the comfor-
tyng of suche as delyght in musicke, it may be permitted that in the
begynning, or in the ende of common prayers, eyther at morning or
evenyng, that there may be song an Hymne, or such like songue, to
the praise of almightie god, in the best sort of melodie that may be
conveniently devised, having respect that the sentence of the Hymne
may be understanded and perceyved.[30]

It was a compromise between the elaborate polyphony of Mary's reign and Cranmer's austere vision for music with one syllable per note – and it allowed musicians to have unprecedented creative freedom. Elizabeth had laid the foundations for the greatest era of church music England had ever seen.

The site of Elizabeth's purest vision for religion was her own private Chapel. Here, music was a vibrant part of the religious culture and two Chapel Royal composers in particular made an indelible mark on music history during her reign: Thomas Tallis, now in his fifties, and his brilliant student, William Byrd. Byrd was a devout Catholic; indeed, when he was employed at Lincoln cathedral, his salary was suspended because his protracted organ playing at services was deemed 'too popish'.[31] After leaving Lincoln, he came to London and was sworn in as a Gentleman of the Chapel Royal in February 1572, where he became joint organist with Tallis. Queen Elizabeth was extremely fond of the composer, and Byrd depended upon her patronage. In one anthem, 'O Lord, Make Thy Servant Elizabeth', Byrd pays sycophantic homage to his queen, adapting a psalm to refer to Elizabeth rather than King David:

O Lord, make thy servant, Elisabeth our Queen, to rejoice in thy strength; give her her heart's desire, and deny not the request of her lips; but prevent her with thine everlasting blessing, and give her a long life, ev'n for ever and ever. Amen.

It's a perfectly symmetrical six-voice anthem and exhibits a finely wrought balance of the ornate Catholic style and the plain austerity of Protestantism. Byrd may have written 'O Lord, Make Thy Servant Elizabeth' just before joining the Chapel Royal in an effort to impress the queen and secure an appointment; or else soon after he had become a member, when he was still trying to get into her good books. It must have worked, since Byrd remained a member of the Chapel for the rest of his life, composing several pieces on the queen's personal orders. After the extraordinary victory over the Spanish Armada in 1588, Elizabeth requested that Byrd set an anthem to her own poem, in which she casts herself as God's handmaid:

Look and bow down thine ear, O Lord:
from thy bright sphere behold and see,
Thy handmaid and thy handywork
amongst thy priests, offering to thee,
Zeal for incense, reaching the skies,
Myself and scepter, sacrifice.

Elizabeth probably ordered the song to be sung at the procession before or after the thanksgiving service at St Paul's Cathedral on

24 November 1588. By all accounts, it was a magnificent occasion, filled with music, crowds lining the streets to watch the victorious queen and her entourage pass, accompanied by heralds and trumpeters. Among the spectators were a band of musicians – shawms, sackbuts and drums – that added to the atmosphere of the procession, and, at St Paul's, Elizabeth heard the choir sing the litany and Te Deum, as well as the playing of the organs and the pealing of bells in celebration.[32] At some point during the procession, a party of boys from Christ's Hospital stepped forward to present Byrd's song, 'Look and Bow Down'. Unfortunately the work survives today only in fragments, but we can still ascertain that it was a composition of great refinement and artistry and would have caused a sensation among the keyed-up crowd.

It was thanks to the queen's special favour that Byrd never found himself seriously in trouble for his Catholicism – and this was a dangerous time for Catholics. In 1581, three Jesuit priests were executed, setting off a deadly chain of Elizabethan religious persecutions. Byrd set a well-known inflammatory poem about the priests' execution, 'Why Do I Use My Paper, Ink and Pen?' to music, scoring it for five-voice part song:

> *Why do I use my paper, ink and pen,*
> *And call my wits to counsel what to say?*
> *Such memories were made for mortal men;*
> *I speak of Saints whose names cannot decay.*
> *An Angel's trump were fitter for to sound*
> *Their glorious death if such on earth were found.*

He was also repeatedly fined for refusing to attend Anglican services and, outside the Chapel Royal, he maintained an almost exclusively Catholic circle of patrons and friends. He composed music for several prominent Catholic families, such as the Earl of Worcester and Sir John Petre, and it was in their houses, as part of clandestine Catholic services, that many of Byrd's best-known works were first performed, in particular his beautiful Latin masses and motets. No one else dared to write and publish music with such obviously Catholic sentiments: in the 1590s, Byrd would actually go as far as to publish three Latin masses, and his name is mentioned on every page of music.

As for Tallis, during these last decades of his life he enjoyed greater musical freedom than ever before, producing some of the greatest works of his career. He composed the 40-part motet *Spem in alium*, written, legend has it, in response to a challenge by the Duke of Arundel to equal a 40-part motet by Italian composer Alessandro Striggio.[33] The first performance of this monumental work – written for five eight-part choirs – was probably heard on Queen Elizabeth's fortieth birthday,[34] and stuns the listener with its sheer weight of sound. Free now to write in both Latin and English, Tallis also contributed nine psalm tunes for a metrical psalter compiled by Archbishop Parker in 1567. Elizabeth's Injunctions of 1559 had allowed psalm singing by the congregation, and it very quickly became a popular part of cathedral and parish church practice, the precursor to the hymn-singing tradition. Tallis's most well-known hymn tune was made famous over 350 years later with Vaughan Williams's *Fantasia on a Theme by Thomas Tallis*, composed in 1910.

Such musical traditions demonstrate one of the most enduring legacies of the Protestant reformation: the power of single-line melody.

❧

While Elizabeth's vision for a Church that was Protestant in doctrine but Catholic in appearance remained unwavering, much of the nation she ruled disagreed. Protestantism had now become a relentless force across the country: in reality, Bloody Mary's brief, fiery reign did little to blunt Edward's legacy of a thoroughly reformed religion.[35] Images, icons, altars and organs – these popish effects that had been reinstated during Mary's reign were once more largely swept away, as Elizabeth's moderate Injunctions were increasingly ignored. Music suffered as a result. Elizabeth's Chapel Royal, the largest and by far the finest in the country – with 32 Gentlemen and 12 Children – was an aberration, where the conditions were cushy and the salaries more than three times the national average.[36] Elsewhere, the influence of growing Puritanism coupled with a general waning of interest in church music had prompted a steep decline in standards, education and resources: a musician of the time named Thomas Whythorne wrote that music had become 'so slenderly maintained in the cathedral churches and colleges and parish churches that, when the old store of musicians be worn out … (which is like to be in short time), ye shall have few or none remaining except a few singing men and players on musical instruments'.[37] In provincial churches, congregants would wait outside while the service music was being performed, and not go in until the sermon and lectures began. For those of a Puritan persuasion, the spoken word was vastly preferable to any 'unnecessary piping and minstrelsy' of choristers and singing men.

The Elizabethan era is now known as the triumphant 'golden age' for English music, and this reputation was built at a single location, the Chapel Royal. Almost all great composers of the age were at one time or another associated with the Chapel Royal – not just Tallis and Byrd, but also Richard Farrant, Robert Parsons, Thomas Morley and John Bull. Composers knew that the only viable place to get the necessary support and resources was at court. As the writer John Boswell observed in 1572: 'If it were not for the queen's majesty that did favour that excellent science, singing men and choristers might go a-begging, together with their master the player of the organs.'[38] Elsewhere, church music may have been in decline but the Chapel Royal acted like an ark, investing in this elite, specialised music and preserving it for future generations. At Hampton Court Chapel – one of several places in which the choir resided – Elizabeth would come to worship in public, each Sunday and during holidays when she was residing at the palace. It was her personal religious space, and she treated it with a possessiveness and idiosyncrasy worthy of her greatest ancestors. The result was that the Reformation had less impact here than anywhere else in England. The Communion table still stood at the east end – draped and arrayed like an altar, and with a pair of massive gilt candlesticks – the crucifix and the great alms dishes. The chapel clergy still wore vestments, the organ still played and the choir still sung, often in Latin. The same went for a handful of other places with powerful royal connections – like St George's Chapel, Windsor, and Westminster Abbey. Otherwise the Chapel

Royal was an island in a hostile sea – inside it was indeed the warm summer of the golden age of English church music. Outside it was the cold, silent winter of Protestant austerity. And the difference was due to the power and preference of one woman.

For Elizabeth, music was not just a pleasing pastime but a political tool: she was adept at turning the theatricality of court life to her advantage, using courtly entertainments to project powerful messages of kingship, harmony and prosperity. At court, music to accompany dining added to the grandeur and impressiveness of the occasion; one spectator reported how the queen dined at Greenwich to the accompaniment of 12 trumpets and 2 kettledrums which 'made the hall ring for half an hour together'.[39] In public, royal musicians were required to follow the queen almost everywhere she went. When Elizabeth made journeys down the Thames, in full view of her subjects, 'her barge was towed by a long galley rowed by 40 men in shirts with a band of music'.[40] Music played a significant role on all royal state occasions, including royal progresses. Progresses made during the summer were the only time of year when Elizabeth's musicians had any time off, as the musicians belonging to the grand houses she visited were expected to entertain her. It was common for the royal household to stay for days or weeks at a time at these houses, lured by a daily timetable of entertainments including balls, courtly masques and musical performances. The cost of these visits was enormous and they were often dreaded by the owners of the houses as a result.

In 1575, Elizabeth travelled to Kenilworth Castle in Warwickshire, the home of her friend and suitor Robert Dudley. Dudley attracted much attention for his close friendship with Elizabeth, for the issue of the 'virgin queen's' beleaguered love life was crucial to the future of the English monarchy, and English religion. To secure the stability of her vision for the English Church – like her half-sister Mary before her – Elizabeth needed an heir who would inherit her vision, and therefore she needed a husband. Dudley believed he could be that husband, and in order to woo her he laid on a spectacular series of entertainments and music for her stay at Kenilworth. 'For the persons, for the place, time, cost, devices, strangeness and abundance of it all ... I saw none anywhere so memorable,' wrote one contemporary.[41] When Elizabeth arrived at the castle on the first day, there were six giant trumpeters to herald her welcome: in fact, there were dummies eight feet tall, dressed in silk, with false trumpets five feet long, but with men with real trumpets behind them.[42] There was a welcome pageant accompanied by a 'delectable harmony of hautbois, shawms, cornets and other such loud music'. The second day was given over entirely to music and dancing; including an instrumental recital which the queen heard from a barge. Music was provided by, among others, Edward Johnson and William Hunnis. Although we don't know precisely what music Johnson wrote, his consort songs, composed for a later royal progress at Elvetham, Hampshire, give us a fair idea – in particular 'Eliza is the fairest quene', which so delighted Elizabeth when she heard it 'that she commanded to here it sung and to be danced three times over'.[43] William Hunnis, then Master of the Chapel Royal Children, was one of the authors of 'The Lady of the Lake', a dramatised entertainment depicting a knight attempting to rape the aforementioned lady, which was performed for Elizabeth during her stay. Dudley nearly bankrupted himself with the cost of the entertainments.

And in the end Elizabeth turned her suitor down. Dudley's previous wife had died in mysterious circumstances, and he was widely spoken of as a murderer and adulterer – and Elizabeth was too savvy to enter into a union with such a notorious figure. She had seen how her half-sister Mary's choice of a husband had sparked dissent and rebellion among her subjects. Elizabeth would never find a suitable husband, and the issue of succession would bedevil her entire reign. In 1601, as the ageing queen's health began to fail, Elizabeth's ministers began to make moves to install James VI of Scotland on the throne. He was the queen's nearest blood relation, with a Catholic mother but brought up by Presbyterians. It remained to be seen what kind of Church Elizabeth's successor would create.

On 24 March 1603, Elizabeth died, leaving the issue unresolved. It is said, appropriately enough, that music was heard at the beginning and end of her life. 'The Te Deum was sung incontinently upon her birth' and legend says that when Elizabeth was dying she called for her musicians to play around her bed, 'so that, she said, she might die as gaily as she had lived, and that the horrors of death might be lessened; she heard the music tranquilly until her last breath'.[44]

It was during Elizabeth's reign that music became an integral component of the ceremony of monarchy – from chapel to court to public occasions – just as it became an integral part of the ceremony of religion. Elizabethan music is the sound of a monarchy that has been sacralised: music for a royal religion, a Church in which the head is the Crown. By preserving the old ceremonial music, the monarchy also preserved most of England's Catholic heritage. The hybrid of Byrd's *Great Service*, but also openly Catholic works such as the same composer's extraordinary Mass for Voices or Tallis's *Lamentations*, regarded as pinnacles of the Tudor church music tradition – this was greatness and superb artistry forged through settlement, toleration and compromise. Such music is Elizabeth's enduring triumph.

REVOLUTIONS

A NEW
GENERATION

Among the entourage of musicians in Queen Elizabeth I's funeral procession on 28 April 1603 were seven violins, all but one of whom had descended from Henry VIII's own court musicians.[1] This group was an heirloom that Elizabeth would leave to her successor, James – previously James VI of Scotland, now James I of England and Ireland under a brand new union of the English and Scottish crowns. Ushering in a new age of Stuart rule, James I's reign was the beginning of a 'century of revolution',[2] an era of great political, religious and social upheaval that would impact heavily on both monarchy and music. For monarchy, it would be a battle over the balance of power between ruler and ruled, a fierce argument over the power, divinity and purpose of kings. For music, the seventeenth century would be one of new sounds, instruments and forms, of experimentation that would elevate instrumental music to a new level of importance. The inheritance of Elizabeth's seven violins was the nucleus of that change – for those seven violins were the beginnings of what would develop into a modern orchestra, an ensemble that had its birth at the courts of Europe and would be the foundation for the greatest classical music of the next two centuries.

The finest English composers of the seventeenth century, almost without exception, were linked with monarchy. Among them was Thomas Tomkins, who, like Tallis the century before, not only witnessed the turbulent reigns of successive monarchs but worked for them and alongside them, commemorating many of their most significant events in music. Born in 1572, Tomkins had been employed first during Elizabeth's reign, but would experience the extravagant reigns of both James I and Charles I, when monarchy was at the zenith of its power. He would also see its dramatic fall,

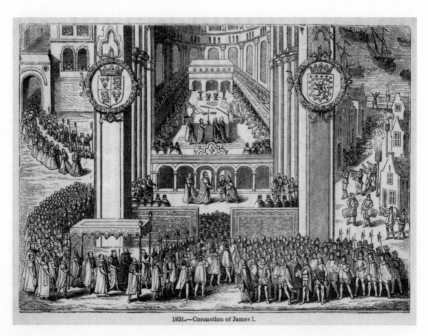

1831.—Coronation of James I.

James I's magnificent coronation which took place on the 25th July 1603. Among the highlights of the musical programme was the rejoicing anthem by court composer Thomas Tomkins 'Be Strong and of a Good Courage', performed by the full forces of the Chapel Royal.

living through the execution of Charles I and the first years of the Commonwealth, with Oliver Cromwell presiding over England as Lord Protector. It was Tomkins who wrote the rejoicing anthem for James I's coronation on 25 July 1603: he would also write a mournful pavan for the death of Charles 50 years later.

James's coronation was, by all accounts, a sumptuous affair, despite the cancelling of the customary coronation procession from the Tower of London to Westminster due to the onset of the plague (the king had ordered 'crowds should not gather'[3]). The coronation was for the most part an Anglican ceremony, although some prayers and important passages were still in Latin,[4] reflecting James's intention to maintain the moderate Elizabethan settlement and reconcile tensions between Catholic and Protestants during his reign. James's accession could have been revolutionary: as a Scot, James was a foreigner, and moreover had been brought up in the Scottish Kirk or Church, which was much more thorough-goingly Protestant than the Church of England. But, instead, James went out of his way to connect himself with his English predecessors. He had already given his eldest children the archetypical Tudor names of Henry and Elizabeth, and when he got to England he erected a large white marble monument to Elizabeth I above her tomb. And – what would probably have pleased her the most – he anglicised musically as well. He left the musicians who had served him hitherto back in Scotland, and took over *en bloc* the Tudor Chapel Royal which included every major composer of the day.

James was not interested in religious reform: his ultimate ambition was to be the peacemaker king – to unite Christianity, but also to end England's debilitating war with Spain, and the ancient, ongoing feud between England and Scotland (his accession united the kingdoms of England and Scotland under one crown, although, despite his best efforts, the two countries continued to maintain separate legislatures, laws and judicial systems during his reign). Moreover, James believed that he derived his authority to implement these ambitions from God and God alone. The monarch's devoutly held belief in the divine right of kings was far from new, but King James went far beyond the views of even Henry VIII by claiming that kings were accountable to no human law at all, only to God's laws. 'Kings are called Gods,' he wrote in 1598. 'They are appointed by God and answerable only to God'. Such beliefs are reflected in Tomkins's anthem 'Be Strong and of a Good Courage', almost certainly heard at the service, in which the text aligns James directly to God:

> *Be strong and of a good courage and observe the commandments of our God, to walk his ways, and keep his ceremonies, testimonies and judgements, and Almighty God prosper thee whithersoever thou goest.*

Once established as King of England, James quickly surrounded himself with a court befitting such a grand mandate: his extravagance was legendary. Between 1603 and 1612 he spent £185,000 on jewels; pensions given as rewards to courtiers rose by £50,000 to £80,000 a year; expenditure on the household doubled. All in all, his annual expenditure reached a peak of £552,000 in 1614.

By contrast, Queen Elizabeth had spent less than £300,000 a year during peacetime.[5] No expense was spared at James's court, and the same applied to music. Although James himself lacked any particular interest or ability in the art,[6] he was not immune to the power of music in royal ceremony, and was responsible for a rapid expansion in the musical establishment: by 1625, when Charles I came to the throne, the court, all told, employed some 140 musicians.[7] There was the Chapel Royal, which at this time employed such undisputed masters as Tomkins and Orlando Gibbons, organist for the Chapel and legendary keyboard composer, called 'the greatest finger of that age'.[8] Gibbons is now regarded as one of the leading composers of the seventeenth century. Born in 1583 and nurtured as a chorister at King's College, Cambridge, he first appears in Chapel Royal records in 1603, the same year that James successfully united the crowns of England and Scotland. Then there was the King's Music, the sovereign's personal body of musicians, which was divided into a number of separate groups, each with its own members, repertory and role in court life. Sixteen trumpeters were used to accompany state occasions with grand fanfares; there were also three groups of wind instruments (including shawms, trombones, flutes and recorders) as well as a string band. Finally, there was the 'Lutes and Voices',[9] an elite group of soloists who provided the royal family with private, personal entertainment in their royal apartments.

James's Lutes and Voices included some of the most famous composers of the period, notably John Dowland, a lutenist who, even during his lifetime, was celebrated throughout Europe. Dowland's court appointment came late in his career: though successful by the 1580s, he was pointedly ignored by the court for many decades, probably because in early life he had been allied with a group of Catholics involved in treasonable activities. He claimed 'never to have loved treason nor treachery, nor never heard any Mass in England'[10] but it did no good. The firmly Protestant court was unwilling to employ a musician with such associations, and, finding no favour among the royals in England, Dowland went to work for the court of Denmark instead. In 1604, he published a self-laceratingly soulful book of consort music called *Lachrimae*, which he dedicated to Anne of Denmark, who was not only the sister of his patron, Christian IV of Denmark, but also James I's new queen. For all its depths of melancholy, *Lachrimae* was also a blatant attempt by Dowland to curry favour with the English court – not only to prove his talent to the king and queen, but also simply to remind them of his availability. But his ruse was not successful. Only a few months later, on 5 November 1605, the Gunpowder Plot was exposed: Guy Fawkes, a Catholic, was discovered in the Houses of Parliament standing guard over 35 barrels of gunpowder with a fuse in his pocket. Had the plot gone as planned, it would have been the ultimate terrorist bombing, wiping out most of the royal family and the entire political establishment: as it was, it had no immediate political consequences, although in the long term it would play an important part in the creation of the anti-Catholic myth in England. For Dowland, it deferred any hopes he had had for a job at court.[11] Seven years later, however, in 1612, he managed to secure a court position, presumably because the passage of time had sufficiently distanced him from such associations.

Thomas Weelkes was also an outsider to the court; a talented composer of church music and madrigals, he was also a rowdy drunkard who was refused a position at the Chapel Royal because of his poor personal conduct, which involved charges of blaspheming and swearing in public. For much of his career he was employed at Chichester cathedral where it was reported that he would often go straight from the pub to sing in the choir:

> *... dyvers tymes & very often come so disguised eyther from the Taverne or Ale house into the quire as is muche to be lamented, for in these humoures he will bothe curse & sweare most dreadfully, & so profane the service of God ... and though he hath bene often tymes admonished ... to refrayne theis humors and reforme hym selfe, yett he daylye continue the same, & is rather worse than better therein.*

Nevertheless, Weelkes was a skilled musician and, moreover, a devout Protestant: after the 5 November Plot was revealed, he was sufficiently moved to write a verse anthem 'for the fifth of November', thanking God for the king's safety. 'O Lord How Joyful Is the King' was probably used at the annual services of thanksgiving for deliverance from the plot in the later years of James's reign, possibly chosen by the king himself. It is easy to imagine the king delighting particularly in such lines as:

> *For why, such mischief did they muse against Thine holy name: yet did they fail, and had no power for to perform the same.*

In 1610, James's 16-year-old son Henry was crowned Prince of Wales at Westminster Palace before a gathering of guests. The ceremony was formal and opulent, and all participants were lavishly robed and formally seated, while the prince wore an ermine-lined gown costing more than £1300.[12] It was a vitally important ceremony since Prince Henry was the first healthy male heir to the throne in a hundred years, a future king who, James hoped, would carry his own vision of divine, peacemaking monarchy forward to the next generation. Befitting the significance of the occasion, a particularly special piece of music was commissioned: a 'cover version' of Tallis's mighty 40-part motet, *Spem in alium*, set with new English words that glorified the young prince:

> *Sing and glorify heaven's high majesty,*
> *Author of this blessed harmony;*
> *Sound divine praises, with melodious graces;*
> *This is the day, holy day, happy day,*
> *For ever give it greeting, love and joy,*
> *heart and voice meeting:*
> *Live Henry princely and mighty,*
> *Harry live in thy creation happy.*

The significance of the piece was twofold: setting such a celebrated, complex piece of Latin polyphony to English words played out James's ambition for a harmonious religious settlement in music, combining the great traditions of Catholicism and Protestantism in one composition. Additionally, by endowing the occasion with that most powerful and elevating element of royal ceremony – music – the newly crowned Prince Henry's divine mandate was further legitimatised.

But Prince Henry was far from being a copy of his father. As a good-looking, masculine, athletic young man he was everything his rather ugly, bookish father was not. His approach to religion was cosmopolitan and European in outlook, and his beliefs were more devoutly Protestant than his father's. This same cosmopolitanism could be seen at his personal court at St James's Palace: a thriving centre of artistic patronage that, as the young prince grew up, became much more popular than the king's. Henry developed what was effectively a second English renaissance at his court; he established important collections of books, paintings and bronzes; he launched the career of the architect Inigo Jones. In music, Henry's tastes were more sophisticated than those of his father, which had tended towards entertainment and dancing, and his court became not only a centre of musical excellence, but of creative experimentation. At the time, ensembles were mostly made up of instruments from the same family, as at James's court: the king would listen, separately, to his flute or recorder consort, to his violin band, to his trumpeters. But Prince Henry took the unprecedented step of employing a single body of musicians, mixing violinists, viol players and an organist with singers and lutenists, and encouraging the musicians to play in new and unusual combinations. Such 'mixed ensembles' had been popular in Italy for several decades; England, however, had been behind the times until young Henry, with his passion for all things Italian, brought the revolutionary new concept to his court.

All was looking bright for the future of the English monarchy – and for English music – until suddenly, in 1612, Prince Henry died. His death, probably caused by typhoid when he ingested bad water while swimming in the Thames,[13] prompted an outpouring of public mourning: Thomas Tomkins, who probably knew the prince personally, wrote an affecting, highly chromatic and expressive anthem, 'Know Ye Not', in his memory:

> *Great Britain mourn, let every family mourn;*
> *O family of David, O family of Levi, sorrowing for him as*
> *for thy first-born, sob and sing, sigh and say:*
> *Ah Lord, ah, his glory!*

Words like these expressed the feelings of a nation that had lost its future king and was now shackled to – it was widely felt – a lesser man, who would make a lesser king: his younger brother, Charles.

Prince Charles was short of stature, weak and shy (even as a teenager, his father nicknamed him Baby Charles); compared to his warrior-like older brother he was no match for the royal title. As a boy he was bookish and introverted – an apocryphal tale has King James scolding Prince Henry for his lack of diligence in studies compared to Charles, and Henry retorting that, in that case 'we'll make him archbishop of Canterbury'.[14] In religion, too, Charles differed from his brother: his preoccupation with the past meant that he was more attached to the splendour and ceremony of the old Catholic ways. Charles was an aesthete: a lover of beauty, elegance and order. Once on the throne, he would play to his strengths as a connoisseur of the arts: he would surround himself with one of the finest collections of artists and musicians in Europe, the warm glow of their talent providing a convenient 'lustre of majesty' that distracted from his personal failings.

But Charles's accession to Prince of Wales was all to the good for music. The aspects of his personality that made him a bad politician – his perfectionism, his rigidity and stubborn belief in his own rightness – made him an ideal artistic patron: he was very musical, with refined tastes and a good eye for spotting talented musicians. He was also, as younger brothers often are, in thrall to the talents of his glamorous elder sibling, and determined to emulate the cultural vibrancy of Henry's court at his own.[15] With that in mind, Charles took on the composers of his late brother's establishment – including Alfonso Ferrabosco the younger and Thomas Lupo – as well as some from his father's – such as Orlando Gibbons, who was employed at Charles's court from 1617. The Prince of Wales's own establishment was second in size only to the king's, but it served a very different purpose. The King's Music provided the music of state, the prince's the music of pleasure. Thus it featured fresh talent, writing new music for novel combinations of instruments and voices, as well as innovative instrumental music in its own right. Prince Charles himself was a talented instrumentalist: he was taught the viol by Ferrabosco, and one contemporary account relates how: 'Charles I ... could play his part exactly well on the Bass-Viol, especially of those Incomparable Fancies of Mr Coperario on the Organ.'[16] A 'Fancy' – now more commonly called a 'fantasia' or 'fantasy', so called because its form and invention sprang 'solely from the fantasy and skill of the author who created it'[17] – was an instrumental genre that grew in importance during the seventeenth century. Thomas Lupo composed many fantasias for viols, in three, four, five and six parts – complex, beautiful and rather mournful-sounding works that require serious listening. Unlike much previous instrumental music, which was written for dancing, or simply to accompany voices, this was an elite, highbrow form, designed for an educated musical audience. It marked the beginning of chamber music as we know it – indeed, the phrase 'chamber music' probably derives from a reference to music played in palace chambers – and was far removed from grand anthems or fanfares used to project the magnificence of the Crown at a state occasion. It was intimate, private, sober and subtle, much like Charles himself.

As court composers began to realise the full potential of instrumental music, accepted forms began breaking up and changing. Following the trend begun at Henry's court, composers under Charles began to write music for new and different combinations: rather than composing for viols alone (as in Lupo's fantasias), they started to introduce other instruments, too, creating what must have seemed completely revolutionary sounds and textures. John Coprario wrote 12 fantasias for two bass viols and organ, probably for Charles himself (it was this form in which Charles could play his part 'exactly well'). Coprario also invented a brand new form specifically for Charles's court: 'the fantasia suite', which was a more dance-like, upbeat form scored not only for organ and bass viol but also for violins.[18] The violin as we know it today was an almost unheard of instrument in England at this time. Coprario's invention was among the very earliest chamber pieces written specifically for this strange new instrument; one that looked so like the viol, but sounded so different, with a percussive, bright and light-hearted tone. Only at court was it possible for composers to pursue this kind of experimentation and the fantasia suite, like so many other musical inventions at court, was eventually taken on by composers outside court, too.

But it wasn't just in string music that the court led the way. In 1613, a year after young Charles became Prince of Wales, a collection of 21 keyboard works named *Parthenia* was presented to Princess Elizabeth (daughter of James I, and Charles's elder sister) in celebration of her marriage to the German Prince Frederick. It was the first music for keyboard ever published in England: these are refined, intricate works that give particular prominence to the notes E (for Elizabeth) and F (for Frederick), as in Gibbons's 'The Queenes Command', where every opening phrase in the top line begins with one of these two notes. The dedication even refers to the 'twin[ing[together [of] … the neighbour letters E and F… that make so sweet a consonant … [and when] wedded together seem lively hieroglyphicks [sic] of the harmony of marriage'.[19] The full title of the collection – *Parthenia or the Maydenhead of the First Musicke that ever was printed for the Virginalls* – is full of clever references, too; the 'Maydenhead' referring not only to what Elizabeth will be giving up on her wedding night, but also to the maiden voyage of keyboard music itself in printed form. It also refers to the instrument this music was originally played upon, a type of keyboard known as the 'virginals'. The pieces in Parthenia are written by three gentlemen who worked at James's Chapel

PARTHENIA,
OR
THE MAYDEN-HEAD
of the firſt Muſicke that ever vvas
printed for the VIRGINALLS.

COMPOSED
By three famous Maſters: *William Byrd*, Dʳ. *John Bull*,
and *Orlando Gibbons*, Gentlemen of his Majeſties Chappell.

Dedicated to all the Maſters and Lovers of Muſick.

Printed for *John Clarke*, at the lower end of Cheapſide,
entring into *Mercers Chappell*. 1651.

Cum Privilegio.

The frontispiece to the collection of 21 keyboard works named
Parthenia, presented to James I's daughter Princess Elizabeth
on her marriage to the German Prince Frederick. It was the first
music for keyboard ever published in England.

Royal: Orlando Gibbons (before he joined Charles's court), William Byrd (now in his seventies) and a man named John Bull, who was not only a composer but one of the leading keyboard players of his time. Bull is less well-known today than perhaps he might have been had his royal patronage not been withdrawn. Shortly after *Parthenia* was published, Bull had to resign from the Chapel Royal and flee Britain, to spend the rest of his life in exile in the Southern Netherlands: he had been found guilty of 'incontinence, fornication, adultery and other grievous crimes'. No less a figure than the archbishop of Canterbury declared: 'the man hath more music than honesty – and is as famous for marring of virginity as he is for fingering of organs and virginals'.[20] His music was as skilful as his crimes were outlandish, and his music had been appreciated by the late Prince Henry: Bull wrote the 'Prince's Galliard'[21] for the prince (who loved dancing) not long before his death. Bull's cheeky, confident personality is noticeable throughout his music – for example 'The King's Hunt', a rollicking jaunty piece that mimics the sounds and sights of one of James I's royal hunts. Deft fingerwork brings the occasion to life in music, complete with echoes of horn calls, the regular trotting of the huntsmen's ponies and small melodies chased from hand to hand like the scrabbling of an animal in flight.

When Bull was forced to flee England, Orlando Gibbons took his place as senior organist of the Chapel Royal, and the leading English keyboard player of the age. He already held several royal posts at the time when, in 1625, James I died and Prince Charles finally succeeded him as king.

THE RETURN
OF CEREMONY

King Charles's reign would be defined by pursuing policies that were the opposite of his father's. Rather than waging a war with the Catholic French, as James had intended, Charles's plan was to secure an alliance with France by marrying (by proxy) a young French princess, Henrietta Maria, who was also a Catholic. Henrietta Maria was petite and lively, with tombstone buckteeth but lovely eyes, and she would be only 15 when she married Charles. Even at that tender age, the princess had already displayed her ferocious will and fierce temper, as well as her fervent commitment to the faith in which she'd been brought up. In May 1625, Charles and his court set out to meet his new bride at Canterbury: Henrietta Maria was known to be travelling in considerable grandeur with a retinue of nearly 4000,[22] and Charles, anxious not to be outdone, summoned a large entourage including the whole Chapel Royal, the royal string band and 12 wind musicians. The cost of such a venture must have been astronomical: enough to pay for the bed and board of the musicians alone, not to mention the clerics, Chapel servants, organists, and all their bags and paraphernalia. Among the musicians was Orlando Gibbons, now in his mid-forties, a Chapel Royal veteran who doubtless provided organ music for religious services en route. There are even records of Charles commissioning an ode by Gibbons for the celebration of his prospective marriage[23] although the music has not survived.

The joyful occasion, coupled with the musical resources at Gibbons's disposal, should have provided him with another highlight of his career. Instead, perhaps worn out by his work on James's funeral, followed so quickly by the need to prepare for another great royal event, Gibbons fell suddenly and dangerously ill. His swift decline caused widespread panic among royal personnel; physicians were quickly summoned amid fears that he had the plague. It was a justifiable fear: that year the bills of mortality recorded 35,428 dead from plague in London alone, with up to 5000 being buried every week. But the doctors – whose grisly medical report has survived in full – assuaged such worries as unfounded:

> *We whose names are here underwritten: having been called to give our counsels to Mr Orlando Gibbons; in the time of his late and sudden sickness … out of which, we could never recover him, neither by inward nor outward medicines, & then instantly he fell in most strong & sharp convulsions which did wring his mouth up to his ears, & his eyes were distorted, as though they would have been thrust out of his head & then suddenly he lost both speech, sight and hearing, & so grew apoplectical & lost the whole motion of every part of his body, & so died. Then here upon … rumours*

were cast out that he did die of the plague, whereupon we together with MR Majors appointment caused his body to be searched by certain women that were sworn to deliver the truth, who did affirm they never saw a fairer corpse. Yet not withstanding we to give full satisfaction to all did cause the skull to be opened in our presence & we carefully viewed the body, which we found also to be very clean without any show or spot of any contagious matter. In the brain we found the whole & sole cause of his sickness namely a great admirable blackness & syderation in the outside of the brain. Within the brain (being opened) there did issue out abundance of water intermixed with blood & this we affirm to be the only cause of his sudden death.[24]

Gibbons's death must have been a great shock to those who knew him, not least to King Charles himself. Charles had grown up with the music of Gibbons in his father's Chapel: the triumphant exuberance of his anthems such as the famous eight-voice 'O Clap Your Hands' (a setting of Psalm 47, originally written for Gibbons's friend and colleague Dr Heather) or the drama of 'Glorious and Powerful God'. The composer was buried at Canterbury cathedral, and his marble bust may be found there today.

Charles's marriage to Henrietta Maria was extremely unpopular: as a princess who was not only French but also Catholic, many of Charles's Protestant subjects – as well as his Protestant parliament – regarded her as a mortal enemy. The marriage did not even succeed, as Charles had intended, in cementing an alliance with France. In the preparations for the king and queen's coronation the following year (postponed due to the plague's appalling death toll), Henrietta Maria refused to accept that the Protestant archbishop of Canterbury should place the crown upon her head, rather than her own Catholic bishop, and in the end she refused – to Charles's fury – even to attend the coronation.[25] Not that this stopped Charles's profligate plans for his own anointing. He believed in the divine right of kings as strongly as his father: moreover, he was the first monarch to be born into the Church of England, and he was devout in his Anglicanism, believing that this ceremony before God would confirm his sacred mandate.

Charles's beliefs in the power of ceremony, and in his own divine right, chimed with those of the up-and-coming cleric William Laud, who organised the service. Laud had been a figure of growing authority within James I's religious establishment – preaching regularly at the Chapel Royal by the end of his reign – and would in turn become an increasingly powerful influence on Charles's vision for the future Church of England. Central to Laud's beliefs was the idea that the 'beauty of holiness' should be employed within the Church, in order to honour its status as a sacred House of God. The beauty of the service would bring the flock to faith as well as the Word. 'It is true,' he wrote, 'that the inward service of the heart is the great service of God, and no service is acceptable without it; but the external worship of God in the sanctuary is the great witness to the world that our hearts stand right in that service to God.' The beauty of holiness should lie, Laud believed, not just in the actual fabric of the church – elaborate altar hangings, candles and rich incense – but also in the ritual and ceremony of the services. Laud and his followers celebrated music as a positive religious value: one polemicist remarked that there was 'nothing of that kinde more powerfull, than melody both vocall and instrumentall, for raising of men's hearts, and sweetening their affections towards God'.[26] Consequently, Laudian beliefs were the antithesis of Puritanism: they aimed to conjure up all the splendour, solemnity and sacred mysteries of the medieval Catholic rite, while still maintaining Protestant doctrine.

It was these beliefs that were implemented with such unbridled zeal at Charles's coronation on 2 February 1626. By all accounts it was an immaculately choreographed affair, perhaps the best-ordered coronation in history – so keen were Laud and Charles to present a perfectly smooth-running ceremony that they even had a dress rehearsal, unprecedented for coronations at this time.[27] It was a highly complex event that demanded rehearsal: the ceremony itself lasted five hours and involved several stages, during which the king processed in; was anointed and presented with the robes and regalia of the last sainted Anglo-Saxon king, Edward the Confessor; and crowned, before processing out again. Details of the service are found in Laud's annotated copy of the coronation of the service; through them it becomes clear that every aspect of the service was invested with sacred meaning, such as Charles's use of the ancient relics, like the sacred sandals and the Anglo-Saxon ivory comb to tidy his hair. And there was lavish music throughout the service, narrating every part of the ceremony, from the procession to the anointing of Charles's head and shoulders with holy oil to the moment when the crown was placed on his head. Specific changes were made to the coronation service, probably implemented by Laud and Charles himself: the anthem traditionally sung for the entrance of the monarch, 'Behold O Lord', was replaced with a new text, Psalm 22:

> *I was glad when they said unto me,*
> *Let us go into the house of the Lord.*
> *Our feet shall stand at thy gates, O Jerusalem.*

It was an appropriate text for Charles, who believed fervently that his accession to the throne was not only sanctioned by God but would elevate him to the status of God's right-hand man on earth. Moreover, this change was one that would endure: the text has been sung at every English coronation up to the present, best-known today for its 1902 setting by Hubert Parry.

Much of the music would have been composed by Thomas Tomkins, who had replaced Gibbons as the chief organist of the Chapel Royal – we know Tomkins was paid 25 shillings for the privilege of 'composing of many songes againste the Coronation of Kinge Charles'.[28] This huge commission was the most important of Tomkins's career. Although many of the pieces have now been lost, still in existence is the little-known anthem 'O Lord Grant the King a Long Life', probably sung at this coronation and perhaps also at James I's.[29] It begins with a long, rather dour-sounding bass solo, accompanied by organ, proclaiming 'O Lord grant the King a long life/that his years may endure throughout our generations', before being taken up by a full choir who declare that 'he shall dwell before God forever/O prepare thy loving mercy and faithfulness' and ending in a festive Hallelujah chorus. Tomkins was already in his fifties by the time of this coronation. Taught by William Byrd, he had grown up surrounded by the Elizabethan traditions of sacred music. By 1625, the style of this music must have sounded conservative, even old-fashioned, to the assembled congregation. For Charles, however, clad in white satin and magnificent robes, perhaps processing towards an elaborate throne as the choir sung this anthem, its text would have confirmed his most fervent beliefs about his duty and role as King of England, illuminated through the solemn, elaborate music that he had grown up with. Listening to it today, the irony of the text is impossible to ignore: for Charles's life was soon to be cut cruelly short, only two decades after coming to the throne.

The coronation was just the beginning for Charles and his new ally. In Laud, the king found a kindred spirit – someone equally unyielding and rigid in his beliefs, who would later advise Charles to 'risk everything rather than yield a jot',[30] and who was equally preoccupied with the power of the old Catholic beauty and ritual in religious ceremonies. The following year, Charles made Laud the dean of his Chapel Royal, which Laud began to use as a testing ground for his ideas of holy beauty. The Chapel Royal was already more ceremonious and richly decorated than most churches and cathedrals elsewhere, filled with tapestry, rich fabrics and costly images. Nevertheless, Laud imposed strict new rules of behaviour and appearance on members of the Chapel, with instructions that 'the gentlemen of the Chapel shall (at all such times as they do attend that service) come in decent manner in their gowns and surplices, and not in cloaks and surplices, nor with boots and spurs'.[31] New rituals, such as the custom of bowing at the altar on entering and leaving the Chapel, were popularised; sermons were increasingly concerned with promoting the beauty of holiness. Above all, music began to return to the High Church tradition of elaborate theatricality. Thomas Tomkins's later work for the Chapel Royal became exceptionally complex: 'Behold, I Bring You Glad Tidings', for example, was written for treble solo, organ and ten-part chorus,[32] while his monumental Third Service was defiantly ornate, full of shifting textures alternating between three, four, five and six parts and a ten-part full choir.

Charles saw himself as the agent of Divine Order, and it was his vision that the entire nation should worship in the same elaborate way as the Chapel Royal. By 1633, his vision was beginning to be enforced: Laud had been promoted to archbishop of Canterbury and his ideas were gradually taking hold across the country. He ordered the reinstatement of stained glass, the regular use of incense and the return of elaborate vestments. He commanded that organs – many of which had been banished during the Reformation – should be built again in churches; the majority of these were constructed by the great organ-building family, the Dallams (who were Catholic), who would continue to build organs across the country until the middle of the eighteenth century. Many of these instruments still survive: Tewkesbury abbey's current organ – originally for Magdalen College, Oxford – was built by members of the Dallam dynasty in 1632. Laud's encouragement prompted a new wave of composers to write church music across England, and fostered a raising in the standards of quality and quantity of music in churches during the 1630s. A military officer from Norwich, Lieutenant Hammond, made a tour of the country in 1634–5 and observed in his journal how delightful the church music was that he heard during his visits to the cathedrals of 26 counties.[33] Experimentation was rife: not only organs, but other, more unexpected instruments were brought into church, such as 'fluits … bag-pipes … tymbrells and tabers'.[34] Along with the 'popish baits', 'glorious pictures' and 'excessive number of wax candles', the new music must have been an assault on the senses for those used to the stark surroundings of the Protestant Church.

Puritans were outraged: one thundered against 'the horrible profanation of both the sacraments with all manner of musick, both instrumentall and vocall, so loud that the Ministers could not be heard'.[35] For many, this new policy was seen as a covert attempt to re-Catholicise the Church. But Charles and Laud would not be deterred: confident of the king's God-given right to implement religion how he pleased, they decided to extend the policy to Scotland, where they attempted to impose a version of the English Book of Common Prayer. This caused riots and full-scale national rebellion. Amid demands that Charles should withdraw what the Scottish saw as a Catholic prayer book, the king merely replied: 'I will rather die than yield to their impertinent and damnable demands.' The battle lines for the Civil War were being drawn.

The more remote from his subjects Charles became, the more vulnerable his position. The king moved in a different world, one of order, decorum and stability, in a court that – with its strict rules of etiquette and ceremony, and waiters whom Charles insisted should serve him on bended knee – was known as 'the most formal in Europe'.[36] As Charles continued to surround himself with wealth and opulence he became increasingly isolated. In 1629 he dispensed with parliament, deciding that he could rule without it, and, since only a parliament could legislate new taxes, he demanded a mandatory and highly unpopular 'free gift' payment from his subjects, which he used to fund his indulgent personal lifestyle. With his sophisticated artistic tastes, Charles poured thousands into his programme of artistic patronage that he had pursued as prince; as a result, his court continued to be a vibrant cultural centre, filled with great artists, architects and musicians. He presided over the largest Royal Music since the time of Henry VIII. It was Charles who employed the first 'Master of the King's Musick' (a post that still exists today), Nicholas Lanier. Lanier was not only a composer, singer and lutenist, but also a connoisseur of art whom Charles trusted enough to send to Italy to negotiate the purchase of a painting for his vast art collection.

The most favoured body of musicians of the King's Music, the Lutes and Voices, was particularly active during Charles's reign. The king introduced more rigorous restrictions on the palace, barring anyone from below the rank of baron from his innermost sanctum, the Privy Chamber. It was here that he would spend hours being entertained by his most trusted musicians, with whom he clearly enjoyed a close personal relationship. There is an account of Nicholas Lanier singing while Charles listened 'with his hand upon his shoulder'; another which describes the lutenist John Wilson, who, 'giving his majesty constant attendance, had oftentimes just opportunities to exercise his hand on the lute – who, while he played, did usually lean or lay his hand on his shoulder'.[37] Such behaviour did nothing to improve Charles's reputation as chilly and remote. In more public spaces, the members of the Lutes and Voices played an important role in court masques, an elaborate mix of theatre, music, comedy, dancing and, above all, propaganda. The multimedia spectacles of their day, masques had been a feature of courtly entertainment since the time of Henry VIII, but it was during Charles's reign that they reached their apogee: they used the full resources of the Royal Music, with spectacular scenery and staging, and dramatic poetry on elaborate allegorical or mythical themes. The Banqueting House at Whitehall was the venue for these sumptuous, bank-breaking productions. The first classical structure built in England since the time of the Romans, the House was designed by Inigo Jones, now one the artistic darlings of the Stuart court. The Banqueting House's order, precision and formality reflect the values that Charles himself believed in: his idea of society was similarly rigid and hierarchical – and on the ceiling inside the building is a glorious painting by Peter Paul Rubens that proclaims, through a central image of Charles's father, James, being crowned by the heavens, the Stuart's God-given right to rule. This view was reinforced by the musical events that the building was primarily built to house.

Masques were not paying concerts for the general public, but exclusive court entertainments, designed for the monarch and about the monarch; since no one but the king and courtiers witnessed them, they were less of an advertisement of Charles's greatness to his subjects and more a private opportunity for the king to bask in the reflected glory of himself on stage. (So irrelevant had his subjects become to him that it would never have occurred to him that the whole performance was simply for his benefit.) There had been public and controversial criticism of the masque genre from Puritan lawyer William Prynne: his notorious thousand-page *Histriomastix* denounced actresses as 'notorious whores' at a time when Charles's Catholic queen, who loved music and dancing, had appeared in a speaking part on the stage. Laud, who hated Prynne, denounced the work as 'infamous treason' and hauled Prynne before the Star Chamber, the royal court of law. There he was served a huge fine and condemned to stand in the pillory, have both his ears cut off, and be imprisoned for life. In the aftermath of the fiasco, King Charles personally requested a masque put on by the Inns of Court – where Prynne had been employed – to prove the institution's love and affection for the Crown. This they did: the masque, entitled *The Triumph of Peace*, was the most expensive (and sycophantic) example of the form during this period. Performed first in 1634, it was dedicated 'To you, Great King and Queen, whose/Smile doth scatter blessing through this isle'.[38] Costing in excess of £21,000, the masque text was written by the dramatist James Shirley, depicting the spirits of Peace, Law and Justice descending to honour the English monarchs. The costumes were rich and fantastic; there were seven changes of scene, which was designed by Inigo Jones, with all lines of perspective culminating at the place where the monarch was seated.[39] Much of the lavish music was provided by one of Charles's favourite personal musicians, William Lawes, and the scoring for the music is as elaborate as the spectacle: the musicians, probably over one hundred in all,[40] included a consort of six lutes, a bass lute, a harp, a violin and three viols. No complete masque score survives, but there exist a number of Lawes's intricate, decorative songs, such as his melancholy 'In Envy of the Night' accompanied by continuo, in which the performer berates the setting of the moon because it signals the end of the festivities. We know that there were also choruses and 'symphonies'; these were not symphonies as we know them today but two-part instrumental dance forms that introduced the songs and also covered the movements of the musicians from the stage to the dance floor. The masque was clearly a success: Queen Henrietta Maria liked it so much she asked it to be performed again two weeks later.

Charles put on 11 masques throughout the 1630s. But despite such outward displays of power and magnificence – or perhaps, in part, because of them – cracks in his reign were beginning to show. His controversial religious policies were gradually bringing Britain to a crisis: parliament was dissenting and a Puritan MP named John Pym was leading the charge against him, while in the background another MP, Oliver Cromwell, was gradually gaining power. Like all musicians at court, William Lawes was in a highly vulnerable position, and in his consort music from around this time, it is surely not too fanciful to hear the nearing thunderous storm clouds of war.

LORD PROTECTOR

By 1642, parliament's disagreements with Charles over his religious policies had developed into full-on rebellion, and the warring factions split into two opposing sides: the royalists, or Cavaliers, insisting on Charles's supremacy over Church and State, and the Parliamentarians, or Roundheads, who believed that the king's powers should be limited, and religion a matter of individual conscience. William Laud had been accused by Parliament of treason for his High Church policies and imprisoned in the Tower of London in 1641. Charles left London in January the following year, in fear of his life and that of his retinue; after assembling a haphazard army he raised the royal standard, first in August at Nottingham, with fewer than 4000 men under his command. For those who had been employed under Charles, there was no hope of remaining at court. Some, like William Lawes, enlisted as soldiers for the royalist cause; others fled to the relative safety of country houses to sit and wait it out under the protection and support of wealthy noble patrons. Thomas Tomkins retreated to his home in Worcester, and his beloved cathedral – where he had been an organist since 1596 – and could only hope the war would not come near his city.

But music was not completely silenced in wartime: indeed, in some forms, it was part of the very fabric of battle. As part of Charles's plan to improve the rather lax standards of the English army during the 1630s, he issued a warrant that a particular traditional 'English March' should be the official march played by drummers throughout his army:

> *Whereas the ancient custom of nations hath ever been to use one certain and constant form of march in the wars, whereby to be distinguished from another. And the march of this our nation so famous in all the honourable achievement and glorious wars of this our kingdom in foreign parts (being by approbation of strangers themselves confessed and acknowledged the best of all marches) was through negligence and carelessness of drummers, and by long discontinuance so alerted and changed from the ancient gravity and majesty thereof, as it was in danger utterly to have been lost and forgotten ... Willing and commanding all drummers within our kingdom of England and principality of Wales exactly and precisely to observe the [playing of the march], as well in this our kingdom, as abroad in the service of any foreign prince or state without any addition or alternative whatsoever. To the end that so ancient, famous and commendable a custom may be preserved as a pattern and precedent to all posterity.*[41]

The march had long been used by the English army, but was ordered to be written down on paper by Prince Henry in 1610, which is the reason for its unusual survival. The warrant betrays Charles's conservative, traditional tastes, which clearly extended from music to militia: he also urged the army to retain the use of the longbow, a weapon that had seen its glory days two centuries earlier during the Hundred Years War.[42] At this time, the military band in England was still in its infancy, but the drum was already an important military instrument in its own right: one contemporary account described how 'in every company there is to be two drums at the least, and over them all a Drum Major, in each regiment. The Drum Major is to be lodged neere or in the Sergeant Majors Lodgings, it being his place to give instructions to the rest, and to take into his custodie the enimyes drums that enter the campe, or garrison ...'[43] There would certainly have been drums on both sides of the battle during the Civil War.

The Roundheads were also known by their fondness for psalms, as were the Puritans, who believed that psalm-singing was the only acceptable form of music in church. There are numerous accounts of the Parliamentarians singing psalms as they marched into battle, demonstrating to the enemy that God was truly on their side: in January 1642, before storming Leeds, a minister led the troops in a rendition of Psalm 68, which begins 'May God arise, may his enemies be scattered/May his foes flee before him'. Later in the war, Oliver Cromwell, having risen fast through the ranks to become a general, led his troops in a coastal conflict at Dunbar, in Scotland. The Parliamentarians triumphed in a dawn attack against the Scottish army, and, as the defeated Scots fled, Cromwell halted his soldiers for a victorious rendition of Psalm 117: 'Oh give you praise to the Lord/ All nations that be'. The Parliamentarians' piety sometimes took more violent forms of expression than singing, however. As they travelled through the country, soldiers often made a point of stopping to dismantle churches that were filled with 'popish' effects, such as organs and elaborate altar tables, and, in August 1642, they descended upon Canterbury cathedral. Here they proceeded to wreck service books and surplices, and one soldier went to the organ and began to play the tune of a popular ballad named 'The Zealous Soldier', but so ham-fistedly that the instrument never sounded right again.[44] Organs across the country were destroyed throughout the war, and the Dallam family of organ builders fled to the safety of Brittany, where they continued to sell their instruments successfully to the French.

Not all musicians were so lucky. In 1645, William Lawes was involved in the deadly siege of Chester, a city that had been in the possession of the royalist army since the beginning of the war. In September of that year King Charles was notified of a new Parliamentarian attack on Chester and travelled with great haste to the city to defend what had become an important royalist stronghold. But at the Battle of Rowton Heath, amid 'a terrible storm, [both sides] firing in the face of one another, hacking and slashing with swords', the royalists gave way altogether and the city was lost. During that final battle, Lawes was killed by a single bullet, one of 600 royalist losses. We know that Charles was in a nearby tower at the time, watching both sides 'exchange some bullets with one another',[45] and it is possible he even witnessed Lawes's death. The king, who had known Lawes since his early twenties, was devastated: he found the time to institute a special period of mourning for the composer, honouring him with the special title of 'Father of Musick'. A more politically pointed epitaph was provided by a fellow young Cavalier, the poet Thomas Jordan: 'Will Lawes was slain by such whose wills were laws'.[46]

Lawes's grief-stricken brother and fellow musician, Henry, would later publish a tribute of his own: a publication of William's three-part psalm settings named *Choice Psalmes*, dedicated not only to his brother 'unfortunately lost in these unnaturall Warres' but also to the persecuted King Charles. It was a brave thing to publish in the charged political atmosphere of 1648, as war was still raging, but Henry was as loyal as his brother to the royalist cause. He also knew the king well: he had been a gentleman of the Chapel Royal in Charles's court, and, as a notable songwriter, was also a member of the elite Lutes and Voices group of musicians. The collection *Choice Psalmes* contains 60 psalms and other devotional songs, half of them by William, and half by Henry. The sixteenth piece in the collection, 'In the Substraction of my Years' by William, is uncannily prophetic. It is a mournful G minor key setting of a verse from Isaiah, including the line 'Cut off by death before my time/and like a flower cropped in my prime'.[47] Perhaps William had suspected all along what was coming for him and his master.

Neither did Thomas Tomkins escape unscathed, even in the comparative safety of rural Worcester: soon after the war began, Parliamentary forces arrived to occupy the city. One contemporary writer reported:

And when their whole army ... came to Worcester, the first thing they there did, was the prophanation of the cathedral, destroying the organ, breaking in pieces divers beautiful windows, wherein the foundation of that church was lively historified with painted glass, and barbarously defacing divers fair monuments of the dead. And as if this was not enough, they brought their horses into the body of the church, keeping fires and courts of guard therein, making the quire and side aisles, with the font, the commons places, wherein they did their easements of nature.[48]

Tomkins had been employed at the cathedral since he was 24 years old; his superb Dallam organ had been in place for nearly as long as he had worked there. Soon after, Parliamentary forces evacuated Worcester and the city was reoccupied by royalist troops. Then, in May 1643, a 3000-man Parliamentary force arrived to try to wreste back control of the city. In the ensuing fight, Tomkins's house was smashed by a cannonade, making it uninhabitable for several weeks. Things must have seemed bleak for the composer: the cathedral locked and silent, his house and city in ruins. In this time of desperation, Tomkins turned to the solace of composing: outraged by the effects of war on his personal circumstances, he made his protest in an enormous, impassioned verse anthem that set the words of Psalm 79: 'O God, the heathen are come into thine inheritance/ thy holy temple have they defiled,/and made Jerusalem a heap of stones'. This anthem – anonymous in its only known source – has only recently been reclaimed as Tomkins's work, and survives in an incomplete form, with only one choral line (the bass) surviving. However, it has recently been reconstructed and recorded for the first time in more than three centuries; on the assumption that if, indeed, it was written in the historical context described above, it would not have been performed by a traditional church or cathedral choir, but by voices and viols in a more intimate setting. The result is a powerful and moving musical response to this pathos-filled text.

∞

On 10 January 1645, an enormous crowd formed around the wooden scaffold on Tower Hill in London to witness the beheading of William Laud. It was a symbolic moment for the Parliamentarian cause: the fall of the man who had been not only Charles's closest ally but also the source of the religious policies that had split the country in two. Tomkins, from his now-restored home in Worcester, composed a solemn tribute in the Elizabethan idiom of his youth, 'The Pavan: Lord Canterbury', adapting the sombre, old-fashioned dance form for keyboard, giving the work an extra dimension of whimsical longing for the past. This pavan, dating from 1647, was written when the Civil War was at its height, when Oliver Cromwell's tough, Bible-thumping New Model Army was bolstering Parliament's cause against the king and would ultimately bring the royalists to defeat. That same year, Charles, who had been taken prisoner by the Scots, was handed over to Parliament, and, in early January 1649, was finally charged with high treason. He was beheaded on 30 January, showing uncharacteristic courage and dignity, in front of the same Banqueting House that had previously staged lavish masques to glorify his name. Tomkins's final tribute to Charles was another keyboard work, the sombre, stately and almost unbearably poignant 'Sad Pavan: for These Distracted Times'. The music is highly reflective and introspective, with its slow-moving, interweaving lines, almost as if the performer is improvising while thinking about other things. It is easy to picture Tomkins playing it while reflecting not only on his own fate, but also that of a king whose own unswerving belief in his divinity had been his ultimate destruction.

∝

Barely two months later, an Act of Parliament was passed decreeing that the office of king should be abolished. The Commonwealth of England was established, and Oliver Cromwell, as Lord Protector, became the most powerful ruler of the British Isles since the fall of Rome. Presiding over the now united kingdoms of England, Scotland and Ireland, with a malleable parliament and the most feared navy and army in Europe, he had all the authority of a dictator. With the help of his so-called major generals who became military governors of the English regions, Cromwell began to impose the Protectorate's strict programme of social reform upon the country: an unrestrainedly puritanical assault on 'social evils' such as drunkenness, swearing and promiscuity, as well as such staples of English life as horse races, playhouses, alehouses, casinos and brothels. Almost all church music was banned (apart from simple psalm-singing) and musical–religious institutions – most of which had been shut down during wartime – remained closed. The most significant composers of that era – including Gibbons and Tomkins – had been raised and educated through such institutions, and there was a fear that their disbandment would mean not only the dearth of musicians of their calibre, but of any professional musicians whatsoever. To that end, a petition was raised in 1657 by those concerned, suggesting the establishment of a school of music:

> *That by reason of the late dissolution of the Quires in the Cathedralls where the study and the practise of the Science of Musick was especially cherished … and there being now noe preferrement or Encouragement in the way of Musick, noe man will breed his child in it soe that it must needes bee that that Science itselfe must dye in this Macion … except some present maintenance and Encouragement bee given for educating of some youth in the study and practice of said science. Wherefore you petitioners must humbly pray that there bee a corporacion or colledge of musitians erected in London with reasonable powers to read and practise publiquely all sorts of Musick.*[49]

Clearly Cromwell remained unmoved by the plea, for no such school was ever established.

But the prospects for performers and composers were not entirely bleak: Puritans were, after all, not against music per se, just its use in church and the theatre. Cromwell himself was a music lover, and although the Royal Music was not returned to anything like its former glory days in the reign of Charles I, the Lord Protector employed a small group of personal musicians – an organist, seven instrumentalists and two singing boys. Cromwell was particularly fond of sacred songs, and even, rather hypocritically, ordered performances of Latin motets by Richard Dering: the Puritans, despite their austere reputation, had no objection to elaborate music as long as it wasn't used in church services. Cromwell had personally intervened to have the fine Dallam organ at Magdalen College, Oxford, moved to Hampton Court, which was now the home of the Protectorate court, where it was probably played by the poet John Milton, who, as well as being Cromwell's private secretary, was a skilled keyboard player. Cromwell's organist and favourite musician, John Hingeston, would have often played the Dallam instrument, too. Most of Hingeston's surviving compositions were in fact written for Cromwell's musical establishment, not just keyboard music but also dance suites for cornetts and sackbuts, wind music (published in a set of part books adorned with Cromwell's personal coat of arms), and instrumental fantasias. Hingeston was also paid to instruct Cromwell's daughters in music; perhaps it was Hingeston's teaching that imparted a particular love of the art in the Lord Protector's youngest daughter, Frances, prompting her to request distinctly unpuritanical musical entertainment at her wedding in November 1658. One account of the raucous celebrations somewhat dispels the straitlaced image of the Commonwealth (although the number of instruments mentioned is almost certainly an exaggeration):

> *On Wednesday last was my Lord Protector's daughter married to the Earl of Warwick's grandson ... on Thursday was the wedding feast kept at Whitehall, where they had 48 violins, 50 trumpets and much mirth with frolics, besides mixt dancing (a thing heretofore accounted profane) till 5 of the clock yesterday morning.*[50]

For musicians outside Cromwell's circle, however, life during the Commonwealth must have been tough. Yet, in the face of adversity, they found ways to adapt and cope imaginatively with the new rules and regulations. In 1656, a notorious rake and dramatist named William Davenant circumvented the blanket ban on play-acting by presenting a 'story sung in recitative music', with music by, among others, Henry Lawes (brother of William). *The Siege of Rhodes*, as it was called, is now known to be the first opera produced in England, invented by happy accident, and anticipating a great flowering of English opera during the later seventeenth century.

At a time when performing religious music could result in the arrest of those playing it, perhaps it is not surprising that instrumental music began to thrive as never before. As the writer Roger North put it: 'When most other good arts languished, Musick held up her head not at Court not – in the cant of those times – profane Theaters but in private society, for many chose to fiddle at home than to goe out and be knockt on the head abroad.'[51] Musicians who had previously worked at court, collegiate churches or cathedrals were now mostly employed at country houses: it was in the parlours, great halls and music rooms of these houses that chamber music – originally played almost exclusively at court – continued to be performed. Composers such as John Jenkins, who during the Commonwealth 'past his time at gentlemen's houses in the country'[52] variously employed by noble patrons across East Anglia, wrote numerous fantasias for imaginatively florid scorings of viols of different pitches, presumably for the 'chests of viols' it was fashionable for wealthy families to own. Jenkins himself was a virtuoso viol player, and had even performed as a bass violist in the opulent masque for Charles I, *The Triumph of Peace*. He also wrote several extraordinary consort works for 'lyra viol'[53] – such as 'The Five Bells' and 'The Six Bells' that imitate the sound of bells, incorporating familiar clock tower melodies used to ring the Hours of the Daily Office.[54] Perhaps Jenkins was remembering the era when musicians regularly heard such bell chimes, working within the hallowed walls of cathedrals, monasteries and collegiate churches. These beautiful, sonorous pieces are certainly filled with an affecting nostalgia and longing, conjuring up the sounds of tolling funeral bells, pealing church bells, and even, to the fanciful listener, the sounds of bell-ringers letting their hair down in the tavern.

From elite country houses, of course, the rich repertory of chamber music would eventually disseminate into the wider community. Thus, in a few short years, chamber music moved from being heard only in palace chambers to becoming an audible presence across the land, a curious unintended consequence of Cromwell's regicide.

RESTORATION

Throughout the years without monarchy, the royalist hopes were kept alive by Charles I's son, Charles II. Young Charles had spent most of the war fighting the royalist cause: after his father's execution in 1649, he was even acknowledged as king by the Scottish Parliament, and assembled a ragged army of Scotsmen to stake his claim to the English throne. But after a crushing defeat by Cromwell's troops, Charles was forced to escape into exile, and now he lay in wait on the Continent, hoping for an opportunity to claim his rightful title. By 1660, that opportunity was drawing near: ever since Oliver Cromwell's death in 1658 and the accession of his son, Richard, the English Parliament had been fractured, its army was in disarray and the support for a new Stuart monarch was widespread and heartfelt. In the spring, Samuel Pepys observed: 'Everybody now drinks the King's health without any fear, whereas before it was very private that a man may do it.' Supporters were not afraid to sing in the streets in support of the man they hoped would be the next king, and they rallied around one ballad in particular, 'When the King Enjoys His Own Again': 'The most famous and popular air ever heard of in this country ... invented to support the declining interest of Charles I, it served afterwards, with more success ... to promote the restoration of his son – an event it was employed to celebrate all over the kingdom.'[55]

> *Though for a time we see Whitehall*
> *With cobwebs hanging on the wall*
> *Instead of gold and silver brave*
> *Which formerly was wont to have*
> *With rich perfume*
> *In every room,*
> *Delightful to that princely train*
> *Yet the old again shall be*
> *When the time you see*
> *That the King enjoys his own again*
> *Yes, this I can tell*
> *That all will be well*
> *When the King enjoys his own again.*

By 1660, the King *did* enjoy his own again – returning at the invitation of parliament, who had finally decided that only a Stuart monarchy had the legitimacy to guarantee known laws and a stable line of succession. In May, Charles made landfall, victorious, on England's shores, and was greeted with joy, dancing and singing, in the streets of London: the diarist John Evelyn reported 'Triumph of above 20,000 horse & foote, brandishing their swords and shouting with unexpressable joye; the wayes strewed with flowers, the bells ringing ... fountains running with wine ... Trumpets, Musick, and (myriads) of people flocking the streetes ...'[56] The following year, on 22 April 1661, the coronation celebrations began. Charles chose to restore – for the last time in England's history – an eve-of-coronation tradition whereby the new king processed from the Tower of London to Westminster. Four vast triumphal arches were specially constructed at strategic points, each topped with musicians. The procession took five hours to pass and was of unparalleled magnificence: Charles had clearly heeded the advice of his supporter William Cavendish, who told him 'when you appear, show yourself gloriously to your people ... for what is a king, more than a subject, but for ceremony and order'.[57] Matthew Locke wrote – probably specifically for this procession – a six-part suite named 'For His Majesty's Sagbutts & Cornetts' to be played by the royal wind musicians, an important commission that shows just how eminent Locke was as a composer by this time. (The leading figures of the pre-war Royal Music – Gibbons, Tomkins and Lawes – had all died before or during the Interregnum.) 'For His Majesty's Sagbutts & Cornetts' is a stately and oddly sober piece, in D minor, which does not convey the celebratory nature of the occasion so much as the solemn nature of the role Charles II was about to undertake.

Musically, Charles II's coronation service the next day was a case of new wine in old bottles. The music was by a new generation of composers: for example, William's Child's anthem 'O Lord, Grant the King a Long Life'. This contrapuntal work for four-part choir and organ would be revived at every coronation up to, and including, George IV's – the first surviving example of a recurring coronation anthem. Everything else was old, or tried to be; after all, this was a Restoration. The same order of service was used, and the same anthem texts (including William Child's) sung, at the coronation of Charles I. The royal regalia – the crown, the orb and the sceptre, which had been destroyed during the Commonwealth – were remade, given their old names and used in the time-honoured way. Even the singing was led, as in the old days, by the Chapel Royal, although, since the last boy treble who had sung for Charles I was now a man of about 30, the choir had been built from scratch with all-new personnel. Alongside them was the reunited King's Music, almost exactly as it had been during Charles I's reign – complete with string band and wind band, as well as trumpets and kettle-drummers; the noise of the instruments, choir and assembled congregation would have been deafening in the echoing chambers of Westminster Abbey. That celebrated lover of music, Samuel Pepys, who was in attendance, complained of 'so great a noise that I could make but little of the Musique, and endeed it was lost to everybody'.[58] Pepys got so tired of the service that he actually left the Abbey.

For those members of the congregation who remembered Charles I's coronation 35 years earlier, the glamour of the occasion, coupled with familiar music, must have made it seem almost as if the Civil War, the Republic and the Protectorate had never been. And, of course, that was exactly the intention. But there would be difficult choices ahead, as the newly crowned King Charles could not have forgotten, even amid the pomp and ceremony of the service: choices over the future of monarchy, of religion and the profound connection between divinity and kingship. Charles II would never feel as secure on the throne as his ancestors before him had: he knew all too well that the king was no longer infallible and all-powerful, and the looming spectre of his father was a constant, sobering reminder of his vulnerability. Outwardly, all may have looked the same, but inwardly Charles and his advisers understood that the British monarchy could never be the same again.

Despite the apparent carefree excesses of Charles's coronation, music had been badly bruised by the effects of the Interregnum as well. At the Westminster Abbey service, the choir were rusty after being so long disbanded, and ambitious choral music was out of the question: the inexperienced choirboys were discreetly reinforced by men singing falsetto,[59] as their more experienced counterparts had long since grown up or died during the bloody civil wars. The pool of musical talent was fast drying up; professional singing men had been some 14 years out of employment, and no new choristers had been trained in the meantime. Much music had been destroyed and organs been taken down. The Chapel Royal, like virtually every other musical institution, had to be started again from scratch.

The man tasked with this responsibility was Captain Henry Cooke, appointed Master of the Chapel Royal Children soon after Charles II acceded to the throne. He was a tough, determined man who had fought for the royalists during the Civil War; he had also seen service as a musician in the former Chapel Royal under Charles I. By all accounts he was an excellent choirmaster and singer – Samuel Pepys credits him with 'the best manner of singing in the world',[60] but he was also an arrogant man inclined to brag, a 'vain coxcomb'. Such innate self-confidence must have come in handy for Cooke in facing such a formidable task that many would surely have balked at. But not Cooke: he rose magnificently to the occasion, riding across the country on horseback, visiting cathedrals, colleges and even parish churches in order to select the best young recruits for the Chapel.[61] It was a huge risk to put such inexperienced singers in such a significant public arena as the Chapel Royal, and, indeed, several early accounts of performances at the Chapel suggest that there were teething problems with this new, raw talent. Pepys (ever the backseat critic) describes hearing a Sunday anthem that was 'ill sung, which made the king laugh'.[62] But ultimately it was a risk that paid off: by luck, or more likely by judgement, Cooke had managed to gather perhaps the single most talented generation of choirboys in Chapel Royal history.

On 22 November 1663, Samuel Pepys recorded in his diary a performance of a setting of Psalm 51, 'made … by one of Captain Cooke's boys, a pretty boy' – a young Pelham Humfrey, who at this time was only 15 or 16 years old. The anthem was 'Have Mercy upon Me O God'. While somewhat self-conscious and laboured in its setting, it is still an astoundingly mature work for a teenager. Humfrey clearly wasn't happy with it, however: he went back to the anthem a few years later and rewrote it.[63] John Blow was also among the choristers purloined by Henry Cooke; by his mid-twenties he would become England's leading musician, his own compositions exerting a powerful influence over several future generations of Chapel Royal composers. Like Humfrey, Blow showed early promise in composition: while he was still a chorister (which he continued to be until he was 16, when his voice broke) at least three of his anthems were regularly performed by the Chapel. One anthem in particular shows what must have been close kinship between the choirboys, who lived, worked, ate and slept together, presided over by their choirmaster (who was paid £30 a year for the task of not only teaching the choristers in the art of music, but also for feeding, clothing and washing them). 'I Will Always Give Thanks' is a 'club anthem' composed jointly by Humfrey, Blow and their fellow chorister William Turner, 'as a memorial of their fraternal esteem and friendship',[64] the homophony of the three voices that open the work perhaps signifying their combined and harmonious creativity.

Despite some hardships – Charles II's chronic lack of cash meant Cooke was continually contending with delays in payments to the Chapel Royal, on one occasion having to keep the Children away from the chapel because their clothes were in tatters[65] – it must have been a golden time in the life of the boys. In the 1660s, being in the Chapel Royal was akin to being at the very best of specialist music schools, surrounded by the most prestigious composing and performing talents, while simultaneously being asked to take part in the most high-profile musical events in the land. There was also the benefit of having personal interaction with the monarch himself: King Charles took a keen interest in the progress of the boys, who were the pride and joy of the Chapel. Fifty years later, a former chorister named Thomas Tudway fondly remembered:

some of the forwardest, & brightest Children of the Chappell, as Mr Humfreys, Mr Blow, &c began to be Masters of a faculty in Composing; This, his Majesty greatly encourag'd, by indulging their youthful fancys, so that ev'ry Month at least, & afterwards oft'ner, they produc'd something New, of this Kind ... for otherwise, it was in vain to hope to please his Majesty.[66]

But Charles II's interests were not, on the whole, devotional. He attended the chapel only on Sunday mornings and on special occasions; and the grave, solemn church music of the past was not to his taste. Charles's reputation as the 'Merry Monarch' is well founded: he was charming, good-humoured and flirtatious, with a practical rather than scholarly intelligence and a love of socialising. He was fond of music, but his tastes had been shaped profoundly by the years he had spent in exile on the Continent, as reflected in the musical innovations introduced at the start of his reign. In most respects Charles had simply re-established the musicians of his father's court: the wind musicians, the Private Music, the trumpets and fifes. But one change was more extreme: Charles radically expanded the royal violin band to 24 players, in emulation of Louis XIV's celebrated '24 Violons du Roi' that Charles had heard perform in France. The 'violin band' was the most up-to-date, fashionable and sought-after ensemble in Europe, and Charles wanted to emulate its magnificence in his own court.

The violin had been growing gradually in importance since the reign of James I, and by Charles's reign there were at least 14 violins employed in his establishment.[67] But while in Europe the violin took hold as the most fashionable string instrument of the day, the English court, perhaps due to the isolating effects of the Civil War and the Interregnum, held on to the more traditional, sober-sounding viol long after it had been abandoned elsewhere.

The seventeenth-century historian Roger North even blames the chests of viols kept by noble families for England's backward tastes: 'the use of chests of violls, which supplyed all instrumental consorts, kept back the English from falling soon into the modes of forrein countrys, where the violin and not the treble viol was in use'.[68] In England, the violin was traditionally associated with more frivolous types of music, and used primarily to accompany dancing. But this suited Charles II, whose tastes were dance-inclined; he detested the contrapuntal fantasies of viol consorts, preferring the 'brisk and arie' sound of the violin, and North observed that the king 'never in his life could endure any [music] that he could not act by keeping the time'[69] – i.e. that he could not tap his foot to. In this, Charles was the opposite of his father: his more 'popular' musical preferences reflected his more 'realist' political inclinations, just as Charles's highbrow tastes were indicative of his strictly hierarchical attitude towards kingship.

In line with his love of all things French, Charles was naturally interested in French dancing, and the court employed a French dancing master who instructed the entire royal family. Pepys witnessed the young Princess Mary, the future queen, practising one afternoon: 'I did see the young Duchess, a little child in hanging sleeves, dance most finely, so as almost to ravish me, her airs were so good – taught by a Frenchman that did heretofore teach the King and all the King's children, and the Queen-mother herself, who doth still dance well.' The skills acquired under the tutelage of the dancing master were shown off at formal balls in front of assembled courtiers as well as informally in private apartments; Pepys records one occasion on which Charles was 'dancing with fiddlers all night long' at the home of his mistress, Lady Castlemaine.[70] The fiddlers in question were undoubtedly a detachment of Charles's beloved 24 violins, which would have accompanied the dancing at most royal occasions. One particularly popular dance was the 'branle' or 'brawl', vividly defined in an English/French dictionary published in 1612:

> [Branle]: *a totter, swing, or swindge; a shake, shog, or shocke; a stirring, an uncertain and inconstant motion; … also, a brawl, or daunce, wherein many (men, and women) holding by the hands sometimes in a ring, and otherwise at length, move all together.*[71]

This is a dance with which Charles would have been very familiar, as would the composers at court. Matthew Locke wrote a cycle of branles in different keys, most likely intended for the 24 Violins, as did the composer John Banister, both of whom were closely connected with the violin ensemble and wrote for it regularly. Locke's 'Suite of Brawls in Bb' opens with a movement that sounds more stately than dance-like, but as the movements progress the tempo increases and the rhythms become more complex, presenting a real dancing challenge for royals and courtiers alike. The sonority of many violins playing together, a sound that is so familiar to modern listeners, would have been surprising, unusual and exotic to seventeenth-century ears.

But the 24 violins were not simply used for dancing. Dissatisfied with the grave and solemn music of the Chapel, Charles II ordered 'the Composers of his Chappell to add Symphonies etc. with Instruments to their Anthems' – in the process inventing a revolutionary new style of music, the 'symphony anthem', where the passages for choir were alternated with sections played by the violins. Since the violin was not traditionally seen as an instrument used in worship, this was a controversial move, and, indeed, the spectators who witnessed the changes were of mixed opinions about the new style. On 7 September 1662, Pepys noted: 'a most excellent Anthem (with Symphony's between)' and, a week later, 'A Symphony between every verse of the Anthem; but the musique more full that it was last Sunday, and very fine it is.' John Evelyn felt differently: 'Instead of the antient grave and solemn wind musique accompanying the organ was introduced a consort of 24 violins betweene every pause, after the French fantastical light way ... better suiting a tavern or a playhouse than a church.'[72] Despite such reservations, Chapel Royal composers were happy to adopt the form. Perhaps the grandest example is Matthew Locke's anthem in celebration of Charles's naval victory during the second Anglo-Dutch war (although the war itself would ultimately end in disaster for the English). 'Be Thou Exalted Lord' is scored for four solo voices, two choral groups, a solo instrumental group (containing two violins, two bass viols and two theorboes) and a five-part string orchestra;[73] visitors to the Chapel would certainly never have heard anything so complex or sumptuous. Charles's revolutionary new symphony author marked another step in the growth of the violin's dominance in English music – and, indeed, its seriousness as an instrument, as composers at court began to realise its potential in works of all kinds. As the violin grew in importance during Charles II's reign, there was a simultaneous decline in the importance of wind music, which had often played at the Chapel Royal since Elizabeth I's reign: in 1663, there were 16 wind players and 24 violins at court, but by 1669 the wind players numbered only five. This change in emphasis from wind to strings, shaped by the monarch's personal tastes, represents perhaps the most important transition in music history, that from Renaissance band to baroque orchestra.

Reflecting the gregarious personality of his Tudor forebear, Charles II was the first monarch since Henry VIII to dine regularly in public,[74] which he did at least three days weekly, and he often called upon the 24 violins to accompany him as he ate. The violin band also followed the king on frequent detachments outside the palace: to Windsor for the summer or to Newmarket for the races. Travelling to Portsmouth in 1662 to meet his new queen, Catherine of Braganza, King Charles took 12 of the 24 violins with him. (When he first saw his unprepossessing looking new wife, he is supposed to have claimed 'they have brought me a bat!'.) In September 1663, the queen herself was accompanied by seven of the violins to Bath to take the waters. For the occasion, John Banister wrote 'The Music at the Bath', a lively dance-like piece in 12 tiny sections in the key of B♭. The bitty nature of the piece was a device by Banister, written to accommodate the whim of the monarch, who might demand the music be started or stopped at any time; the very small sections mean that the music can begin or leave off almost anywhere without sounding unfinished.[75]

In 1670, after the bitter loss suffered by the English in the second Anglo-Dutch war, King Charles went to Dover to form an alliance with France against the Dutch, signing a secret treaty with the Catholic king, Louis XIV. On the journey Charles took all 24 violins, at great cost, probably in an effort to impress Louis whom Charles admired fervently. The treaty helped to exacerbate the ongoing tensions between Protestants and Catholics that dominated Charles's reign. On the one hand were the Anglicans who made up the majority of his parliament, and zealously supported the restored monarchy; on the other were the Catholics and persistent rumours that Charles himself was dangerously partial to their faith. It was not a baseless concern either: as part of this new deal with France, Charles secretly promised that he would indeed convert to Catholicism. The English king's open alliance with Catholic France would not only prompt the third Anglo-Dutch war – ending, again, in triumph for the Dutch and embarrassment for Charles – but also fuel the nation's, and parliament's, ever-growing hysteria about the rising Catholic influence in England.

⌘

Charles II reigned for 25 turbulent years; aside from the constant sparring between Protestant and Catholics and a series of humiliating defeats by the Dutch, a plague arrived in London from Amsterdam in 1665, killing 70,000 Londoners, followed shortly by the Great Fire in 1666, which required substantial rebuilding of the entire capital city. As London began to emerge from the rubble and ashes, a young boy name Henry Purcell, aged seven or eight years old, became a Child of the Chapel Royal. Born in Westminster into a family of musicians – Purcell's father (Henry Purcell the elder), and his uncle Thomas were both professional singers – perhaps it was natural that Purcell would also grow up to be musical. What no one could have predicted, however, was that Purcell would become what many regard as England's greatest ever composer, creating a body of work during his short life that many composers could not have equalled in twice the time. By the time young Purcell became a chorister, the Chapel Royal had been restored to all its former glory; that meant that – as it had been for the last 300 years – it was the best music school in the land. He was tutored by Captain Henry Cooke, and later Pelham Humfrey; from them he learned to sing at sight, to perform confidently on the grandest occasions and to understand the basic principles of composition, as well as how to play the keyboard, lute and violin. Although none of Purcell's childhood compositions have survived, the works he was creating in his teenage years are miraculous in their assurance: his natural talent is undeniable, but it was his rigorous apprenticeship with the Chapel Royal that made such works possible. After leaving the choir in 1673, he studied with composers such as John Blow and Matthew Locke, both of whom would become lifelong influences on his music. In 1677, upon Locke's death, Purcell replaced him as the composer for the 24 violins (Purcell commemorated Locke in a heartfelt elegy *What hope for us remains now he is gone?*); and it was around this time that he probably wrote 'My Beloved Spake', the vivacious symphony anthem that is one of his earliest surviving works. This anthem marks Purcell as an extraordinary teenage talent: it is remarkable for its technical skill and emotional maturity, bringing the text to life with vivid word painting and a highly developed sense of the dramatic, making it a pleasure both to sing and to listen to. Utilising the Old Testament text 'The Song of Solomon', the work is in five substantial parts, depicting the end of winter and the arrival of spring with suspense-filled discords followed by a skilful move to a bright major key and a jubilant chorus of 'Hallelujah!'. It is hard to believe that such a work was written by an 18-year-old.

The quality of this work, and others like it, prompted Purcell's star to rise at court: in 1680 he received a prestigious and very public commission to compose a 'court ode' to celebrate Charles II's return to London. Odes were a significant musical custom at court; ever since the early years of the Restoration, they had been commissioned to celebrate major secular state occasions, such as New Year's Day, the king's birthday, and his return to court after the summer remove to Windsor. (By now, the royal calendar was no longer organised around religious feasts, for fear it would look far too Catholic.) On these occasions there would be a formal reception at court, during which the Lord Mayor and other leading dignitaries would make speeches proclaiming their loyalty to the king. A poem would be penned for the occasion by one of the court poets and set to music by the court composer; this would be performed as part of the service by the Chapel Royal choir and the instrumentalists of the King's Music. Various composers of the Chapel Royal had written odes in the past – Cooke, Locke and Humfrey among them – but the duty now fell to Purcell, who, along with his friend and mentor John Blow, would write at least one a year for the rest of his life.

Purcell's first ode, 'Welcome Vicegerent of the Mighty King', sets a spectacularly terrible, highly sycophantic text:

Welcome Vicegerent of the Mighty King.
that made and governs everything
Welcome from rural pleasures to the busy throne
In this head city, this imperial town,
The seat and centre of the crown

His absence was autumn, his presence is spring
That ever new life and new pleasure does bring
Then all that have voices, let 'em cheerfully sing,
And those that have none may say 'God save the King!'

The text should not perhaps be judged on its artistic merits so much as its political capital: it is, of course, designed to flatter the monarch in the highest terms possible at a large and influential public gathering. For the ambitious 21-year-old Purcell, it was also an opportunity to show off his talents in a very public context, using the resources of the entire Chapel Royal along with the king's Private Music and the 24 violins. He rises triumphantly to the occasion with 'Welcome Vicegerent', with a setting that is elegant, spritely and sensitive, conveying a tone of joyful celebration but nevertheless befitting the dignity of what must have been a solemn ceremony for the king's return.

By the early 1680s, the political temperature of Charles II's reign had risen to boiling point. Anti-Catholic hysteria was at its height, not just over Charles's suspected sympathies towards the faith, but those of his younger brother, James, the heir to the throne – who, it turned out, had previously converted to Catholicism. The hysteria extended to parliament, where the Exclusionists (or Whigs, as they became known) were violently opposed to James's accession, and were desperately looking for another candidate to put in his place, the primary choice being the Duke of Monmouth, Charles II's illegitimate – but Protestant – son. Ballads from the time in support of Monmouth show the divisions that existed even on the street, such as the pointedly named 'England's Darling: or Great Britain's Joy and Hope in that noble Prince James, Duke of Monmouth':

> *Brave Monmouth, England's glory*
> *Hated of none but Papist and Tory*
> *May'st thou in thy noble father's love remain*
> *Who happily over this land doth reign.*[76]

In 1683, a desperate Whig faction plotted to assassinate Charles and his brother James and put Monmouth on the throne: the Rye House Plot, as it became known, was, however, badly planned and failed miserably. Monmouth went into hiding, and two Whig lords were publicly beheaded. But the royal propaganda machine went into overdrive as a result: this triumph for Charles and the Tories who supported him was expressed in music, through a symphony anthem by John Blow, 'Hear My Voice O God', setting a wrathful text about God's vengeance on conspirators, performed in the Chapel Royal only a week before the executions of the hapless plotters. Purcell's welcome ode for that autumn, 'Fly Bold Rebellion', is on the same subject, crowing over Charles's victory and chiding the mob that had previously been against him:

Fly Bold Rebellion! Make haste and be gone!
Victorious in Council, great Charles is return'd
The Plot is display'd, and the traitors, some flow
And some to Avernus by Justice thrown down

Come then, change your notes, disloyal crowd
You that already have been too loud
With importunate follies and clamours
Tis no business of yours
to dispute the high powers
As if you were the government framers.

This was a high point for the monarchy: the rebels were, it seemed, defeated; the Tories were triumphant, and Charles's throne appeared to be secure. It was also a peak for music of the time. Charles had rebuilt an unprecedented thriving musical culture out of the ashes of the Civil War, just as he had rebuilt the city of London out of the ashes of the Great Fire. The Chapel Royal in particular was at the height of its powers, regularly packed with eager crowds of spectators, who were drawn to see the king, of course, but also to see and hear the extraordinary music. Purcell's music was a star attraction; so were the 24 violins that accompanied the lavish symphony anthems, as well as performances from celebrity singers like John Gostling, 'that stupendious bass',[77] and John Abell, 'the famous Trebble', whose voice one observed could have sworn 'had been a Woman's – it was so high and so well and skilfully managed'.[78]

Then, on 6 February 1685, King Charles II died, quite unexpectedly, aged 55, having converted to Catholicism on his deathbed. The country mourned, and musicians at court looked on nervously. As always, the royal musical establishment depended upon the passion and personal enthusiasm of the monarch who was on the throne. Under James – an unknown entity, and, most worryingly, a Catholic – its future suddenly looked far from certain.

Charles had been acutely aware of the rumblings of anti-Catholic sentiment in England, and he had prophesied that his younger brother, James, would last no longer than three years on the throne. But James II acceded surprisingly smoothly: there were no riots in the streets, no rebellions or resistance. Londoners cheered and toasted him with free wine. James himself was stunned and believed this to be a divinely ordained miracle; hoping to capitalise on this stability, and to further legitimise his position, he ordered a magnificent coronation that he commanded should do 'All that Art, Ornament and Expense could do to the making of the Spectacle Dazzling and Stupendous'. There was, however, one fundamental omission: James, being Catholic, had asked 'with expresse command' to leave out the customary Anglican Communion that had always formed part of the coronation. The night before the official enthronement, he and his queen had attended a secret Catholic ceremony at Whitehall Palace, and James lent far more significance to this private service conducted in his preferred religion. The public coronation, then, was an elaborate formality, an exercise in political spin designed to exhibit his divine mandate and legitimacy in full public view of the nation.

The entire choir of Westminster Abbey as well the Gentlemen and Children of the Chapel Royal participated in the ceremony; accompanying them were no fewer than 35 instrumentalists, in addition to the royal trumpeters,[79] and the entire entourage of the 24 violins. There were eight anthems in all, of which Purcell provided two and Blow three. Purcell clearly relished this opportunity for length and spectacle: his extraordinary anthem 'My heart is inditing' is over 15 minutes long and scored for a massive eight solo voices, eight-part choir and string accompaniment. It was performed as James's queen, Mary of Modena, was crowned, accompanied by the 'whole consort of voices and instruments'. There had never before been an anthem at this point in the service, but in 1685 it was instigated to fill the gaping hole in the programme left by the omission of the Anglican Communion. Purcell's anthem must have been an extraordinary climax to the highly elaborate ceremony, the sensuous, radiant textures echoing through the crowded Westminster Abbey as the anthem built to its final 'Alleluia'. This anthem for the queen was distinctly delicate and feminine in comparison to John Blow's more masculine, warlike 'God Spake Sometime in Visions'. Blow's anthem, written for the point in the service when the king was crowned, was a clear and pointed warning to James's enemies, elucidated through spectacular music: the text hints that James is God's servant, David, and claims that God's 'hand shall hold him fast, and my arm shall strengthen him/The enemy shall not be able to do him violence, the son of wickedness shall not hurt him'.

This coronation was also the first in which the scholars of Westminster School greeted the king and queen during their procession into the Abbey with the traditional call of *Vivat Rex!* (God Save the King!) and *Vivat Regina!* (God Save the Queen!), probably shouted or sung to a simple tune – this feature was very likely a relic of the medieval Latin coronation service that had been out of use for many years. This Latin tradition would have chimed with James's Catholic sensibilities, but that wasn't the only reason he ordered them to be included. In fact, James was 'so doubtful of his subjects' loyalty that he ordered the schoolboys to be present and acclaim him in case there should be any lack of cheering'.[80] Luckily for James, the gorgeous, lavish service pleased Protestant Londoners, and, adorned with music by the most glamorous stars of the Chapel Royal, was a complete success.

But the fortunes of the Chapel Royal were about to change dramatically. James II was a man on a mission: inspired by the successes of his Catholic ancestor Mary Tudor, he was determined to convert the nation back to what he considered to be the 'true faith'. Moreover, he felt that his ambition was bolstered by divine right; an open Catholic had acceded to the throne in a nation with an inbred hostility to Catholicism – what clearer sign could there be from God that He supported the Catholic cause? As part of his grand plan, James ordered a new Catholic chapel to be built in Whitehall Palace, at great expense. The building was beautifully decorated in keeping with the Catholic tradition, featuring ornate architectural decorations carved in marble, statues of the saints, coloured frescos and a conspicuously costly throne. Filled with the candles and incense, it provided an intimidating yet theatrical backdrop for bishops and priests to create their world of mysterious ceremony. In it, the clergy were able to employ a whole new raft of musicians: organists, seven boy choristers and a famous *castrato* (at this time a phenomenon as yet unheard of in England) named Giovanni Francesco Grossi who had been purloined from the papal choir in Rome. Italian composers attracted to the chapel included Bartolomeo Albrici and Innocenzo Fede; the latter became a court music master and was also employed to teach Italian to the royal children, James and Louise.[81]

The arrival of this new popish chapel was a rude shock to members of the Anglican Chapel Royal, and more than one ego must have been bruised as the Chapel's great composers, previously so much in demand, found themselves rather underemployed. Indeed, the Chapel narrowly escaped complete closure: it was only maintained for the use of James's Protestant daughter, Princess Anne. With money and resources diverted, Purcell, Blow and their colleagues found themselves with less motivation to produce great work, and there is more than one account of standards declining. On one occasion in 1687, Anne complained that instrumentalists had not turned up to play at the Chapel. The musicians were chided and ordered that at least when she was present the violins should attend 'as formerly they did'.[82] There must also have been a considerable amount of rivalry between the musicians of the two chapels. Purcell continued to write regular anthems, and some – such as 'Thy Way O God Is Holy' – are so grand and powerful that it is tempting to speculate that Purcell was deliberately writing to eclipse the papal theatricality of the chapel across the way.[83]

But the situation would be by no means permanent: James's reign was already on rocky ground. As James made conspicuous moves to ease the burdens on English Catholics – opening monastic houses, filling official positions with popish candidates – he became increasingly unpopular. In 1688, he issued a 'Declaration of Indulgence' which proposed universal religious toleration, arguing that it was a guarantee of economic prosperity, as opposed to persecution, which 'spoiled trade, depopulated countries and discouraged strangers'; and, in the process, suspended the ban on Catholics from holding public office. On 27 April of that year, James ordered that the clergy read the Declaration from their pulpits; seven prominent bishops refused, amid a wave of public sympathy and popular demonstrations of support for their cause. The bishops were promptly thrown in the Tower of London, and during their controversial trial – in which they were charged with seditious libel against the king – an extraordinary rebellion broke forth within the king's own stronghold, a rebellion *in music* that was sung at Whitehall Chapel four days into trial. It was a new anthem by Blow, sung by John Gostling, and it caused a sensation:

> *O God, thou art my God: I will exalt thee …*
> *For thou hast been a strength to the poor: a strength to the*
> *needy in his distress*
> *A refuge from the storm: a shadow from the heat, when the blast*
> *of the terrible ones is as a great storm against the wall*
> *He shall bring down the noise of strangers: the branch of the*
> *terrible ones shall be brought low*
> *He will swallow up death in victory*

And it shall be said in that day, Lo, this is our God: we have
waited for him and he will save us: This is the Lord:
We have waited for him, we will be glad and rejoice in his
salvation.

As the bishops' trial continued in the huge space of Westminster Hall, it would have been devastatingly obvious to those listening that the 'terrible ones' referred to members of the Catholic faith; it has even been suggested that the 'noise of strangers' was a dig at the Italian musicians of James's Catholic chapel.[84] It is impossible to know who among the Anglican priests of the Chapel Royal selected these texts – though we can surmise from the lively musical settings that Blow himself took pleasure in setting them – but for the monarch's own chapel to go against the sovereign in such a deliberate manner was an unprecedented act of rebellion and demonstrates just how fragile James's position had become. Purcell possibly got in on the act, too; around the same time he composed a verse anthem, 'O Sing Unto the Lord', which includes the rather politically pointed lines:

The Lord is great, and cannot worthily be praised:
he is more to be feared than all gods.
As for the gods of the heathen, they are but idols:
but it is the Lord that made the heavens.

This anthem shows clear Italian influences, with its light imitative texture and vigorous alternating sections between voices and instruments; clearly, even amid the rivalry, the ever-inventive Purcell could not help but absorb the influences of the Italian musicians of the Catholic chapel.

These dramatic events at the Chapel Royal were compounded by the announcement, only a few days later, that the bishops were found 'not guilty'; James's government had been condemned instead. James was furious and two of the four judges who had sat on the case were summarily dismissed. As for the mere court musicians, Blow and Purcell, their punishment was more subtle yet nevertheless disdainful: they did not attend James's summer remove to Windsor that year.[85]

By now James was in open conflict with parliament, bishops and even the judiciary. He was deeply unpopular among his subjects, and anti-Catholic feeling was more pronounced than ever. Moreover, across the Channel his nephew-in-law, William of Orange, ruler of Holland and a hardened Protestant, was preparing an invasion, having assembled a formidable armada of 60 warships, 700 transports, 15,000 troops, 4000 horses and 21 guns. William was married to Mary, James's first (and Protestant) daughter, and William had always expected that Mary would eventually inherit the throne – an invaluable opportunity to unite the Netherlands and England in a Protestant crusade against the Catholic power of France. But a new development had halted William's ambitions in their tracks: James's second, Catholic wife – Mary of Modena – had given birth unexpectedly six months earlier. Ugly rumours began – spread by James's many opponents – that the child was illegitimate, and had been smuggled into the queen's bed in a warming pan. Illegitimate or not, William could not stand calmly by while his designs on the English throne were snatched from his grasp.

In November 1688, William arrived in Devon, with cheering crowds of Protestants to welcome him. Perhaps they were even whistling the ballad that had, in the past few months, been sung across the kingdom: a tune named 'Lilliburlero'. Today, 'Lilliburlero' might be recognised as a British army regimental march, and the theme tune to the BBC World Service. In James's reign, however, it had been published as a 'new Irish jig' by Henry Purcell, who probably adapted it from a traditional melody. Amid the growing hostility towards King James, the tune acquired satirical – and wildly popular – lyrics in a mock-Irish dialect. The first ten verses satirise the characteristically overblown hopes of Irish Catholics following James's unheard of appointment of the Irish Catholic Richard Talbot, Earl of Tyrconnell, as the Governor of Ireland. The last two verses deliver a damning and, as it turned out, prophetic verdict on Talbot and his brother, the Archbishop of Dublin, denouncing the one as a dog (a feature of the Talbot coat of arms) and the other as an ass. The text, as well as the melody that accompanied it, turned out to be devastatingly catchy:

> *There was an old prophecy found in a bog*
> *Lilliburlero bullen a la*
> *The Ireland be ruled by an ass and a dog*
> *Lilliburlero bullen a la*
>
> *Refrain: Lero Lero Lilliburlero etc.*

The prophecy's true and now come to pass
Lilliburlero bullen a la
For Talbot's a dog and Tyrconnell's an ass
Lilliburlero bullen a la

Refrain: Lero Lero Lilliburlero etc.[86]

It was said that 'Lilliburlero' played an important part in swaying public opinion against James:

A foolish ballad was made at that time treating the Papists, and chiefly the Irish, in a very ridiculous manner which has a burden said to be Irish words – lero lero, lilliburlero – that made an impression on the army that cannot be well imagined by those who saw it not. The whole army, and at last all people in city and country were singing it perpetually. And perhaps never had so slight a thing so great an effect.[87]

Another source from 1715 observed: 'it so perfectly stuck in with the humour of the people that we feel some consequence of it to this very day ... that ballad was highly instrumental in singing out a bad monarch.'

By December there was little support left for James. In Scotland, this was strikingly evident when a Protestant mob overtook the Palace of Holyrood in Edinburgh. James II had ordered the Chapel Royal at the Palace – like his Chapel at Whitehall – to be turned into a place of Catholic worship, furnished and equipped with popish elaboration, including a state-of-the-art organ. But before it was even finished and consecrated, it became one of the first victims of James's fall: the furious mob burst in, tore out the fine wooden fittings and ripped up the marble pavement. They even desecrated the ancient tombs of the Scottish kings. The chapel was left unrepaired, exposed to the elements, setting it on the path to ruin, a potent symbol of James's failed mission to Catholicise Britain, and, above all, the decline of the Chapel Royal as the greatest musical institution in the land.

When James II fled from England on 23 December 1688, the ballad printers – who had previously held back – took immediate advantage: copies of 'Lilliburlero' were published and distributed that very month.[88]

DECIMATION

In the wake of the Glorious Revolution that put William and Mary on the throne, Parliament decreed that British monarchs must now be Protestant. This new law meant that the heir to the throne, James II's newborn son, could not be officially acknowledged because of his Catholicism. Instead, it would be William's Protestant wife, and James's eldest daughter, Mary. William, however, who had led the revolution to victory, would not accept being a mere 'prince consort' to his wife; nor did Mary want to be queen alone. As a result, the king and queen were crowned – on 11 April 1689 – as joint monarchs, a state of affairs unprecedented in the history of the British monarchy. Although in principle William and Mary were equal, in practice the exercise of sovereignty would be vested solely in William.

Their coronation was a far cry from the magnificent displays seen at James's crowning only four years earlier. William was a strict Calvinist, and had no time for fancy ritual and redundant ceremony. Once king, he would refuse to participate in traditional ceremonies that English monarchs had participated in for centuries: he would not wash the feet of the poor on Maundy Thursday; he would also abolish the tradition of touching people afflicted with scrofula (the so called 'King's Evil'; it was believed by many that the king's hands could banish the disease), which he regarded as superstitious absurdity. The coronation, though adhering to some aspects of tradition in order to maintain legitimacy, was changed and pared down to suit William's austere tastes. The coronation oath and sermon were altered to suit a new, modern idea of monarchical power: there was no elevated pontificating over the divine role of monarch and his God-given sanctity, rather a prosaic down-to-earth description that rejoiced in England's 'middle way' between despotic power – as in Louis XIV's France – and the 'wildness' of a republic, as England had been during the Civil War and Commonwealth. The music, too, was less lavish – probably in deference to the wishes of the new king. Only 12 Chapel Royal Gentlemen took part in the event – as compared to 32 at James II's coronation[89] (although the instrumental forces of the King's Music were employed to the full force), and in general the anthems were modestly scored, shorter, and for fewer voices. John Blow's anthem 'The Lord God Is a Sun and a Shield' is eight minutes long, a third shorter than the anthem sung at the same point in James II's coronation service. Purcell's anthem 'Praise the Lord O Jerusalem' is written for five voices, compared to eight in his coronation anthem for James II, and is half as long in duration. Though filled with rich harmonic sonorities, it is in many ways a restrained setting: the opening is sombre and serious in a D minor key, and the first vocal entry is not sung by full choir but by a quintet of solo singers. The significance of the second line of text, 'For kings shall be thy nursing fathers, and queens thy nursing mothers', which refers implicitly to Mary and William's status as joint monarchs, is emphasised by Purcell's setting: he clearly states that this line should be sung by 'voices only', making the line more audible for those listening, and adorning it with delicious harmonic suspensions for extra emphasis.

Despite all this, the newly crowned Queen Mary was not pleased with how the service went. After the event, she complained that 'there was so much pomp and vanity in all the ceremony that left little time for devotion'.[90] Perhaps she felt that, despite its comparative austerity, the music had been too elaborate and fanciful, although she was probably also referring to the taking of Communion, which she and her husband disapproved of. The new queen was in fact fond of music, and Purcell, still in employment at court, would continue to write birthday odes for her for the rest of her life. Within a few weeks of the coronation, around 30 April 1690, he wrote her an ode named 'Arise My Muse'. But this was no ordinary birthday ode. Musically speaking, it was completely revolutionary: it had a setting for a full baroque orchestra, with independent parts for two trumpets, two oboes and recorders, as well as the usual strings and continuo. It was a palate of richness and variety that composers were beginning to realise was full of endless possibilities – a far cry from the limited textures and tones of single-instrument consorts that were the norm at the beginning of the century. In 'Arise My Muse', Purcell exploits the potential of this new ensemble to the fullest extent: his grand, fanfare-like opening, which pairs oboes and trumpets over a string accompaniment, creates a rich and complex sound. He uses an 'antiphonal' texture that would become characteristic of English orchestral writing over the next few decades, with alternating parts for wind, string and brass. This is one of the first pieces Purcell wrote for full orchestra, and it is testament to the composer's extraordinary talent that he understood orchestration instinctively – how to balance the different instrumental groups and play them off each other, when to employ them for colour and tonal effects, and when to let them carry melody and harmony. It was an art form that great musicians over the next three centuries would spend lifetimes attempting to perfect. The date of its first performance was also symbolic: by extraordinary coincidence, 'Arise My Muse' was performed almost exactly 150 years after the first string consort – the ancestor of the 24 violins – was taken on at Henry VIII's court.[91]

Ironically, Purcell owed his talent to two particular developments of the previous Catholic regime under James II. During his brief reign, James had formally and decisively reorganised the structure of the Royal Music: no longer were there separate consorts special-ising in different types of instruments, such as a wind band and a string band. Now the ensembles were streamlined into one single body called the Private Music, which was effectively an up-to-date baroque orchestra, complete with strings, wind and continuo, the ensemble that Purcell utilised for Queen Mary's birthday ode. The second development was a piece that had been written by the organ-ist of James's controversial Catholic Chapel in 1687, a composer named Giovanni Draghi. His 'Song for St Cecilia's Day' was scored for five-part strings and also used recorders and trumpets; it was this work, in a modern Italian style, that would influence Purcell's orchestral writing for the rest of his life.

This was revolutionary music for revolutionary times – and, far from encouraging the new style, the new king took steps to quash it. Two days after 'Arise My Muse' was first performed, on 2 May 1690, he ordered the Lord Chamberlain to cut the size of the Royal Music by a third, to just 24 musicians plus an instrument keeper. Purcell lost his position as a harpsichordist, although he continued to be a member of the Chapel Royal and a keeper of the royal instruments, a post that he had held since the age of 14. The only ensemble of the Royal Music that remained untouched was the king's trumpeters: there were still 16, a number that had remained consistent at court since the time of Henry VIII. The trumpeters – previously used mostly in ceremonial functions – were now liable to find themselves on active service with King William, who had declared war against France within days of his coronation. There is even an account of the trumpeters suffering a 'loss' of sorts on campaign: one William Shore, of his Majesty's 1st Troop of Horse Guards, was robbed of his trumpet while in Flanders in 1694.[92] William also liked the sound of the oboe, an instrument at this time mostly associated with military activities. One writer probably had the king in mind when he wrote of the oboe: 'Besides its Inimitable charming Sweetness of Sound (when well play'd upon) is also Majestical and Stately, and not much Inferiour to the Trumpet; and for that reason, the greatest Heroes of the Age (who sometimes despise String Instruments) are infinitely please with This for its brave and sprightly Tone.' The Dutch 'hero of the age' William III did indeed equip his regiments with oboe bands, and ordered that they should be played at court balls instead of stringed instruments.[93] Bands of oboes and trumpeters were also seen as suitable to accompany ambassadors abroad.

William and Mary were not entirely deprived of artistic sensitivity, after all. Within months of coming to the throne, they had ordered Christopher Wren to do a makeover of Hampton Court, their favourite rural palace. But this, too, was proof of a very different direction for the monarchy: out went the opulent private apartments of Henry VIII and his queens; in came William's plain baroque style – sober, practical and, above all, modern, rather like William himself. But where music was concerned, William was mostly uninterested, and towards religious music he was actively hostile. To him, religious music was synonymous with foolish 'popish' ceremonies: the rituals, which often centred on the Chapel Royal, followed the ancient rhythms of the Church calendar, and – to him – seemed close to blasphemy. Queen Mary evidently agreed: on 23 February 1689 – only ten days after she and her husband had come to the throne – she decreed that instruments should no longer be used in services at Whitehall. After that, only one more symphony anthem – the distinctively and gloriously British form created and nourished by Charles II himself – was composed: Purcell's 'My Song Shall Be Alway of the Loving-kindness of the Lord'. The king himself evidently saw fit to intervene the following year and ordered that 'The King's Chapell shall be all the year through kept both morning and evening with solemn music like a collegiate church'. Thereafter the Chapel Royal was accompanied by orchestras only on great state occasions.[94]

This was a watershed for the King's Music, not just in putting musicians out of work, but also altering the musical culture of the court. It was the beginning of a decline in morale and enthusiasm, and a deterioration in musical standards. The discipline in the choir grew lax – on one occasion 'the Queen was offended' by a poor performance at the service[95] – and in 1694 it was necessary for the sub-dean to remind the Gentlemen of their obligation to attend choir practices. The Chapel Royal went from being an innovative showcase for the nation's best music to a musical backwater: royal musicians became increasingly part-time, used only for the occasional ball and special state occasions. This is reflected in the career of Purcell, who had long since sensed the tide was turning and had established a successful career outside court. Between 1680 and 1688, he had composed some 50 anthems for the Chapel Royal. Between the Glorious Revolution and his death in 1695, he composed only five. Instead he wrote for the commercial theatre: in less than five years he had written music for over 40 stage plays produced by the United Company – until 1695 the only company in London licensed to perform plays.[96] They were hugely successful. Purcell no longer needed the court, although he continued to compose regular birthday odes for Queen Mary, sumptuous orchestral settings which often, symbolically, exhibited the talents of great singing stars from the theatres as well as the Royal Music. Odes such as 'Love's Goddess Sure Was Blind' and 'Come Ye Sons of Art' were the final burst of musical magnificence from an establishment falling into decay.

In the end, the monarchy's loss was the public's gain. The kind of music that had once been the preserve of an exclusive royal circle – from balls and intimate court concerts to grandiose royal masques –

could now be heard by a much larger audience. As the monarchy lost its power, and stopped investing in its musical establishment, the market stepped in, providing, as it turned out, eager, music-loving consumers who, enjoying new affluence amidst an economic boom, were willing to pay. Yet Purcell had not entirely left behind the royal tradition that shaped him. The subjects of his major theatrical works from the 1690s are often royal in theme: *King Arthur*, *The Fairy Queen*, *The Indian Queen*. Moreover, the works themselves are curious mixes of drama, dance, music, extravagant effects and symbolism, the text serving as a framework on which to hang a succession of visual spectaculars and musically complex scenes involving the use of movable scenery – the latest in theatrical technology of the time. In short, these works were public masques; the once highly elite form for exclusive royal performance had become mass entertainment. Masques weren't the only ones: the smash-hit semi-opera *Dioclesian*, for example, was Purcell's first full orchestral score for theatre, and here the composer employs the skills and expertise he developed at court, including elements of ceremonial and military-style music, as well as magical instrumental music, scored elaborately for strings, trumpets and oboe band.[97] Like the masque, the orchestra was no longer the pet project of a passionate monarch, but was becoming an ensemble for, and by, the public, let loose to influence and be influenced by public taste and artistic vision from further afield than court; it would form the mainstay of a new form of musical entertainment called 'the public concert'. In one sense, at least, William and Mary did more for English music than any other monarchs in history: they set it free.

Purcell was kept busy by his theatre commitments, though his annual birthday odes for Queen Mary came to an end after 1694, when the queen caught smallpox and died suddenly in December, aged only 32. In keeping with her aversion to elaborate ceremony, Mary had specifically stated in her will that she did not want a large funeral; grief-stricken William, initially set on respecting her wishes, was forced to bow to public demand for a state funeral. Queen Mary, it seemed, had been more deeply loved by her subjects than she ever imagined: her embalmed corpse lay in state at Whitehall from 21 February 1695, and thousands came to pay their respects. On a cold, snowy 5 March two months later, an enormous funeral procession made its way to Westminster Abbey, and, among the royal heralds, the horse guards, the government members, the queen's ladies-in-waiting and, of course, the members of the Chapel Royal, was a consort of four slide trumpets sounding Purcell's 'Funeral March for Flat Trumpets'. The march might well have been accompanied by a solemn and ancient tattoo on military drums[98] that spectators would have recognised as the traditional 'English March' often played during battle campaigns. Whether William had a hand in the music is not known, but the distinctly military feeling of the music suggests that Purcell was bearing the tastes of his patron in mind as he wrote it (the procession also included one of William's beloved oboe bands). These were not ordinary 'natural' trumpets, however, such as William might have heard on military campaigns or at court, sounding blasts of victory or celebration; these 'flat trumpets', with their unusual sliding devices, were able to play a whole extra range of chromatic notes in 'flat' or minor keys.[99] This sombre minor tonality, so suited to a funeral procession, was used to emotive effect in Purcell's March, which is slow-moving and almost unbearably poignant in its simplicity.

Inside the abbey, the choir sung funeral sentences by Thomas Morley, and flat trumpets played Purcell's restrained polyphonic Canzona. Those trumpets probably also accompanied Purcell's tiny anthem 'Thou Knowest Lord the Secret of Our Hearts'. Composer Thomas Tudway was present at the occasion and captured the solemnity of its performance in a later description:

> [the anthem was] compos'd by Mr Henry Purcell after ye old way; and sung at ye interment of Queen Mary in Westminster Abbey; a great Queen, and extremely Lamented, being there to be interr'd, every body present was dispos'd and serious at so solemn a Service, as indeed they ought to be at all parts of divine Worship; I appear to all yt were present, as well as such as understood Music, as thost yet did not, whither they heard anything so rapturously fine, so solemn and so Heavenly in ye Operation, wch drew tears from all; and yet a plain Naturall Composition, which shews ye pow'r of Music, when 'tis rightly fitted and Adapted to devotional purposes.[100]

As Tudway rightly points out, the simplicity of Purcell's funeral music is its beauty: the simple chordal style evokes 'ye old way' of the most dignified Tudor settings of the burial sentences. His music, moreover, leaves us in little doubt of his own personal grief: he had known the queen since she had acceded to the throne six years earlier and worked closely alongside her. Later that year, Purcell and his old friend and mentor John Blow published 'Three Elegies upon the Much-Lamented Loss of Our Late Most Gracious Queen Mary'. Listening to Purcell's heartrending setting of a duet, *O Dive Custos, Auriacae Domus* – in which God is called upon to witness the grief of the royal household – there can be no doubt of the integrity of his intentions.[101]

No one could have predicted that, just a few months later, Purcell's funeral music for Queen Mary would be played at his own. Purcell died suddenly, aged only 36, on 21 November 1695 – the nature of his final illness, discussed and wrangled over by historians for centuries, is still unknown. One story which has persisted is that Purcell caught a cold as a result of being locked out of the house by his wife after spending too much time at a local tavern; this is possible, as his rate of work up to September gives no hint that he was unwell, suggesting that an apparently minor infection took an unexpected turn for the worse. On the evening of 26 November, 'the whole Chapter assisting with their vestment, together with all the Lovers of that Noble Science, with the united Choyres of that and the Chappel Royal',[102] Henry Purcell was laid to rest in Westminster Abbey to the sound of his own music. It was fitting that he should have a royal burial: he had been employed at court for almost his entire life.

Three years later, the Palace of Whitehall – where the Chapel Royal had been based for centuries, and where so many royal odes had been heard, burned to the ground – the blaze reputedly caused by a Dutch laundress whose laundry had caught alight after she left it to dry over a charcoal fire. John Evelyn recorded the event neatly and simply in his diary: 'Whitehall burnt: nothing but walls and ruins left'.[103] It was truly the end of an era. For centuries, music had been used to sanctify the monarch, to reinforce the message that our rulers were chosen by God, and placed our kings and queens at the heart of holy ceremony. Now, monarchy was no longer sacred. King William had created a new kind of English monarchy – one that was founded on modern English values of cosmopolitanism, commercialism and tolerance – a world apart from the old ways of mysterious ceremonial and divine right. Its primary role lay in tatters, its former home in ruins, its musicians cast out from court into the public sphere. And the future for royal music looked bleak indeed.

THE SOUND OF GREAT BRITAIN

UNION

By the eighteenth century, thanks to trade and vigorous mercantile expansion, London was fast becoming the wealthiest city in Europe, and buildings that symbolised the capital's new prosperity and power were filling its skyline. Most iconic among them was St Paul's Cathedral, built by Christopher Wren to rival St Peter's Basilica in Rome. St Paul's was officially completed in 1711 after 35 years of work, but was in use for several years before that, and leading the worshippers was Queen Anne, who had acceded to the throne in 1702 after King William's untimely death aged only 51. St Paul's would provide the backdrop for the high points of her 12-year reign. The nation would win a series of glorious military victories against the French – under the command of Anne's general, the Duke of Marlborough – and St Paul's was the centrepiece for a series of church services in thanksgiving for Marlborough's successes. These services were attended by the great and good of London, and the highlight of each service was specially composed music by the leading English composers of Anne's Chapel Royal.

The Royal Music was no longer the glorious institution it had been only a few years before – now shorn of its greatest star, Henry

Purcell, and depleted in numbers – and the home of the Chapel Royal was now St James's Palace after the catastrophic fire that had destroyed Whitehall. But Queen Anne, unlike her predecessors William and Mary, was at least interested in music; as a girl she had learned to sing and play the harpsichord, and as princess during the reign of King William she had even possessed her own personal group of musicians.[1] On acceding to the throne, she ensured that the various vacancies in the choir accrued during previous years were filled, and took an interest in the music that was performed at her thanksgiving services. She may have had some hand in choosing the texts that should be set to music, or at the very least the composers who should write it, such as William Croft. Formerly one of the Children of the Chapel Royal, tutored and mentored by the great John Blow, Croft was now a respected, if not ground-breaking, royal composer and organist. His anthem 'I Will Give Thanks', written for the victory at Oudenade in 1708, is inscribed by the composer: 'The words of this Anthem were [chosen] and given to me by Her Most Excellent Majesty Queen Anne …' Croft also wrote a large-scale *Te Deum and Jubilate* for soloists, choir and large orchestra, performed at three different thanksgiving services, and notable in particular for its militaristic use of brass.

But the greatest achievement of Anne's reign was the unification of England and Scotland in 1707. The Act of Union forged a new nation that not only protected the interests of both countries, but also protected against rival Catholic claimants to the throne. The Union would prove to be a success, and it was the nation of Great Britain that would become a leading world power over the next century. It was Great Britain that would kick-start the Industrial Revolution and become known as the workshop of the world. By the end of the eighteenth century, and with the accumulation of a major portion of the British Empire, Britannia would truly rule the waves.

The Union was celebrated with another grand ceremonial service at St Paul's Cathedral on 1 May 1707. Wishing to denote the significance of the event in music, Anne turned to not just one composer, but three: William Croft, John Blow and Jeremiah Clarke, all of whom held posts in the Chapel Royal. By this time, Blow – who had participated in the glory days of the Chapel Royal under Charles II – was nearing 60 and he would die the following year. Jeremiah Clarke, a gentleman-extraordinary of the Chapel since 1700, would meet a far more tragic end only a few months later: in December he would commit suicide by shooting himself, the result of a disastrous love affair.[2] But in the happier days leading up to May 1707, Clarke, Blow and William Croft collaborated to write a so-called club anthem, 'Behold How Good and Joyful', to commemorate the Thanksgiving Union, the piece forming a central part of the St Paul's service. Anne attended wearing the combined orders of the English Garter and the Scottish thistle, processing through the streets of London in her carriage, where 'the Balconies and Windows of the Houses were hung with Tapestry, and crowded with Multitudes of Spectators'. After the service, 'the Great Guns of the Tower and those at St James's Park were thrice discharged the first time, when her Majesty parted from St James's, the second at the Singing the Te Deum, and the third when her Majesty came back to her Palace. The public

Demonstrations of Joy were suitable to so great an Occasion; and the Day was concluded with Bonfires, Illuminations and all other Expressions of a General Satisfaction.'[3]

Yet, incredibly, given the significance of this occasion, the club anthem written by the three composers has not been performed in public since. In fact, most of it has been lost. Only a fragment remains – the section by Croft – stored for centuries in the annals of the British Library, and this three-minute-long fragment, as well as the surviving text, shows how intent the composers were on emphasising the theme of unity and harmony. The text runs:

> *Let him fly from evil and do good*
> *Let him seek peace and ensue it*
> *Love as brethren*
> *Live in peace and y-God of love and peace shall be with you*
> *Hallelujah.*

The music, in a bright major tonality throughout, contrasts solo voices with unified full choir, and emphasises the words 'let him seek peace' with long tranquil legato passages, ending on a joyful, imitative section declaiming 'Hallelujah'. The Union was a major landmark in our constitutional history: it begged for a musical landmark to match, perhaps even one that might have become a national anthem. But, instead, 'Behold How Good and Joyful' has faded into obscurity, as have the names of William Croft and Jeremiah Clarke. The quality of the piece itself is perhaps one reason for this – Croft and Clarke were competent composers but not game-changers – and the text is banal in the extreme and fails to set the world alight. But neither did the event itself. The Union of 1707 was of major constitutional and political significance, but it was also the result of hard political bargaining; unlike spectacular military victories, this was hardly the stuff of musical inspiration. But there are also deeper, structural reasons. The grand celebrations of 1707 might look like business as usual, both for the monarchy and the musicians of the Chapel Royal, but, in fact, they were the last gasps of a dying tradition. After Anne's reign, St Paul's was barely used for royal musical events until the end of the century; much of the eighteenth-century music we now think of as so quintessentially British, and traditionally royal, would no longer be created from either the religious or royal institutions which had proved so important in the past.

The root of the problem was with the queen herself: repeated failed pregnancies had broken her health. She was also in personal and political turmoil. Anne had become disillusioned with Marlborough's seemingly never-ending war with France; was quarrelling bitterly with Marlborough's wife, Sarah, hitherto her closest friend; and felt imprisoned by her own government, dominated by the Whig party with their partisan commitment to the French war. To cap it all, her dull and dreary husband, Prince George of Denmark, to whom she was nevertheless devoted, died in 1708. In these circumstances, the musical life of the court – already weakened by the Glorious Revolution and William III's dour Protestantism – flickered and very nearly died. But rich, vibrant London abhorred a vacuum; and, in any case, real power was shifting elsewhere –

religiously, politically and culturally. Ultimately it would be the commercial theatre and new influences from abroad which would transform royal music in the eighteenth century.

Perhaps the most pervasive influence of them all was that 'exotic and irrational import',[4] Italian opera. This first arrived in London in 1705 with productions at Drury Lane and the architect-cum-playwright John Vanbrugh's new Queen's Theatre in Haymarket. This was opera as the English public had never seen it before, with its dramatic, lavish staging and vocal acrobatics. The plots were often long and complex – and entirely in Italian – and the music was a vehicle for the individual singers – imported from Italy, of course – who were regarded as glamorous celebrities and were the focus of much adoration, gossip and speculation by opera-goers. The rules of performance etiquette would perhaps seem strange and unfamiliar to modern audiences: eighteenth-century theatres were noisy and chaotic and audiences were lively. There were reports of riots in the cheaper seats; in the expensive boxes prostitutes could find good business; and the aisles in the pit were known as 'Fops' Alley', the place for young rakes to cruise and flirt with ladies. The audiences in the auditorium were as well lit as the performers on stage, and spectators would walk around, chat and play card games, stopping occasionally to listen to the more famous arias before resuming their conversation, game or salacious gossip. In short, the opera was a place to see and be seen: a social hub for London's elite, and a demonstration of the opera-goer's exotic, cosmopolitan cultural tastes, the sort of tastes that young men and women of opportunity cultivated on the Grand Tour.

The German composer George Frideric Handel came to London in 1710 to take advantage of this fashionable new craze. He had become an accomplished opera composer during the three years he had spent studying and working in Italy, but was currently employed by the Elector of Hanover. He was not just a talented musician but a savvy commercial operator: he understood the artistic opportunities that might arise from being involved in the emerging London scene. On his arrival in the capital, he had a stroke of luck – the first of many – and teamed up with the even younger Aaron Hill, who was the manager of the Queen's Theatre that season. It was the perfect combination: Hill came up with the libretto and Handel wrote the music (speedily, in two weeks flat) to the opera, *Rinaldo*, which premiered in February 1711. 'Let me weep my cruel fate and sigh for liberty': this great lament is sung by Almirana, the heroine of the opera, who has just been trapped along with the hero, Rinaldo, by the wicked sorceress, Armida, Queen of Damascus. It's a tale of derring-do and high passion set amidst the delights of the fabled East. It gave Handel the opportunity to show his talents not just as composer, but also as musical director and harpsichord soloist. With a famous and talented castrato, Nicolini, in the title role and Handel's colourful musical score with its elaborate vocal lines – designed to show off Nicolini's talents to the full – the opera was an instant hit. The production was by all accounts spectacular: the effects included thunder and lightning, illuminations and fireworks, and at one point a flock of live sparrows and chaffinches was released into the audience.[5] Handel was praised as 'the Orpheus of our century':[6] *Rinaldo* played for 15 performances, and the reviews were almost unanimously positive.

Rinaldo was the first Italian opera to be specifically written for the English stage. Handel's librettist-cum-impresario, Aaron Hill, made the most of the fact in his dedication of the opera to the queen herself, proclaiming that 'this opera is a native of her majesty's dominions, and was consequently born your subject', although, of course, this 'British' subject was sung in Italian and written by a German. In February 1711, Handel was summoned to court to lead a command performance of extracts from *Rinaldo* at St James's Palace on Queen Anne's birthday (she must have enjoyed it, because within a few weeks Handel and his opera singers were back again). The opera

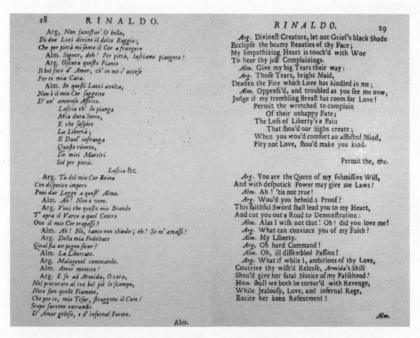

A programme (left) and translated libretto for Rinaldo (1711), Handel's first Italian opera for the English stage, and his first big hit. The production was lavish and spectacular – at one point featuring a flock of live sparrows and chaffinches that were released into the audience – and ran for 15 performances to rave reviews.

came to the queen for practical reasons, too, since even at this time her ill health stopped her from going out to such events frequently. Although there is some dispute over the cause of her ailments, she was probably a chronic sufferer of lupus, an auto-immune disease that would have caused her severe joint pain (at the time incorrectly diagnosed as gout) as well as giving her a disfiguring facial rash that was known colloquially and cruelly as 'corned-beef skin'. The same month that *Rinaldo* premiered, Handel had already secured his position by writing a 'Dialogue in Italian, in Her Majesty's Praise' (unfortunately it no longer survives) performed at the palace for the queen's birthday on 6 February.

But not everyone was so enamoured. Many saw this new form of opera as effeminate, and – with its fanciful staging and ornate music – possessing a whiff of European tastes. The essayist, politician and co-founder of the *Spectator*, politician Richard Steele, attacked Italian opera from the start as 'popery in wit'.

> *Arise, for shame, ye conquering Britons rise*
> *Such unadorned effeminacy despise.*

Instead, Steele invoked Britain's new greatness and called for a native culture whose distinction would match its military power:

> *Let Anna's soil be known for all its charms;*
> *As famed for liberal sciences as arms:*
> *Let those derision meet, who would advance*
> *Manners or speech, from Italy or France.*

Let them learn you, who would your favour find,
And English be the language of mankind.

This search for a native music worthy of Great Britain – as a formally united nation, but also as the new military and economic superpower in Europe – would be one of the crucial factors determining the development of music in the eighteenth century, and the monarchy would be involved at every step along the way.

But the composer who took up the challenge most successfully was not, at this time, British at all: Handel would capture the hearts of the royals, successfully eclipsing the English composers of the old tradition, and in the process almost writing many of them out of musical history. In 1713, on returning to London after another long stay in Hanover – where he was still officially in the employ of the Hanoverian court – he was awarded a grand commission that kickstarted his persistent trend of supplanting court musicians. The royal birthday ode, which was a time-honoured custom imported from France at the beginning of Charles II's reign, was traditionally written by a composer in the employ of the English court, and had been duly served up by Purcell and Blow throughout their careers. Anne had abandoned it, along with most other forms of musical patronage, in her mid-reign crisis: none seems to have been written after 1707 and, in despair, the rather talented master of the Queen's Music, John Eccles, retired to Hampton Wick where he spent his time fishing. But in February 1713, with a new Tory government in office, and peace with France in the bag, Anne felt in celebratory mood once more and Handel was asked to provide the ode.

For a foreigner with no official role within the court bureaucracy to perform the birthday duties was a radical break with tradition – it was not only a tremendous honour for Handel, who was fast being recognised as the most exciting composer in London, but also a pointed snub towards existing royal composers such as Eccles and William Croft.

The ode itself – 'Eternal Source of Light Divine' – is based loosely on the traditional English form. The words are English, written by the sentimental poet Ambrose Phillips. Even the musical forces were English, too, since Handel originally wrote this for a favourite counter-tenor of the Chapel Royal, accompanied by trumpet in the manner of Purcell. But the melodic genius, which has led the piece to be appropriated by great sopranos and sung with gusto, was Handel's own. It owes much to the traditional ode form, but updates it for the eighteenth century, making it longer and more harmonically adventurous than the traditional church anthems written by the English Chapel Royal composers. Nine movements long – made up of arias, duets and choruses – the ode demonstrates Handel's great skill in quickly assimilating English traditions into his own distinctive musical voice, a skill that would secure his enduring popularity with the English people. It is also a sublime piece of musical flattery that praises the queen's virtues as a peacemaker, constantly returning to the line 'The Day that gave great Anna birth/who fixed a lasting peace on earth'.

Indeed, Anne's peace-making reputation was confirmed by the event for which Handel wrote another grand composition around the same time. The Peace of Utrecht was established in the spring of 1713, ending the lengthy, bloody War of the Spanish Succession and marking England's eclipse of the two powers, France and the Netherlands, that only half a century earlier had overshadowed her. The Peace was celebrated by a grand thanksgiving service at St Paul's on 7 July: it was a spectacular occasion for which crowds lined the streets, including – according to contemporary newspaper accounts – 4000 charity children singing specially composed hymns in honour of Queen Anne and peace.[7] Handel made his contribution to the service in the form of a magnificent work known as the 'Utrecht Te Deum and Jubilate' – the first important religious composition written by him that used English words – and the warm popular reception it received succeeded in overshadowing William Croft's anthem, 'This Is the Day', which was written for the same occasion. This was the first major public work Handel had written since *Rinaldo*, and newspaper coverage of the time enthusiastically reports on Handel's 'Utrecht Canticles' while barely mentioning Croft; an added sting in the tail for poor Croft was that Handel probably studied the native-born composer's own Te Deums to familiarise himself with the form before he composed his own. How Croft reacted to all this is not recorded, although we do know that he published an imposing volume of his own work that same year, *Musicus Apparatus Academicus*, that included two odes celebrating the Treaty of Utrecht, and it is possible that this book was an attempt to maintain the native composer's reputation.[8] Unfortunately, the attempt more or less failed: for all his considerable talents, Croft is a mere footnote to the life of the German composer who, in 1713, was fast being adopted by the English as their own.

Queen Anne showed her appreciation to Handel for his royal work: although, as a foreigner, it wasn't possible for Handel to attain an official court post, the queen granted him an extremely generous royal pension of £200 per annum, more than twice as much as Croft earned.[9] It was highly unusual for the queen to take such an interest in her musicians or composers. Normally, she 'was too busy or too careless to listen to her own band, and had no thought of hearing and paying new players however great their genius or vast their skill'.[10] But with Handel, Queen Anne had another motive. Although he was now spending the majority of his time in England, the composer was still employed by the dynasty of German nobles that would take over the throne at Anne's death: the north German House of Hanover. There has been much speculation over why Handel was allowed by his employer to spend so much time in England during this period; but for the future king, Elector George Ludwig, it was probably useful to have a strong presence from his own court in Anne's, particularly since the queen – mindful of the threat of opposition – refused to let any member of the electoral family set foot in England while she lived. From September 1710, a resident of the Hanoverian court, Christoph Friedrich Kreienberg, was stationed in London, along with a succession of Hanoverian diplomats whose duty was presumably to report back to the Hanoverian Elector. Handel's presence similarly suited the foreign policy of the Hanoverian court, paving the way for the German entourage's arrival: Kreienberg even mentions that Handel had been useful in supplying reports on Anne's ailing health, obtained through his friendship with the queen's doctor, John Arbuthnot.[11] But Anne's official endorsement of Handel with a pension was a claim of ownership for him: this, coupled with Handel's involvement in the Utrecht celebrations – the treaty which was against Hanoverian interests – must have stretched the patience of officials a notch too far. Handel's appointment at Hanover was summarily terminated in June 1713.

But Handel's association with Hanover was far from over. In the summer of 1714, Queen Anne suffered two violent strokes which left her barely able to speak, apart from the words 'yes' and 'no'. Two days later, at the age of 49, she was dead, leaving behind no children who had lived into adulthood. Her reign had been defined by a single paradox: an ailing, feeble woman who could barely stand was the ruler of the most powerful country in Europe. At her funeral it is possible that William Croft's sombre and deeply affecting setting of the burial service was performed.[12] Fittingly, this is one work by Croft that has endured to the present day, having been performed at state funerals ever since, including that of Princess Diana in 1997 and Queen Elizabeth the Queen Mother in 2002. It was appropriate that Croft – who had worked in the dedicated service of Queen Anne and the Chapel Royal throughout her reign, detailing her triumphs in music – should write the music that sung the queen to her final resting place. The music – which is deeply indebted in its style and form to the 'Great Master' (as Croft refers to Henry Purcell in the preface) – thus seems to hold a deeper symbolism; it represents the death of the old ways, a distinct break with the past and the beginning of a new chapter for music and for monarchy.

But who would succeed to the throne? Parliament had ruled out the possibility of Great Britain ever being headed by a Catholic successor; passing over more than 50 popish claimants who stood legitimately in the line of succession, the throne was now inherited by the insignificant north-German principality of Hanover, and the Elector George Ludwig – James I's grandson, and Anne's closest living Protestant relation. King George embodied the foreign character of the eighteenth-century monarchy that was already coming to define eighteenth-century English music. The gradual Anglicisation of the Hanoverian dynasty over the next century was mirrored by Handel – the German's adaptation of foreign influences and forging of a new musical style that was entirely his own would come to be considered, with the aid of royal influences, entirely English. The Hanoverian dynasty would forge a new national and cultural identity for the British nation that would endure far beyond the Georgian era.

THE HOUSE
OF HANOVER

In September 1714, the new king travelled up the Thames and was
dropped off in Greenwich. The north wall of the Painted Hall at the
old Royal Naval College in Greenwich depicts the event: George I,
bedecked in Roman splendour, arrives in a chariot, flanked by cherubs
and attended by such symbolic personages as Justice and Peace. It
is grandiloquent and faintly preposterous to modern eyes, and the
reality of the event was somewhat different: George arrived at night
and in rather plain travelling clothes. Such dour sobriety would in
many ways define George I's reign. He was a good and modest man,
and he would preside over a good and modest monarchy. In music,
however, his tastes were as magnificent as James Thornhill's fantastic vision in this painting; and, as king of the newly formed Great
Britain, he would not only indulge his tastes, but manipulate them
for his own gain. German George would use music as a convenient
method to ingratiate himself with his British public.

The British were not as enthusiastic about their new German king
as they were about the music of Handel. George was unremittingly

German: he never learned more than a few words of broken English, and came accompanied by German ministers, German-speaking servants and even German mistresses (who were known, somewhat cruelly, by the nicknames inspired by their figures: 'the Elephant' and 'the Maypole'). Though not a 'dunce', as history has sometimes mistakenly labelled him, the new monarch was modest and introverted: he kept to himself; enjoyed long walks, going hunting and intimate, informal dinners with German friends; and disliked fuss and ostentation. As Elector of Hanover, he had forbidden the use of trumpets and drums to greet him on his return from military campaigns;[13] he certainly wasn't the type to go in for the grand pageantry that might have boosted his popularity among the British people. He did, however, like music: moreover, in the early years of his reign, George made the politically expedient move of patronising British musicians over and above his fellow Germans for official royal occasions. For William Croft, this was good news: the indefatigable composer provided much of the music for George I's modest coronation in 1714, including the coronation anthem 'The Lord Is a Sun and a Shield'. (Whether this move boosted the king's popularity in any way is doubtful; on the day of the service, banners mocking the new king were displayed throughout the country.) Handel was not involved at all: indeed, he would not make a contribution to a Chapel Royal service for another eight years.

The coronation, however, did little to convince the people of Britain that George was rightful king. Within a year of taking the throne, the new sovereign faced an armed rebellion from the Jacobites, the supporters of the exiled, Catholic line of James II. To make matters worse, there was a dispute festering within the German royal family. George's eldest son, George Augustus, Prince of Wales, was a much more attractive character than his father. Fun-loving and vivacious, he adored public pomp and ceremony as keenly as his father detested it. He was married to an intelligent, charismatic wife named Caroline, and the prince and princess had set up a lively, open court at Hampton Court Palace which had a reputation for good parties and attracting interesting people, from poets, such as Alexander Pope, to scientists like Isaac Newton and Edward Halley. Prince George and Princess Caroline were seen regularly in public by their subjects; most mornings, they would 'take the air upon the river' in their crimson-decked barge, rowed by watermen attired in royal livery. Sometimes the boat would pause for those on board to listen to the music of the prince's personal string band, or stop on the banks while lords and ladies sang to them.[14]

George was furiously jealous of his son's increasing popularity. Under pressure from all sides, the king badly needed to break with his reclusive habits and make a bold public statement – the grander the better. During the summer of 1717, he took decisive action, planning a very public concert party on the Thames – inspired, perhaps, by his son's frequent boat trips, or the long tradition of monarchs listening to music on the water. George turned to his fellow German and brother-in-law, Baron von Kielmansegge, to deal with the details; it was Kielmansegge (holding the court office of 'Master of the Horse', which was responsible for organising the king's public appearances) who made the inspired choice that would result in one of the most famous performances in musical history. The music, Kielmansegge decided, should be by George Frideric Handel.

Despite Handel's acrimonious break with his Hanoverian employers in 1713, their relationship had by now been reconciled. George liked Handel – not least because he was German – and as soon as George had become king, Handel had become part of the court's entourage, providing an easy introduction into London's musical scene for the monarch. Handel's music was certainly to George's taste, since he had previously found favour at the king's Hanoverian court. In 1715, the king had attended a revival of Handel's opera *Rinaldo*; in 1716, Handel may even have accompanied the royal party back to Hanover for a visit.[15] George had retained native-born musicians in official positions at court for political reasons, but now, with Handel taking London by storm, the German composer had political capital of his own. So at around eight o'clock on the beautiful, tranquil evening of 17 July 1717, King George embarked on his royal barge, alongside another boat that held 50 musicians. The subsequent journey to Chelsea and back would see the premiere of Handel's *Water Music*.

This time, at the request of Kielmansegge, Handel was to make his music bigger, better – and louder. Although this is essentially a series of elegant short movements suitable for dancing, the *Water Music* is no ordinary dance suite. Handel skilfully scored the work for instruments loud enough to carry across the water – trumpets, horns, oboes, bassoons, flutes, violins and bass – for the benefit not only of the king, but also for the hundreds of spectators who lined the banks and crowded onto nearby vessels (a Prussian visitor to London reported, 'The number of barges and above all of boats filled with people desirous of hearing was beyond counting'[16]). This combination of instruments was unusual, not just for its particularly large number of wind and brass instruments, but also for its lack of harpsichord or timpani, both staples of the baroque orchestra, which were too bulky and heavy to be accommodated on a barge. The result was a rich and distinctive sound lacking the 'grounding effect' normally provided by those instruments. The tone of the *Water Music* is consequently more ethereal and sonorous, while also being stately, elegant and upliftingly expansive. It is easy to imagine the suite's alternately jaunty and meditative movements carrying effortlessly across the water on that still, beautiful evening in central London: it is an inspired piece of outdoor music and remains one of the most popular of Handel's works.

King George approved of the *Water Music* so much that he demanded the entire composition – lasting an hour – be repeated three times: once on the way to supper at Chelsea, once during supper, and again on the return journey. It was an immediate hit with the public, quickly taken up at playhouses and performed by the theatre orchestras before curtain-up and during the interval.[17] Before long, most of London had at least a nodding acquaintance with the work. The success of the event must have caused some discomfort to the king's son, Prince George: he and his wife Caroline were conspicuously absent from the *Water Music* festivities. But for King George (and for Kielmansegge) it was not only a successful exercise in propaganda, it was also a turning point for royal music. The *Water Music* was the first example of royal music being deployed for the purposes of spectacle, with no spiritual or even obvious ceremonial purpose. Instead, what George had done was to transform the River Thames into a theatre-cum-concert hall, with himself and his subjects as an enthusiastic audience.

This trend towards purely theatrical royal music would magnify throughout the eighteenth century, and the reasons for this are inextricably linked to certain unprecedented political developments – the rise of a second parallel monarchy in Britain known as the premiership. With the gradual transferral of power from palace to parliament, the House of Hanover would become increasingly irrelevant, and so too would its awkward, unattractive kings. For George, as for his Hanoverian successors, royal ceremony and its musical accompaniment, shorn of any kind of religious or – even very much national – *raison d'être*, would increasingly become merely, if gloriously, theatrical.

∞

And in a literal sense, too, the monarchy was now moving into the theatre. Despite his reclusive tendencies, George I was a great fan of the opera and attended it as often as he could. In Hanover, Italian opera had been all the rage while the young prince was growing up, and his favourite composer had been the Italian Agostino Steffani, the predecessor to Handel as Kapellmeister, who had helped initiate the new musical fashion at court. George also witnessed his father, Duke Ernst August, use opera to political ends – the duke regarded opera as a symbol of power and an instrument of propaganda[18] – and this would profoundly influence his own attitudes towards the possibilities of royal music. Steffani understood, perhaps better than anyone, the need for projection of the right political message; he was not just a musician, but also an important court diplomat who played a crucial role in negotiations with Brussels over the state of Hanover as an electoral power, as well as participating in the delicate political manoeuvres preceding the War of the Spanish Succession. He must have been a powerful presence at the Hanoverian court: King George liked Steffani's work so much that he brought a collection of his opera scores with him to London. (They remain in the British Library archives today.)

The king was clearly determined to continue his passion for Italian opera once ensconced in London. During the 1714–15 season, for example, he went to half of the 44 performances on offer.[19] In previous centuries, the best music – secular as well as sacred – had been performed in court, but since the vast palace of Whitehall had burned down during the reign of Queen Anne, the monarchy no longer had large spaces suitable for performance. So George came up with a more cost-effective method of sponsoring his favourite art form, partly for his own pleasure and enjoyment, but also as a way of securing his popularity among the opera-loving elite. The result was a new opera company: the Royal Academy of Music.[20]

The Academy dominated London musical life for nearly a decade, and the bulk of the music was Handel's: out of 487 performances, 240 were by the German composer and the rest by other foreign composers.[21] An opera by an Englishman wouldn't get a look-in for the entire time that the Academy was in existence. Nevertheless, the Academy was an artistic triumph, and it was made possible by George I who contributed £1000 a year for seven years.

It was his patronage that helped secure further investments in the form of subscriptions from many of the country's leading aristocrats: the Prince of Wales also donated a large sum, and a host of other patrons – from Britain and from Hanover – put in shares of £100 each. This was not a fully royal-funded court opera like those in Europe; it was effectively a joint stock company.

Handel's life was subsumed by the Academy for the next decade – financially, emotionally, artistically – leaving him little spare time for other projects. Such was the public's insatiable appetite and desire for novelty that he was constantly having to write new works. During the eight-year life of the Academy, he wrote 12 new operas. In earlier eras, it had been the musicians of the Chapel Royal who had been subject to the testing demands of daily composition: now it was the commercial market for theatre that beat the drum, that made and broke careers, and set the standards of excellence in both composition and performance. Luckily for Handel, who possessed the ability to turn out an opera in weeks, rather than months, his genius seemed designed to thrive in such a heady, cut-throat environment. He was appointed 'master of the Orchester with a Sallary' and was sent overseas 'by Order of his Majesty, to Collect a Company of the choicest Singers in Europe for the Opera in Hay-Market'[22] – returning with a selection of celebrity singers from abroad, a crucial selling point in the staging of any new opera.

Handel's first Academy opera, *Radamisto*, was an intensely dramatic tale of nobility in the face of aggression. It was dedicated to the king, in predictably sycophantic fashion:

The protection which your Majesty has been graciously pleased to allow both to the art of musick in general, and to one of the lowest though not the least dutiful of your Majesty's servants, has emboldened me to present to your Majesty, with all due humility and respect, this my first essay to that design. I have been still the more encouraged to say this, by the particular Approbation Your Majesty has been pleased to give to the Musick of this Drama ...[23]

King George had evidently already heard and approved of Handel's work. *Radamisto*'s first performance in April 1720 was a storming success and the theatre was unusually crowded, as related somewhat breathlessly by John Mainwaring, Handel's first biographer:

In so splendid and fashionable an assembly of ladies (to the excellence of their taste we must impute it), there was no shadow of form, or ceremony, scarce indeed any appearance of order or regularity, politeness or decency. Many, who had forc'd their way into the house with an impetuosity ill suited to their rank and sex, actually fainted through the excessive heat and closeness of it. Several gentlemen were turned back, who had offered forty shillings for a seat in the gallery, after having despaired of getting any in the pit or boxes.[24]

Despite the 'excellence of their taste', the crowds were almost certainly drawn by more than Handel's music alone. They were drawn by gossip: across London, tongues were wagging that King George and the Prince of Wales – who had been estranged since 1717, and whose rival courts were mutually exclusive – were coming to a formal reconciliation. It can surely be no coincidence that the crowds jostled so closely on the night that king and prince made their first formal attendance together at the opera, and the fact that its premiere was such an important court occasion can only have enhanced the reputation of the opera itself. Its popularity was lasting, and Handel saw the financial rewards of that popularity when the king granted him a 14-year copyright on the piece.

The most famous singer of the day was Senesino, the Italian castrato. The best castrati possessed unnaturally beautiful voices that combined the purity of boy sopranos with the power of the mature male voice. Lured to London with the offer of a salary of a thousand pounds for a single season, Senesino sang with the Academy in 32 different operas, including 13 by Handel, and his performances were apparently 'beyond all criticism'.[25] When he wasn't singing, Senesino spent his money living like a lord, accumulating paintings and rare books. However, his arrogant personality clearly clashed with Handel's as early as 1720, when one eyewitness witnessed the composer calling Senesino 'a damned fool'. In fact, Handel, who was hot-tempered, had frequent arguments with several of the singers he worked with, on one occasion threatening to throw the soprano Francesca Cuzzoni out of the window after she refused to sing an aria he wanted.[26] But the success of performances depended wholly on these prima donnas, and so in general their wishes and objections had to be appeased.

When Handel wasn't fighting with the talent, they were fighting with one another. Cuzzoni and another great soprano, Faustina Bordoni, developed a fierce rivalry: in the opera *Alessandro*, which featured both prima donnas at once, Handel took great pains to ensure that they each had equally important and challenging singing roles. Tensions rose to boiling point one night in June 1727, when ovations, whistles and catcalls from the audience culminated in an all-out fight on stage during a performance.[27] Unsurprisingly, the spectacle prompted a public scandal – causing great offence in particular to Princess Caroline, who was present at the performance – and Cuzzoni was summarily dismissed from the Academy, after six long years of service. But King George was such a fan of the great soprano – of whom it was said that 'her high notes were unrivalled in clearness and sweetness, and her intonations were so just and fixed, that it seemed as if it was not in her power to sing out of tune'[28] – that he threatened to withdraw his subsidy. She was quickly reinstated.

It was a heady, riotous time for opera in London and the success of this new musical culture was largely down to the patronage of King George I. Although monarchs had long patronised music and musicians, what George achieved with the Royal Academy was unprecedented. Unlike the Tudors and Stuarts, who had primarily supported music that not only glorified the monarch, but was often directly about the monarchy, George was spending time and money on something that gave him pleasure. Occasionally his attendance at the opera – as with the premiere of *Radamisto* – had a political significance, but this was a rarity. Usually the king went to the opera because he wanted to: it is estimated that the king turned out to around half of all the opera performances given in London during his reign (a great number of which would have been by Handel).[29] George, it has been nicely observed, was either a genuine lover of

Handel's operas or an extreme masochist. At the same time, the Academy was the making of Handel as a composer: it secured his position as the leading light of London's musical scene, and gained him financial security, allowing him to take a lease on a grand house in Brook Street, conveniently situated for not only the opera in Haymarket, but also the royal court at St James's.

Handel now had a foot in both worlds, making a tidy profit from the opera business while also working sporadically at court and for private patrons. Unlike composers of previous generations, he was dependent on no particular patron, and could pick and choose the commissions and the projects he wished to work on. His connections at court were recognised in 1723, when a specially created post – 'Composer of Music for His Majesty's Chapel Royal – was awarded to him. Over the next few years he would supply occasional works for the Chapel Royal and become music master to King George's granddaughters, Princesses Anne and Caroline. But Handel remained his own music tutor, working when and for whom he pleased, ruled only by the tastes and whims of the British public. The confirmation that the British had adopted him as one of their own came through in 1727, when Handel's application to become a naturalised British subject was accepted and approved by an Act of Parliament. It was one of the very last public acts of George I's reign.

King George died unexpectedly in June of that same year, 1727: fittingly, he died in Germany and was buried in Hanover, the place his heart had never really left. While Handel had embraced life in Britain, George had never become remotely British, and neither had his musical tastes. The reason for this was not – as in the legend of much British historiography – that he was a stubborn German boor, but because, like Handel himself, George was a product of the international court culture that made love, war and peace in French (which George spoke perfectly) and sang in Italian, as in the operas that George adored.

Unfortunately, the high drama of his beloved Academy couldn't last: in the end it outlived him only by a year, being declared bankrupt in 1728, eight years after it had begun. The great castrato Senesino is said to have invested the extortionate earnings he received from his time at the Academy in a grand house in Siena with an inscription across the door claiming 'the folly of the English had laid the foundation of it'.[30] But however financially disastrous the Academy might have been, its lifespan is regarded as one of the golden eras in the history of opera. It is too often forgotten that one of our least-loved kings was largely responsible for its success.

The hopes of the British people were higher for King George's son and successor, George II. He spoke English, and loved ceremony and theatrical display, a fact neatly demonstrated by his magnificent coronation that took place at Westminster Abbey on 11 October 1727. It was an event marked with perhaps the greatest ceremonial music of all time: Handel's coronation anthems.

As a newly naturalised British citizen, Handel was able to participate in the ceremony, but, even so, for a foreign-born composer to be the star musical attraction was a controversial break with tradition. At all previous coronations, music had always been the responsibility of a senior figure of the Chapel Royal or the Royal Music. Veteran William Croft had finally died on 14 August that year, and was succeeded by an even lesser-known composer named Maurice Greene, who, rather unusually, had no previous connection with the Chapel Royal. The Hanoverians seem to have had a rather low opinion of his abilities: George III later described him as 'a wretched little crooked ill natured insignificant writer, player and musician'.[31] Precedent dictated that the choice should fall on Greene, but Handel was well-placed, too, having written all the music for special occasions in the Chapel Royal for the past five years. Talent was now more important than protocol, however – in addition to George II's characteristically extreme partisanship – and it is quite possible that the new King George intervened personally in order to ensure that Handel got the top job.

Music lovers down the centuries have been thankful that he did. For the occasion, Handel produced four coronation anthems on a larger scale than any church music he had previously written: he clearly relished the opportunity, utilising the full resources of the King's Music in a way that was simply not on offer to him at the opera house. The public quickly anticipated what was coming, for even the rehearsals of the anthems aroused excitement: 'The Time will be kept private', *Parker's Penny Post* reported smugly on 4 October 'lest the Crowd of People should be an obstruction to the Performers.'[32] Indeed, the performers themselves made up a considerable crowd: 40 voices along with an extraordinary 160 instrumentalists. According to one commentator, the coronation music may well have involved every professional orchestral musician and every professional singer then in London: the combined choirs of the Abbey and Chapel Royal augmented by 47 further singers, most likely professional Italians from Handel's opera company. The musical forces probably represented the largest performing group of players and singers ever seen in the whole of Europe at this time.[33]

Handel appears to have regarded the coronation as a musical rather than a liturgical occasion. He complained that the position of the altar adversely affected communication between his musicians – many of whom were stuck in separate galleries – and demanded (unsuccessfully) that it be moved. The texts of the coronation anthems are made up of arrangements of verses from the two great achievements of the English Reformation – the Book of Common Prayer and the King James Bible. The arrangements were traditional and were re-edited by the archbishop of Canterbury to suit the circumstances of each coronation. But in 1727, so the story goes, the archbishop was stunned to be told by Handel: 'I have read my Bible very well, and shall chuse for myself'.[34] And he did, ruthlessly editing down the text and rearranging the verses to serve his own musical ends. The composer was not prepared to devolve any authority over his beloved music: this was Handel's concert, not the Church's. And that is precisely what makes these coronation anthems so revolutionary. Though Handel had probably attended the coronation of George I in 1714, and studied previous coronation anthems by composers like Croft, Purcell and Blow, he didn't simply conform to the traditions of the past. These anthems were not only unprecedented in scale, but also in orchestration: they were the first coronation anthems ever to include timpani, and with an innovative

The original score for Handel's coronation anthems: the four movements have becomes some of the most famous and frequently performed ceremonial works of all time, in particular 'Zadok the Priest', which has featured in the programme of every coronation since 1727.

scoring for three trumpets as well as oboes and bassoons, created a new and modern orchestral sound utterly distinct from the more solemn church music previously heard at religious royal ceremonies.

English Protestantism – with its single-minded emphasis on the pure, unadulterated word of God – had historically been a great enemy of music. But Handel responded more imaginatively than any Englishman to the power and poetry of the English of the King James Bible and Prayer Book, to create a new musical language. In the coronation anthems he put the new language at the service of the Hanoverian monarchy, and the anthems were an instant hit – in particular 'Zadok the Priest', which remains the most celebrated and most frequently played of the four. The movement is distinctive for its 23-bar string introduction, which tantalises with its slow build-up and almost unbearable harmonic tension, before the entry of the seven-part choir, accompanied by trumpets, in a dazzling blaze of sound. Nowhere is Handel's extraordinary gift for the dramatic more evident than here – honed by all those operas written for the Royal Academy – for 'Zadok the Priest' is pure theatre. The text it uses is a biblical passage describing the anointing of King Solomon, which has been used at coronations since Anglo-Saxon times – although over the centuries new musical accompaniments had been composed for it. Once Handel produced his version, however, no one felt able to better it. It has been used at every single coronation since. Moreover, repeated acclamations of 'God save the king' would make 'Zadok the Priest' the perfect national anthem – if it weren't so difficult to sing – and, indeed, for decades afterwards it filled much of the purpose of the yet-to-be-written 'God Save the

King', and headed the programme of countless concerts, where it was described as 'the Coronation Anthem', or even the anthem 'God Save the King'.

While George I had spent much of his reign listening to Handel in London theatres, George II went one step further: with the aid of Handel's music, he brought the sensibility of the theatre into the very heart of royal ceremony. Handel's unashamedly dramatic music, echoing around the cavernous acoustic of the enormous Westminster Abbey, must have been utterly breathtaking for the assembled audience. It wasn't just the music that was showy, either. George II's wife, Queen Caroline, wore a petticoat adorned with £2,400,000 worth of precious stones, as well as carrying a sceptre and ivory rod (she later declared that 'the weight of jewelled dress was the worst thing I had to bear'[35]). The king himself wore a magnificent crown set with hundreds of diamonds hired specially for the occasion. This was truly coronation as spectacle, monarchy as performance.

The coronation was a success, and Handel's anthems a palpable hit – used in innumerable charity concerts and services throughout the eighteenth century – but ultimately none of it helped George II's reputation. He started off with great ambitions to rule as a 'British King, not a reluctant German', but ultimately his love of, and allegiance to, Hanover cost him political capital and personal popularity, amid constant Continental wars to defend Hanoverian interests. He conducted a large part of his court life in French and never visited much of his kingdom. He complained that he had little power, moaning 'Ministers are Kings in this Country': and when he visited Hanover much later, in 1755, he very nearly didn't go back to

England. 'There are Kings enough in England,' he said. 'I am nothing there. I am old and want rest and should only go to be plagued and teased there about the damned House of Commons.'

His fiercest critic, in fact, was not the Commons but his own flesh and blood – his son Frederick, the Prince of Wales and heir to the throne. Making true the old dictum that 'Hanoverians, like pigs, trample their young', Frederick's relationship with George was so acrimonious that he was forbidden from attending his own father's coronation. Frederick, who was inclined to be rebellious and disagree with his father on everything from politics to music, was kept on a tight rein by his parents, who restricted his income and snubbed him in various ways, including – in George II's absence on a trip to Hanover – naming Caroline, his mother, 'regent' rather than him. But Frederick would not be quelled; attempting to assert his independence from his parents, he made contacts within the nobility, and began to advertise his cultural and musical interests – building up his art collection and hosting theatrical performances. Indeed, the first painter he employed at his court was an artist named Philip Mercier, who was responsible for a now famous painting called *The Music Party*; it depicts Frederick playing the cello in the company of his sisters Anne (who plays the harpsichord), Amelia (who strums the mandolino, a type of bass lute) and Caroline (who was rather unmusical and is simply reading from a book of Milton poems[36]). But on closer inspection the painting, which dates from 1733, is highly revealing: tensions among the figures betray some kind of quarrel between them, none of them acknowledging his or her siblings. Indeed, Frederick turns his back on Amelia – who in turn seems almost to elbow her brother away.

The source of this tension is easily located in history. During the creation of the portrait, the royal family was involved in a musical feud: Frederick had recently announced his support for a new opera company, which was based in a theatre on the edge of Lincoln's Inn Fields in central London. The company was known, somewhat meaningfully, as the 'Opera of the Nobility' (set up and funded by a group of wealthy aristocrats along with Frederick himself) and it was in direct rivalry with Handel's company – the so-called Second Academy at Haymarket that was opened after the closure of the first Royal Academy, and continued to be patronised by George II. What followed was a fierce opera war that was destined to end badly for both companies. The Nobility Opera mounted 52 performances in the first season, while Handel's company mounted 60[37] – both companies insisting on Tuesday and Saturday nights in direct competition with each other. On 13 December, a patron and landowner named Charles Jennens wrote: 'How two Opera Houses will subsist after Christmas, I can't tell; but at present we are at some difficulty for the support of One; & Mr Handel has been forc'd to drop his Opera three nights for want of company.'[38] At the end of 1733, the Opera of the Nobility moved to the King's Theatre at Haymarket, and Handel reposted by moving to the beautiful new theatre at Covent Garden, the first time the opera had ever been performed there.

Competition is supposed to be a good thing, but, according to courtier and gossip Lord Hervey, George II took as dim a view of his son's operatic challenge as he did of his political one:

[The King and Queen] were both Handelists and sat freezing constantly to that of Lincoln's Inn Fields. The affair grew as serious as that of the Greens and the Blues under Justinian at Constantinople. An anti-Handelist was looked upon as an anti-courtier, and voting against the Court in Parliament was hardly a less remissible or more venial sin than speaking against Handel or going to Lincoln's Inn Fields Opera. The Princess Royal said she expected in a little while to see half the House of Lords playing in the orchestra in their robes and coronets; and the King (though he declared he took no other part in this affair than subscribing £1000 a year to Handel) often added at the same time he did not think setting oneself at the head of a faction of fiddlers a very honourable occupation for people of quality ...[39]

However, Lord Hervey was severely biased against Frederick – who had previously poached one of his mistresses – and it was in his interests to present the prince in a negative light. In reality, the situation was probably not quite so polarised. In fact, in several of the seasons when the two companies presented rival productions, each company received a £250 bounty from the prince;[40] perhaps it suited Frederick sometimes to be identified with the younger generation of aristocrats who supported the new opera, but ultimately the prince couldn't afford to offend London's most popular composer. Indeed, in April 1736, Handel even provided the music for Frederick's wedding – an anthem, 'Sing unto God', as well as the opera *Atalanta*, a pastoral, almost masque-like production that was designed to flatter the Prince of Wales. It was yet another example of how Handel's independence worked to his advantage.

But that advantage, unfortunately, didn't hold for long: as Jennens had predicted, London simply couldn't support two opera houses. In 1737, both companies went bankrupt and the great opera war was over. There is an account of a conversation between George II and Handel – when Handel's fortunes were at a low ebb – where the king told him that 'these Italian discords' were finished in London.[41] His words had turned out to be remarkably prescient. It was a year of endings: on 20 November, George II's wife, Caroline, died suddenly, leaving the king distraught, and Handel set about preparing the music for her funeral. 'The Ways of Zion Do Mourn' is a moving anthem for four-part choir and orchestra, giving expression to genuine grief which surely Handel shared with the king. He had known the queen for many years, and she had become an important supporter of his work. Princess Anne, in mourning for her mother, later described hearing the rehearsal for the anthem: 'We had Handel's anthem last Wednesday in ye French chapel that ye king might hear it … and it's ye finest cruel touching thing that ever was heard.'[42] Mozart must have agreed: he later borrowed material from its first chorus for the opening movement of his own famous requiem.

Caroline's death did nothing to improve relations between father and son: on her deathbed, far from forgiving all, she had in fact reiterated her hatred of Prince Frederick. But Frederick was still intent on presenting himself as the 'people's prince': a thoroughly modern, thoroughly English, prospect for the throne. He knew that the collapse of the London opera scene wasn't due just to over-supply – in fact, its foreignness, once seen as exotic and fashionable, was increasingly viewed with suspicion. A new craze for ballad opera had been prompted with the premiere in 1728 of John Gay's *The Beggar's Opera*, a satirical play in English, spun around already popular ballad tunes. The opera's totally unprecedented success changed the face of London entertainment. This was the antithesis of the high-art, foreign-language, pompous Italian opera – indeed, it even mocked the fastidious conventions of that form, and depicted characters from all sections of contemporary society, from thieves and whores to courtiers, lawyers and priests, moralising and commenting on the state of society. The opera's astonishing popularity – it ran

A depiction by William Hogarth of a scene from John Gay's *The Beggar's Opera*. This comic opera in English – featuring familiar ballad and folk tunes – was hugely popular from its premiere in 1728, and prompted a new craze for operas in the vernacular, and a move away from high-art, elaborate Italian opera.

for 62 performances in its first season – prompted a new craving by audiences for a return to musical forms that were familiar and – crucially – English. National tastes were changing, and with that change, the monarchy, which was perceived as too foreign, now saw itself placed in an increasingly vulnerable position'.

What was needed now was truly British music.

PATRIOTIC
ANTHEMS

Thomas Arne was a native-born Englishman who had established himself away from the world of the court and the Chapel Royal. Originally apprenticed as a lawyer, he abandoned the legal world for the musical one, writing music for plays and pantomimes as well as various operas. In 1738 his adaptation of John Milton's *Comus* was a storming success; it held the stage beyond the end of the century, a fact that had much to do with Arne's charming, accessible music. He had a knack for writing catchy tunes that appealed to a more middle-brow taste and, crucially, he wrote works that were performed in English.

Thomas Arne became the one composer in the land whose popularity rivalled Handel's at the time. It was only much later that Handel's music eclipsed Arne's, as one Keats poem from 1816 demonstrates. The poet excuses himself for his bad verses, explaining that he has been out of reach of inspiring influences:

> *But many days have past since last my heart*
> *was warm'd luxuriously by divine Mozart*

By Arne delightd, or by Handel madden'd,
Or by the song of Erin perced and sadden'd.[43]

Put on a plane equal to Handel and Mozart, this poem demonstrates just how highly the English composer was regarded in the early nineteenth century. Perhaps Keats was thinking of Arne's opera *Artaxerxes*, which was such a hit that it was regularly revived for decades: Jane Austen complained in 1814 that she was 'very tired' of hearing it.[44]

In 1740, Arne was commissioned by Frederick, Prince of Wales, to write the music for an event staged at the prince's country estate at Cliveden. The event was supposed to celebrate the birthday of Frederick's three-year-old daughter Augusta, but in reality it had much more to do with Frederick's own political ambitions. Frederick, now openly estranged from his father, was in the midst of launching a carefully orchestrated campaign promoting himself as the patriot prince, supporting British manufacturers at home and a ruthless expansion of British power abroad. The lease on Cliveden, a grand country house, was all part of Frederick's attempts to style himself as an English country gentleman. He went hunting, played cricket and attended the races at Epsom. He also patronised English theatre and music, and the grounds of Cliveden House – which included a cliffside amphitheatre overlooking the Thames – lent themselves beautifully to theatrical performances. The *London Evening Post* reported how:

For the representation of these Pieces a long Walk in the Gardens
was properly decorated, and lighted up with a great Number of

Lamps, at the End of which was erected a great Number of Benches
for the Company. In the Front of which were placed Chairs for the
Prince and Princess of Wales, Prince George and Princess Augusta.

When the company – including the royals – was assembled, what they
witnessed was a veritable onslaught of theatrical Englishness. The
tickets were engraved by no less a figure than William Hogarth; the
form of the piece was English masque rather than Italian opera;
the actor and manager hired by Prince Frederick, John Rich, was
English and experienced in English productions. (Rich became
successful thanks to his work with John Gay on *The Beggar's Opera*,
inspiring the delightful axiom that *The Beggar's Opera* 'made Gay
rich and Rich gay'.) Above all, Arne's music was quintessentially
English, and so was the very subject matter – England's legendary Anglo-Saxon monarch, King Alfred. In Arne's opera, Alfred was
cultured and learned, a heroic defender of his people against a
barbarian invader – the Danes – the patron of towns and commerce,
and the founder of the Navy. Alfred, the only English king to be
called 'Great', would be Frederick's model. Only Frederick would
be greater, because he would be ruler, not of England, but of Britain
– Great Britain.[45]

Of the seven musical numbers contained in Arne's masque, the
most famous by far is 'Rule, Britannia!', with its iconic opening lyrics:

When Britain first, at Heaven's command
Arose from out the azure main;
This was the charter of the land,

And guardian angels sang this strain:
'Rule, Britannia! rule the waves:
Britons never will be slaves.'

When this piece is sung at the Last Night of the Proms, few of the people joining in the chorus realise that it was actually a potent attack on the king, a song that reinforced the beliefs of politicians who supported the Prince of Wales. These politicians felt that Britain should adopt a more aggressive foreign policy by using the Royal Navy to assert the country's power against the Spanish, as a pair of recently discovered letters at Oxford University's Bodleian Library confirm. One of these letters, written by a Welsh aristocrat to a fellow audience member, Lord Guildford, recalls, 'Methinks I saw you stretching your Melodious Throat in the Greatest Extasy, pronouncing Those Delightful Words; Britons Never Will Be Slaves.' What seems like simple patriotism today – 'Britannia, rule the waves' – was actually intended as an argument for increasing naval spending and a vision for a new kind of king that Prince Frederick exemplified. Swiftly, the tune transformed from something only heard by a tiny circle of Frederick's associates and supporters to one of the most famous anthems in history.

Never had the nation been more in need of it. Throughout the 1740s, Britain was heavily involved in the War of the Austrian Succession (also known as 'King George's War') defending Austria against the French, but also defending the French from invading the king's beloved Hanover. After a sensational victory at Dettingen in 1743 – led by King George II himself, now aged 60 – all seemed hopeful, but by 1745 a defeat at the great Battle of Fontenoy put Britain, and the Hanoverian monarchy, in a highly vulnerable position. It laid open the way for an invasion by 'Bonnie Prince Charlie', or Charles Edward Stuart, another descendant of Catholic James II. The Jacobites gathered an army in Scotland and, as they headed south, they sang Arne's anthem to rouse their spirits. Some of them even adapted the words to a more suitable – if metrically suspect – Jacobite theme:

> *When Royal Charles by Heaven's command*
> *Arrived in Scotland's noble Plain*
> *Thus spoke the Warrior, the Warrior of the Land*
> *And Guardian Angels sung this strain;*
> *Go on Brave Youth, go combat & succeed*
> *For Thou shall't conquer, tis decreed.*[46]

But the Hanoverian army sung the song, too. Arne's tune was so emotionally uplifting – and its text was specifically about *nation* rather than king – that it could cross the political divide.

'Rule, Britannia!' wasn't the only song that Arne wrote at this time. In the midst of this state of emergency, as the Jacobite troops marched south for England, the composer would come up with an even more widely known statement of Britishness in support of the embattled monarch. It was an old tune set to new words in a new arrangement by Arne; but the crucial moment that cemented it in English hearts and minds came on 28 September 1745 at the old Theatre Royal in Drury Lane. The *Daily Advertiser* of the time described it thus:

On Saturday night last, the audience of the Theatre Royal Drury Lane were agreeably surprised by the Gentlemen belonging to that House performing the Anthem of God Save Our noble King. The Anthem was repeated nightly till nearly the end of November, and the managers of Covent Garden Theatre followed suit. The arrangement of the Anthem for Drury Lane was made by Arne, who had for principal singers Mrs Cibber, Mr Beard and Mr Reinhold ... Benjamin Victor, in a letter he wrote to Garrick on the 10th October 1745, said 'the stage at both houses is the most pious, as well as the most loyal place in the three kingdoms. Twenty men appear at the end of every play; and one, stepping forward from the rest, with uplifted hands and eyes, begins singing to an old anthem tune, the following word – God save the King'.[47]

The tune of 'God Save the King' is in rhythm and style a 'galliard': a lively, triple-metre court dance that originated in the sixteenth century. The origin of the melody is unknown – there are similar versions dotted across the English musical landscape, including one by John Bull and a seventeenth-century Christmas carol – but it certainly would have been familiar to audiences hearing it at the Drury Lane Theatre in 1745. As with 'Rule, Britannia!', the song was picked up by both Jacobites and Hanoverians who sang it on their way to battle.

By the end of the eighteenth century, 'God Save the King' was firmly established as the national anthem, making Britain the first country in Europe to have such a patriotic hymn, and over the centuries the tune would be borrowed by twenty different countries across the world as their official national song.[48] It had originated not in an official commission, but instead in an instantaneous response to a political and military crisis, by the ever fertile, ever creative world of the London theatre. It must have been a glorious moment for Arne – and perhaps prompted Handel, with a constantly roving eye for popular taste and mood, to get in on the act, for he penned a popular song at the same time. The song was named '"Stand Round My Brave Boys": a Chorus Song for the Gentleman Volunteers of the City of London'. Its rousing lyrics began:

> *Stand round, my brave boys*
> *With heart, and with voice*
> *And all in full chorus agree*
> *We'll fight for our King*
> *And as loyally sing*
> *And let all the world know we'll be free.*

Despite these and its uplifting melody, the song never caught on quite like Arne's.

Composers everywhere, it seemed, were writing songs in an attempt to capture the patriotic atmosphere of the time. The famous old song 'The Roast Beef of Old England' has its origins around this time, written first by the novelist Henry Fielding for one of the 'ballad operas' that were all the rage in 1731. But after a new setting penned by the bass singer Richard Leveridge, it became customary for theatre audiences to sing the song before, after – and occasionally during – any new play. Its lyrics revel in being English – but betray in particular a nostalgia for the 'good old days' and the military glory of Elizabeth I's reign. Two of the middle verses run:

When good Queen Elizabeth sat on the throne
Ere coffee and tea and such slipslops were known
The world was in terror if e'en she did frown
Oh the roast beef of Old England
And Oh, for old England's roast beef!

In those days if fleets did presume on the main
They seldom or never return'd back again
As witness the vaunting Armada of Spain
Oh the roast beef of Old England
And Oh, for old England's roast beef!

Yet the song makes no bones about the fact that monarchy was by now losing power. No longer did Britain possess an absolute monarch with dictatorial powers, who could inspire terror with their frown. Those days were long past, and Prime Minister Robert Walpole could inspire more fear and terror than King George II ever could.

The War of the Austrian Succession had begun with the high hopes expressed in Thomas Arne's 'Rule, Britannia!', but it ended with a whimper. The highly unpopular peace treaty of 'Aix-La-Chapelle' was signed in October 1748, returning Britain's colonial conquests to France. To win over popular opinion, the government tried a well-worn technique of bread and circuses and decided to throw a grand fireworks party, a ceremony to reassure the public that Britain was still a great military power despite having accepted this ignoble peace. As Horace Walpole sardonically observed: 'The Peace is signed between us, France, and Holland, but does not give the least joy; the stocks do not rise, and the merchants are unsatisfied … in short there has not been the least symptom of public rejoicing, but the government is to give a "magnificent firework".'[49] The fireworks were to be designed by a pair of Italians, and the enormous architectural structure from which they were to be launched was the work of a French stage designer: the kind of team, in fact, that produced Italian operas. The music commissioned was, too, something of an afterthought: originally the king had wanted no music whatsoever. But if there was to be music – to add burnish to the proceedings – it would naturally be by Handel, the king of Italian opera. Even its title – *Music for the Royal Fireworks* – was propaganda, with its pointed use of the word 'royal' to give it additional authority. Handel had simply wanted to call the work *Ouverture*.

By November, workmen had begun to build a magnificent wooden structure (410 foot long and 114 foot high) in Green Park. It had a central triumphal arch, elaborate scenery and a giant bas-relief of George II as the Sun, which was to burn for five hours with the words *Vivat Rex* – God Save the King. As the structure rose, the newspapers excitedly reported prospective plans for the show, due in April the following year. The rehearsal took place at Vauxhall Pleasure Gardens, whose verdant avenues and pretty pavilions were the principal place of public entertainment in eighteenth-century London. The capital came to a near standstill as some 12,000 people struggled to get there to hear the music, probably the largest audience to gather for such a purpose anywhere in Europe at this time. The *Gentleman's Magazine* for April 1749 commented, 'So Great a resort occasioned such a stoppage on London Bridge that no carriage could pass for 3 hours'.[50]

Pleasure gardens were Arcadian retreats from the chaos of the city, a mixture of elegant park, art gallery and open-air music hall. What made Vauxhall particularly unusual as a musical venue was that the audience was drawn from all levels of society; since the entrance fee was only a shilling, almost anyone could afford it, and Horace Walpole praised the way 'the Princes and Peeresses mixed with the tradesmen and their wives, with apprentices and women of pleasure'. Vauxhall was equipped with bandstands and decorated 'supper boxes', and although the food was described by some as stingy – some complained that the ham was so thinly sliced that the programme could be read through it[51] – the musical offerings were more generous, and the work of Handel was frequently played. Vauxhall was designed as a heady experience to tickle the senses. Punters came to enjoy the gardens, to smell the flowers, to admire the buildings, to indulge in the food, to listen to music, and above all to see and be seen. Anywhere else in Europe this would have been a royal park, or a great princely garden, but in London – the workshop of the world – it was a commercial venture, and a very successful one at that.

Handel was the embodiment of that success, perhaps the world's first truly cosmopolitan composer, who regarded music as a business and himself as a businessman. It was those attitudes that allowed him to survive and thrive in London's market-driven environment, and London rewarded him in return. In 1738, at Vauxhall Pleasure

Gardens, Handel was the first artist in England to be publicly honoured in stone, as the *Daily Post* of the time reported:

> *We are informed from very good Authority; that there is now near finished a Statue of the justly celebrated Mr Handel exquisitely done by the ingenious Mr Raubillac of St Martin's Lane Statuary out of one entire Block of white marble, which is to be placed in a grand Nich erected on Purpose in the great Grove at Vauxhall Gardens ...*[52]

Louis-François Roubiliac – a well-known French sculptor of the time – actually created several sculptures of Handel, including a bust of the composer and memorial at Westminster Abbey where he is buried. But the one put up at Vauxhall was particularly remarkable. As a full-length statue – an honour at that time reserved only for monarchs, noblemen and military leaders – it caused a sensation when it was revealed. Moreover, the depiction of Handel's relaxed attitude – his informal clothes and lack of wig – is highly unusual, though in keeping with the carefree atmosphere of Vauxhall at the time. It demonstrates just how highly Handel was respected in his time, by kings and princes, and also by the general public. In this statue, Handel is the king of music – and he is the king of Vauxhall, too.

Far more people heard Handel's works at Vauxhall than in the expensive opera houses of the elite, and his *Music for the Royal Fireworks* was written as a crowd-pleaser. Although it was supposed to commemorate peace, the six-movement suite was written in the martial style, and scored for military instruments including horns, trumpets and kettledrums. For some, though, the sound was not military enough. A letter from the Duke of Montague (in charge of operations for the fireworks display) to a colleague reveals the arguments between stubborn Handel, determined as always to have his way, and the organisers who were keen to stick to a 'military' style of music:

I think Hendel now proposes to have but 12 trumpets and 12 french horns; at first there was to have been sixteen of each, and I remember I told the King so, who, at that time, objected to their being any musick, but when I told him the quantity and nomber of martial musick there was to be, he was better satisfied and said he hoped there would be no fidles. Now Hendel proposes to lessen the nomber of trumpets &c, and to have violeens. I don't at all doubt but when the King hears it he will be very much displeased ...[53]

But despite the worries of the bureaucratic officials, Handel nevertheless came up with a masterful piece of outdoor music for the occasion. The final scoring for the overture was for 9 trumpets, 9 horns, 24 oboes, 12 bassoons and 3 pairs of kettledrums, and described as 'a grand Overture of Warlike Instruments'. The sheer volume of the *Music for the Royal Fireworks* is impressive, and must have effectively carried over the noise of the enormous crowds assembled at Vauxhall for the rehearsal. The six movements are sonorous and stately, and convey a sense of grandeur that was sadly lacking from the fireworks display itself; the ceremony took place six days later in Green Park and turned out to be rather a damp squib. There is, in fact, no contemporary description of Handel's music surviving from the night of the fireworks, so sidelined was it by the series of the disasters that took place. Horace Walpole, clearly disapproving of the whole sorry affair, later described it in withering terms:

> *The next day were the fire-works, which by no means answered the expense, the length of preparation and the expectation that had been raised ... the rockets and whatever was thrown up into the air succeeded mighty well, but the wheels and all that was to compose the principal part, were pitiful and ill-conducted, with no changes of coloured fires and shapes: the illumination was mean, and lighted so slowly that scarce anybody had patience to wait the finishing; and then what contributed to the awkwardness of the whole, was the right pavilion catching fire, and being burned down in the middle of the show.*[54]

The royal fireworks had begun as theatre and ended as farce, with a panicked crowd and a stampede that resulted in three deaths. In spite of its popularity at Vauxhall, the *Music for Royal Fireworks* failed to enter the repertory during the eighteenth and nineteenth centuries. The result is that the music is royal in name only, and has none of the accretions of history, patriotism and long ceremonial usage that 'Zadok' and 'Rule, Britannia!' enjoy. Handel wrote nothing else in the same grandiloquent style. He sensed what truly royal music required – genuine integrity of purpose, passion and feeling – and he knew exactly how to provide it. The next, and most enduring, phase of royal music was about to begin.

THE CULT
OF HANDEL

By the end of 1741, Handel had stopped writing Italian opera altogether. He had devoted three decades of his life to the genre, channelling nearly all his creative energies into the near constant production of new works, but, after the spectacular failure of an opera called *Deidamia*, he was left finally financially and emotionally exhausted. Instead, he began to concentrate on English oratorios, which were usually unstaged, performed without sets, costume or action, and therefore much cheaper to produce. Oratorios could be performed on religious feast days, when the theatres were otherwise dark, while the biblical stories on which they were usually based appealed to the religiosity of an important new audience: not the cosmopolitan aristocracy who had been the great patrons of Handel's Italian operas, but the ever more prosperous, numerous and politically powerful middle class, who grew and thrived in the lengthy economic boom of Georgian England.

Oratorios had long been popular in Europe and especially in Italy, where they had originated. When he had first come to

England, Handel was surprised to find that audiences were hardly at all familiar with the form. So he created a new kind of oratorio for the English, distinct from those of the Italian tradition and entirely his own. Oratorio was effectively opera without the acting, and the variation that Handel introduced to England was a cosmopolitan synthesis of English masque, religious anthem and French classical drama, with elements, even, of the German Protestant oratorio thrown in. It was notable for its three-act dramatic text (in English), a combination of choruses and solo sections, with the choruses in particular being an important focal point for the entire work. These choruses would often become the popular 'hits' of the composition, and were performed on other occasions in their own right. (The 'Hallelujah' chorus from *Messiah* is the most famous example.) And it was a form that grew out of the circumstances and creative will of one composer – with the help of direct royal involvement.

Back in 1718, Handel had written a work called *Esther*, based on the biblical drama by the French playwright Jean Racine. It had been presented for Handel's birthday in 1732 as a staged performance – with the Children of the Chapel Royal (along with members of the choirs of St James's and Westminster) acting and singing in costume under the direction of the Master of the Chapel Royal Children, Bernard Gates. There were three performances in all, which took place at the Crown and Anchor tavern in the Strand – a well-known inn that housed the Academy of Ancient Music, set up to study and perform the works of great British composers of the past. The concerts were clearly a success, for George II's daughter Anne, the Princess Royal – and Handel's pupil – expressed a desire to see the work put on again. The tavern was not an appropriate concert venue for a member of the royal family to attend, so Handel set about organising a performance at the Opera House in Haymarket instead. For the clerical authorities in London, the thought of performing a religious-themed work in the theatre was more than a little unseemly – particularly with the involvement of the young Chapel Royal boys – and the Bishop of London, Edmund Gibson, intervened to prevent Handel from staging the work there. Obliged to compromise, Handel instead presented *Esther* in an unstaged form by mature professional musicians. A London newspaper, the *Daily Journal*, reported pointedly:

> *By His Majesty's Command. At the King's theatre in the Hay-Market on Tuesday the 2d day of may, will be performed The Sacred Story of Esther an Oratorio in English. Formerly composed by Mr Handel and now revised by him, with several Additions, and to be performed by a great Number of the best Voices and Instruments. NB There will be no Action on the Stage but the House will be fitted up in a decent Manner, for the Audience ...*[55]

The ruse worked. The oratorio was a complete success, running for six performances, and it set a precedent for the popularity of the unstaged form in future.

Between 1741 and the end of his life, Handel composed 16 oratorios, using not only the opera theatres for his performances but – for a while – the same star performers who had performed in his Italian operas. These oratorios had strong militaristic and nationalistic themes: for example, *The Occasional Oratorio*, first performed in 1746, was an act of encouragement to the Hanoverian regime in its suppression of the Jacobite rising and the invasion of Bonnie Prince Charlie and his army. At the time Handel wrote the piece, the uprising had not been defeated and the Hanoverian troops needed all the help they could get: Prince Charles's army had done an about-turn at Derby, withdrawing back to Scotland to gather more troops, although the Battle of Culloden – where the Duke of Cumberland's army would finally crush the Jacobites – was yet to come. But Handel anticipated that true victory was on the horizon. On 8 February 1746, an acquaintance of Handel's, the Reverend William Harris wrote: 'Yesterday morning I was at Handel's House to hear the rehearsal of his new occasional Oratorio. It is extremely worthy of him ... The words of the Oratorio are scriptural but taken from various parts, and are expressive of the rebel's flight and our pursuit of them. Had not the Duke carried his point triumphant, this Oratorio could not have been brought on.'[56]

There were some fears that Handel had been too hasty in his predications: Charles Jennens grumbled: ''Tis a triumph for a Victory not yet gain'd, and if the Duke [of Cumberland] does not make haste, it may not be gain'd at the time of performance'. Jennens's prediction was right, in fact: the first performances were given in February and the decisive victory at Culloden didn't happen until mid-April, which may explain the oratorio's somewhat lukewarm reception. The work is a series of victorious biblical tableaux – its lack of narrative drive or plot another reason it has often received a bad press – but it includes a series of fine choruses, attractive arias and rousing orchestral movements. As the title suggests, it celebrates 'occasion' – pageantry, ceremony, and the glorification of George II – more than drama, almost like a royal ode or religious anthem. In this sense, it is more in the tradition of royal music of the past: here Handel somewhat uncharacteristically compromises his sense of the dramatic to make a political point, the overarching themes of the work being the misery of war, the anticipation of peace and the praise of God for the victories of the righteous over those who are evil. Unfortunately, it was precisely this lack of drama which made *The Occasional Oratorio* less successful as a work of art, and a good deal less popular.

Handel's subsequent oratorios, however – *Judas Maccabaeus*, *Alexander Balus* and *Joshua* – caught the public mood perfectly. This was especially true of *Judas Maccabaeus*, which would go on to be one of Handel's most successful, most frequently performed and best-loved works. It was written amid the celebrations of the victory at Culloden in 1746, although it was not performed until the following year. The debut 'went off with very great Applause' according to Lord Shaftsbury, who was present at the occasion, and Handel made a large sum of money from its packed first performances. The oratorio was inspired by an Old Testament story: the beleaguered Israelites, under threat of persecution, are led by the military leader Judas Maccabaeus who heroically defeats a rebellion and unites a doubting people. (The libretto was written by one Reverend Thomas Morrell, a Fellow of King's College, Cambridge, who had been recommended to Handel personally by Prince Frederick.) The text, with its barely concealed metaphor for the recently failed Jacobite invasion, was designed as a compliment to the Duke of Cumberland: and, indeed, the parallel is made explicit in the dedication of the piece, which hails the Duke as a 'Truly Wise, Valiant and Virtuous Commander'. The audience would have understood the plot fully: such a devout, middle-class section of society could be trusted to know the story of Judas Maccabaeus, and at each performance they were given a booklet containing all the words so they could read along to the singing. Thus they would also have understood the obvious parallels between the Israelites and the modern English nation: these were a nationalistic people who regarded themselves under the special protection of God, and the 'just wars' Israelites waged with their enemies would have immediately chimed with English audiences.

Several of the movements from *Judas Maccabaeus* became popular hits, including the glorious chorus 'See the Conquering Hero Comes!' (which was actually incorporated from another oratorio, *Joshua*). The melody, in fact, is well known today, made famous by its conversion into one of the more enduring Victorian hymns, 'Thine Be the Glory'. Another movement from *Judas*, the aria 'Tis Liberty', was sung at Covent Garden four times in one month, and was even arranged for barrel organ. The wonderful image of Handel's aria being cranked through the streets of eighteenth-century London – heard by everyone from beggars to merchants, from shopkeepers to noblemen – shows just how far things had come for royal music by the mid-eighteenth century. And Handel's *Judas Maccabaeus* is indisputably royal music, composed to celebrate the prevention of the fall of the Hanoverian dynasty. George II probably attended its performance, and would surely have appreciated the dissemination of such general rejoicing in the securing of his lineage. But Handel's oratorio is above all written for the people, heard by the people, and giving voice to the nation's sense of relief and triumph far more effectively than any pomp-filled thanksgiving service.

In the years that followed, Handel would write a series of oratorios that would each present a new instalment of the ancient story of God's chosen people – the story of ancient Israel. But it was also the story of God's new chosen people in a new Holy Land named Great Britain. The idea of a divinely ordained monarchy no longer held sway in Hanoverian England: instead, it had been replaced by the idea of a 'divinely ordained' nation. Oratorio was the soundtrack for this new ideology, combining religious zeal with a strident national pride. It defied the old Puritan objection to religious music by bringing the religion triumphantly into the theatre. It was oratorio musical form that would be elevated into a new national cult, and given royal endorsement by the next Hanoverian king.

⟨∞⟩

Unlike all the previous Hanoverian kings, George III had actually been born in Britain. When he acceded to the throne in 1760, he proclaimed to parliament: 'Born and educated in this country, I glory in the name of Britain.'[57] George was English through and through by both birth and inclination, and he was determined to fulfil his duties as a patriotic British king. History has often viewed him, wrongly, as 'politically orthodox and personally conventional';[58] quite to the contrary, George III understood – as Georges I and II had failed fully to appreciate – that the power of monarchy was in how the king appeared to his subjects. Like Frederick, George believed that the key to a secure and popular monarchy was one that projected a picture of cosy domesticity burnished by nationalistic royal splendour. To achieve that burnish, he would turn to music.

The new king's coronation on 22 September 1761 demonstrated these aspirations. While many of the ceremonial aspects were badly organised, the music was well planned, well organised and well executed. It was also the first coronation in history where almost all the music was written by a single composer: William Boyce, born and bred in London, and a stalwart member of the Chapel Royal since 1736. Though now a much neglected figure of music history, Boyce was a well-respected composer in his day, in particular for his editing of a Cathedral Music collection which created a new canon of the nation's greatest church music. He was also responsible for penning the popular national song 'Heart of Oak' inspired by a series of naval victories against France – which even today is still the official march of the Royal Navy. In qualifications and in nationalistic sentiments, Boyce was an appropriate choice for George III's new vision of monarchy. But Boyce – as he himself must surely have known – was not George III's first choice as composer for the coronation. Boyce was only selected for the job because the composer who had been the leading light of royal music for five decades – Handel – had died two years earlier. Not only was Boyce playing second fiddle to a dead composer, but, humiliatingly, he was in the employ of a royal patron who was utterly in thrall to Handel.

For George III was no mere tub-thumping nationalist. He was a genuinely cultured man and intensely musical, playing the flute, harpsichord and piano. It was his musicality that would help to

The vast 'Three Choirs Festival' in 1844; such festivals were an important feature of musical culture during the Victorian period, featuring gargantuan choirs, orchestras and massed spectators playing enormous versions of popular works, in particular religious-themed oratorios like Handel's Messiah and Mendelssohn's Elijah.

bond him with with his wife Queen Charlotte, who herself played the piano and the guitar, and whose music master was J. C. Bach (the youngest son of Johann Sebastian, and often known as the 'London Bach'). Indeed, Bach – lured to London by the opportunity of employment as Queen Charlotte's music master – was almost single-handedly responsible for establishing the first ever regular public concerts in London, a development that would consolidate the city's reputation as the music capital of Europe. While Charlotte dedicated herself to her music practice with Bach – his harpsichord concertos of 1763 are dedicated to Charlotte, one of which ends on a series of variations of the tune of 'God Save the King' – her husband concentrated on his grand ideas about Britain's role as an artistic power. George III believed that Britain's cultural reputation should rival its aspirations to military might. During his reign, he would set about fulfilling these ambitions: renovating Somerset House and insisting that a north block be added to the building in order to house a club house-cum-exhibition space for the elite of Britain's scientists, artists and historians. George would become patron of the Academy of Ancient Music in 1784, he regularly attended 'Concerts of Antient Music' performed by the Academy, and from 1785 he even chose the programmes for the concerts. In 1788, he visited Worcester for the reputable 'Three Choirs Festival', lending his own private band to the orchestra for their use. But it was a German-born composer who George particularly revered; it was Handel who represented the zenith of the king's national cultural project. Handel himself had said of George – when the king was still a young prince: 'While that boy lives, my music will never want a protector.'[59] His words were more prophetic than Handel could have imagined.

The ghost of Handel is ever present in the music that William Boyce provided for George III's coronation. And no wonder: not only did Handel remain, even in death, even, the most enduringly popular (if adopted) English composer, but the previous coronation, that of George II, had given the world Handel's coronation anthems, which had already proved to be the finest and most revolutionary music of its kind of all time. Boyce wrote eight anthems for the event, all of which set out to emulate the lustre and scale of Handel's own anthems. His version of 'The King Shall Rejoice', for example, with its bouncing rhythms, use of kettledrums and bright, major harmonies, is in its opening so Handelian that, as the music filled the vast acoustic of Westminster Abbey, it must have seemed as though the German composer had been reincarnated for the occasion.

But William Boyce possessed both pride and dignity when it came to acknowledging Handel's superior talents, demonstrated by the one coronation anthem for which he refused to compose a new setting. The archbishop had asked for the text of 'Zadok the Priest' to be reset; in a return note, Boyce politely explained that 'the Anthem Zadock the Priest cannot be more properly set than it has already been by Mr Handel'.[60] The reply promptly came: 'His Majesty hath signified his Pleasure, that the 4th Anthem, Zadok the Priest &c should be performed as it was set for the last Coronation.' And so it was: Boyce performed Handel's 'Zadok' for George III, and it must have been as much of a crowd-pleaser at this coronation as it had been at the last. The coronation would be the high point of Boyce's public career, but it was also symbolic: despite his own undoubted worth as a composer, he would forever be in the shadows – along with many other English composers of the period – eclipsed by the great and powerful light of Handel.

❧

When the nation's favourite composer died in 1759, his passing was marked with something close to a state funeral: he was buried in Westminster Abbey, on a regal scale, with 3000 people in attendance. Remarkably, death would not diminish Handel's popularity – instead his music continued to reach an ever wider audience. And Handel's enduring reputation was cemented for posterity by George III. The king had loved Handel since he was a child: one story tells how the composer was at court one day, improvising on the organ, when the young prince crept up behind him and listened with fixed and rapt attention. Handel turned to notice the boy, and said, in his broken English: 'Goot boy, goot boy, you shall care for my fame when I am dead.'[61] But George's childish obsession with the composer did not fade once he was on the throne: far from it. He exasperated the music historian Dr Charles Burney by insisting that the praise accorded to Handel in his *General History of Music* be increased.[62] He possessed a bust of Handel by Roubiliac which he kept at the Queen's House in Greenwich, and among George's proudest possessions were a harpsichord owned by Handel and many autograph scores by the composer, which were probably presented to him by Handel's friend and assistant, J. C. Smith the Younger. The king even owned a copy of John Mainwaring's biography of Handel, which he had read closely and annotated with his own thoughts. The copy was unfortunately destroyed during the Blitz, but we still have records of what the notations said. One comment runs:

G.F Handel was ever honest, nay excessively polite, but like all men of sense would talk all, and hear none and scorned the advice of any but the Woman He loved, but his Amours were rather of short duration, always within the pale of his own profession, but He knew that without Harmony of souls neither love nor the creation would have been created and Discord ends here as certainly as the last Trumpet will call us from our various Pleasures.[63]

George III kept a private band of musicians to play for him in both London and his favoured residence of Windsor Castle. His leader was the accomplished German violinist George Griesbach, one of four musical brothers in the king's service. Each day it seems the king would give him a playlist of the music he wanted to hear. A handful of these playlists – scribbled on any scrap of paper that came to hand – have survived in the family's possession. They consist, simply, of Handel, Handel and Handel. And not any old Handel: but a wide range of his music, including overtures, *concerti grossi* and movements from operas and oratorios of every period. These little scraps are hands-on evidence, in George's own handwriting, that the king not only loved Handel but really knew his music.

In 1784, George's obsession came to a head with the championing of a massive concert in Westminster Abbey in honour of the centenary of Handel's birth (although, in fact, they got the year wrong). Four thousand of the richest, most powerful and fashionable people in London poured into the newly decorated Abbey: it was the biggest national event since George III's own coronation 25-odd years earlier. George III, second to none in his enthusiasm for Handel, quickly took the lead in the celebrations. He was patron of the centenary; he secured the use of the Abbey – unheard of for such an event – he personally approved the architect James Wyatt's Gothic designs for the temporary galleries and stands; he insisted that a third day be added to the celebrations, because the two originally planned couldn't do justice to Handel's music. And each day, sitting in a great Gothic throne and surrounded by the royal family, the bishops, the nobility, the great officers of state and the judges, he led the nation's homage to the man who had given it its musical voice.

The jewel in the crown of the programme had to be Handel's most famous oratorio, *Messiah*: it was suggested that the entire festival should culminate in a huge performance of that work before the royal family and a packed abbey. *Messiah* is, of course, the work that most epitomises Handel, a glorious fusion of astonishing music, compelling entertainment and profound sacred message. Its theme is an extended reflection on Jesus Christ, setting to music extracts from the King James Bible, the Book of Psalms and the Book of Common Prayer. It was the only oratorio to have been performed during Handel's lifetime in a consecrated building, although *Messiah* was first and foremost written as entertainment. In fact it was this very dichotomy that confused listeners when it was first performed in 1742: one journalist of the day asked whether or not an oratorio 'is an Act of Religion ... if it is, I ask if the Playhouse Is a fit Temple to perform it in'. He continued, if it is 'for Diversion and Amusement only ... what a Prophanation of God's Name and Word it is, to make so light Use of them?'[64] But during successive decades *Messiah* became an increasingly regular choice in theatres, at festivals, for charity performances and – in extracted form – for use during church services. As Charles Burney put it: 'And from that time to the present, this great work has been heard in all parts of the kingdom with increasing reverence and delight; it has fed the hungry, clothed the naked, fostered the orphan, and enriches succeeding managers of the Oratorios, more than any single production in this or any country.'[65]

In combining entertainment and religion so neatly, Handel had hit upon a winning formula: the work contains many choruses for full choir – more than almost any of his other oratorios – and these choruses appealed to the conservative British audiences who were familiar with Anglican anthems from everyday church services; the choruses were relatively simple and easy to sing – melodious, bright and full of word painting – an appealing choice for choral festivals and amateur choirs; and the subject matter was universally familiar and compelling. George's very visible approval of the work, along with all of Handel's oratorios – he would bring his queen to the Covent Garden oratorio performances at least once a week – sustained and fuelled the fashion for the musical form, and it remained the most substantial fare of concert programmes throughout the eighteenth century and into the nineteenth.

As *Messiah* grew in popularity, the forces it was written for grew, too. Originally composed for a modest choir and simple orchestration (strings, trumpets and timpani), the numbers of performers began to increase in relation to its growing cultural importance. In 1771, a performance at the Foundling Hospital used 56 singers, the first recorded instance of there being more singers than instrumentalists. By the time of the Handel commemoration in 1784, the numbers of performers had reached around 500: 250 singers and 250 members of the orchestra. The sheer size of the forces made this an entirely different musical experience. King George was responsible for effectively turning Westminster Abbey into a concert hall for the glorification of Handel. The significance of this was historic and unprecedented. For nearly a thousand years, Westminster Abbey had been the heart of religious ceremonies celebrating monarchy. For generations, it was where monarchy and religion had always met, with music being part of what bound them together, whether at coronations, weddings, funerals or other royal services. At these services, however, music had always been a subservient part of royal ceremony. But with the centenary of Handel, the focus of the ceremony had entirely changed: it wasn't the monarch but the music that was being worshipped, as well as the composer and the idea of Britishness he had come to represent.

The extraordinary popularity of the first day of celebrations was described vividly by a London newspaper:

The Commemorative Entertainments in honor of Handel began yesterday morning. By seven o'clock the several doorways of the

A statue of Queen Anne has stood outside St Paul's Cathedral since 1712. Anne was on the throne when the magnificent building was officially completed in 1711, and it was home to many important thanksgiving services – adorned with music – throughout her reign.

St Paul's Cathedral was built by the brilliant scientist, mathematician and architect Sir Christopher Wren, and was designed to replace the old cathedral, destroyed in the Great Fire of 1666. It took 35 years to build, and as it rose above the London skyline it became a powerful symbol of the emerging empire of the newly-unified Great Britain.

The north wall of the impressive Painted Hall at the Old Royal Naval College in Greenwich. It depicts George I arriving in ancient Roman magnificence to claim the throne, riding in a chariot and attended by winged cherubs. The reality was somewhat different: he arrived by boat late at night and in sober travelling clothes.

This statue by the French sculptor Roubiliac depicts eighteenth-century Britain's favourite composer, George Frideric Handel. Designed to stand in Vauxhall Pleasure Gardens – and now at the V&A museum – the memorialisation of a musician in stone was unprecedented at this time, an honour previously only reserved for monarchs, noblemen and military leaders.

Canaletto's depiction of Westminster Bridge on Lord Mayor's Day gives a flavour of what the Thames might have looked like on the day that Handel's *Water Music* was first performed for King George I in 1717, when 'the number of barges and above all of boats filled with people desirous of hearing was beyond counting.'

A portrait of George II, the king responsible for commissioning some of Handel's best-loved works, including his magnificent coronation anthems and *Music for the Royal Fireworks*.

The Music Party by Philip Mercier depicts Prince Frederick playing the cello in the company of his sisters Anne, Amelia and Caroline. But all is not as it seems: the tense nature of the figures and their lack of eye contact with one another reveals the deep family feud that was raging at the time the painting was created.

Thomas Arne, the English composer who, during the eighteenth century, rivalled Handel for fame and reputation, and indeed his most famous works are even more widely known today than Handel's. He was responsible for penning both 'Rule Britannia' and 'God Save the Queen'.

A contemporary depiction of the imposing machine in Green Park that was built to launch the fireworks at George II's public firework party: Handel's *Music for the Royal Fireworks* was performed at the same occasion.

Musicians and members of the eighteenth-century public at Vauxhall Pleasure Gardens.
The Pleasure Gardens were a popular place of entertainment from 1661 until the early
nineteenth century, offering the combined sensual experience of music, dancing, beautiful
gardens, fireworks, food and drink. Handel's music – along with that of other popular
composers of the day – was often performed here.

The extraordinarily lavish Music Room at the Royal Pavilion in Brighton, built at the
request of George IV between 1818 and 1820 to house his personal, private band.

German-born Mendelssohn was the most popular composer in Britain during the early nineteenth century. He was also a close friend of Queen Victoria and Prince Albert, rearranging some of his own compositions as piano duets specifically for the royal couple to play together.

The Albert Hall and the Albert Memorial are two monuments to Prince Albert's vision for a cultural and scientific community at South Kensington: he also envisaged a series of museums (the V&A, the Science Museum and the Museum of Natural History) and a musical conservatoire (the Royal College of Music). Sadly Albert did not live long enough to see any of them completed.

St George's Chapel, Windsor: legendary organist and leading figure in the English Musical Renaissance, Walter Parratt, worked here for half his life, providing daily services of extraordinary music for Queen Victoria herself. During the course of his time here, the queen became a close personal friend and Parratt was eventually appointed as her private organist.

Crowds gather on the steps of St Paul's during Victoria's Diamond Jubilee in June 1897. This service marked a turning point in nineteenth-century royal music – as with every subsequent jubilee, it was celebrated with pageantry and elaborate, lavish music.

Queen Victoria's magnificent gold piano still stands in the White Drawing Room of Buckingham Palace. It is sumptuously gilded, and decorated with dancing cherubs, animals, birds and foliage, and cost around 175 guineas to make (around a quarter of a million pounds today).

Elizabeth II's coronation service in 1953 marked the culmination of the British monarchy's bid to reinvent royal ceremony: an extraordinarily lavish music programme included composers old and new, from Tallis and Gibbons to Elgar, Holst and Bax. The order of service shown here lists the reworking by Vaughan Williams of the ancient 'Old Hundredth' hymn tune to the text of 'All People That on Earth Do Dwell.'

THE FORM AND ORDER
OF THE SERVICE THAT IS TO BE
PERFORMED AND THE CEREMONIES
THAT ARE TO BE OBSERVED IN THE

CORONATION

OF HER MAJESTY

QUEEN ELIZABETH II

IN THE ABBEY CHURCH
OF ST PETER WESTMINSTER
ON TUESDAY THE SECOND DAY OF JUNE 1953

soul live, and it shall praise thee. For thine is the kingdom, the power, and the glory, for evermore. Thou wilt keep him in perfect peace, whose mind is stayed on thee.
SAMUEL SEBASTIAN WESLEY

When the Homage is ended, the drums shall beat, and the trumpets sound, and all the people shout, crying out:

GOD SAVE QUEEN ELIZABETH.
LONG LIVE QUEEN ELIZABETH.
MAY THE QUEEN LIVE FOR EVER.

Then shall the Archbishop leave the Queen in her Throne and go to the Altar.

XV. THE COMMUNION

Then shall the organ play and the people shall with one voice sing this hymn:

All people that on earth do dwell,
  Sing to the Lord with cheerful voice;
Him serve with fear, his praise forth tell,
  Come ye before him, and rejoice.

Abbey were thronged with the subscribers of both sexes, who thought
no sacrifice of time too great for a priority of situation at a Concert
so grand and novel. Whether it was from any miscalculation in issu-
ing tickets than there were places, we know not; but by half after ten
o'clock, every gallery &c overflowed, and in consequence thereof, some
hundreds were under the necessity of returning home, or contenting
themselves with the dark stations under the several structures ... a
few gentleman indeed, not inclined to brooke the disappointment their
female parties most thus sustain, cut down the whole canvas partition
at the back of the pit near the choir, and by this justifiable manoeuvre
at last commanded one of the most desirable stations ...[66]

From the start, the commemoration was seen in nationalistic as well as religious terms. The same newspaper described, 'The performance of Sacred Musick as ... a flattering and novel instance of national taste.'[67] A member of the audience, Reverend Robert Hall, described it as 'like a great act of national assent to the fundamental truths of religion'.[68]

With the Handel commemoration, a tradition of mass Handel worship had been established and the commemoration was repeated the following year. The number of performers was increased to 616 and it kept on growing. Next time it was 640 performers (which gave Horace Walpole a headache). By 1791 there were 1068. One important guest at the 1791 celebrations was the German composer Joseph Haydn. Haydn, who would take up the baton from Handel in the 1790s as the nation's most popular living composer, was struck by the sheer size of the performances, and found that it confirmed 'that deep reverence for the might genius of Handel, which ... he was even prone to avow'. Haydn was inspired by the experience and it prompted his own masterpiece oratorio, *The Creation*. Memorial concerts for Handel spread throughout the country with similar festivals in Manchester, Birmingham, Sheffield and York. In the nineteenth century Handel worship would increase still more. Handel's music, performed with ever increasing firepower, became the dominant musical expression of our national identity.

George III's 60-year reign was rocked by revolutions in America and France, but the overthrow of the monarchy in other countries only served to bolster it in Britain. It was a gradual shift in popularity that is marked neatly in music: between George's accession in 1760 and 1781, records show that 'God Save the King' received only four formal performances, but over the following 20 years there were more than 90.[69] Cartoons depicting George become kinder, portraying him as a gentle, kindly, frugal farmer. The shift was partly due to the king's recurring mental illness – possibly the debilitating effect of the genetic disease porphyria – that made him appear deeply vulnerable. But it was also a national reaction of horror to the bloody events occurring across the English Channel. The French Revolution, it turned out, was the best thing that ever happened to the British monarchy: for the first time in the history of the Hanoverian dynasty it made the British love their king.

During the 1790s, there was a surge of popular support for the monarchy, expressed through the music of the time. The market was flooded with ballads and songs to this effect: at Vauxhall Plea-sure Gardens, the official composer James Hook provided a steady stream of songs like 'The Good Ship Britannia' (which stresses that 'Britannia's our Country, her Captain's our King, and while she keeps the Sea and he bears kind Command' the nation will flourish) and 'The King and Constitution', which warns:

> *Warm in the great, the glorious cause*
> *Of our religion and our Laws*
> *Ye great and good with pious hand*
> *Support your King and save the land.*[70]

Hook's political songs provide a musical commentary on political events as they affected England during the 1780s and 1790s. As composer-in-residence at the Pleasure Gardens, however, Hook's job was not to present a radical political view – that might jar with the calm and easy atmosphere of merry-making – but simply to reflect the popular opinions of the public as he understood them. Consequently, these songs are a valuable insight into the attitude towards the 'glorious cause' of monarchy at this time.

As for George himself, he was ageing, and as his health was declining he turned increasingly to the music of his beloved Handel for strength and support. His own musicality and love of music remained, even during his descent into madness. As he grew blind and deaf, he played movements from Handel's oratorio *Jephtha*, including Jephtha's lament on the loss of his daughter. In his final years, he played Delilah's mad love song from the oratorio *Samson* (one of Handel's finest dramatic works, with an obvious, poignant parallel with George: the work begins with Samson, the fallen hero, blind and in chains, bemoaning his fate). The king even arranged imaginary concerts, and would try futilely to grasp a tune from Handel in order to sing it. By the end, the King of Great Britain had no knowledge of who he was.

It was a sad demise for the man who had worked hard to promote the idea of Britishness and to forge a British cultural identity, and the canonisation and adoption of Handel as our own was an integral part of that process. This is the extraordinary achievement of the eighteenth-century monarchy: despite being a surprisingly fragile institution that had lost much of its political and religious power, it helped to create not only a new and powerful nation but also a patriotic national soundtrack to accompany it.

REVIVAL

MONARCHY IN
CONFUSION

'I Vow to Thee, My Country' is one of our greatest national hymns, performed regularly at royal events throughout the twentieth century. It was sung at St Paul's Cathedral for the Silver Jubilee of George V in 1935; Lady Diana Spencer called it one of her favourite hymns from childhood, and it was sung at her wedding to Prince Charles in 1981 and her funeral 16 years later. The words, by the poet and diplomat Sir Cecil Spring Rice, fuse a fervent love of country with a fervent love of God:

> *I vow to thee, my country, all earthly things above,*
> *Entire and whole and perfect, the service of my love ...*
> *The love that asks no question, the love that stands the test,*
> *That lays upon the altar the dearest and the best.*

This combination of patriotism and Christian devotion has been the foundation and continuing inspiration of royal music from the beginning of our story. The music, too, follows a long British tradition: it was written by Gustav Holst, who took the melody from the 'Jupiter' theme in his well-known orchestral suite *The Planets*. It combines a dignified grandeur and poignancy with a pervasive nostalgia characteristic of our best royal music.

But, remarkably, though the hymn seems so much part of our national fabric, 'I Vow to Thee, My Country' dates only from 1921; its themes and the imperial sweep of its music captured the public imagination in the aftermath of the First World War. But, then, Elgar's 'Land of Hope and Glory' is only 20 years older, while Parry's 'Jerusalem' dates from 1916, the same year that the House of Windsor itself came into being. The twentieth century was far from being the dying gasp of either the British monarchy or its music. It was an age of revival, in which Crown and nation found a new unity and a new form of self-expression.

But the story might have been very different. At the beginning of the nineteenth century, the monarchy was in a troubled state. The British nation had held on steadfastly to their monarchy – the institution's continuing popularity founded largely on the personality of the touchingly humble, vulnerable George III – while, across the Channel, France had waged bloody revolution and chosen the path of a republic. But George had long since begun his descent into a permanent twilight of madness, and his son George, the Prince of Wales (known as 'Prinny' to his cronies), was effectively left in charge. The prince was a very different man from his father. Frivolous and lazy, he enjoyed gambling, and his extravagant tastes meant he ran up almost incalculably large debts; on one occasion, he had to be bailed out by the House of Commons. He was by his own admission 'rather too fond of wine and women';[1] he had a disastrous affair with an older, widowed woman named Maria Fitzherbert, which caused a national scandal. He was deeply unpopular with the British public, and regularly and viciously caricatured in the press by cartoonists like Gillray and Cruikshank. Suddenly the monarchy, bereft of its political and sacred power, and without a popular figurehead to rally around, was in danger of becoming an irrelevance.

Prince George was no good at the business side of monarchy – that was too much like hard work. But he was far from talentless. He was imaginative and creative, and he was probably the greatest royal builder since Henry VIII. He was responsible for encouraging the complete redesign of central London by Regency architect John Nash, including the remodelling of Buckingham House into a new royal residence named Buckingham Palace, as well as the rebuild of Windsor into one of the world's most distinctive castles. He was also deeply passionate about music, a passion inherited from his father. But while George III's tastes had barely extended beyond Handel, his son was fond of up-to-date, fashionable composers in the classical style, such as Mozart, Beethoven and Haydn. Haydn in particular became a close acquaintance of the prince while staying in London: the prince organised several concerts of Haydn's music, and even had a portrait painted of the composer which he ordered to be hung in his bedroom.[2] Prinny played the cello so well, indeed, that one contemporary observed that 'few amateurs could equal him';[3] he also enjoyed singing, and had a pleasant voice. His two passions – for building and music – came together in spectacular fashion at the extraordinary Marine Pavilion in Brighton, where he had moved to pursue his affair with Mrs Fitzherbert in relative privacy. Originally designed in a Greco-Roman style by the architect Henry Holland, the Pavilion was transformed by John Nash into an exotic oriental palace: 'a mixture of Moorish, Tartar, gothic and Chinese'[4] styles, adorned with minarets, domes and pinnacles on the exterior and an interior decorated with opulent decoration and exquisite furnishings, including a lavish music room. The prince's oriental fantasy was – and remains – an incongruous and utterly bizarre addition to Brighton's seafront, but it is in keeping with his love of theatrical pageantry and sensual pleasure.

In the Pavilion's fanciful music room – lit by nine lotus-shaped chandeliers, and decorated with opulent Chinese dragons and Eastern designs – Prinny maintained his own private band. It was not an official royal band – by the early nineteenth century such a thing barely existed – but, rather, a personally funded passion project, containing the finest hand-picked musicians. It included a total of 34 players from the woodwind, brass and percussion families, and was essentially what we recognise today as a military band. The opulence of the room's furnishings extended to the band itself: their trumpets and drums were made of solid silver, and their uniforms were covered in gold lace.

George entertained a stream of guests at the Pavilion – feeding them in his magnificent banqueting hall before showing off his favourite musical toy to the assembled party. It was here that he received the great opera composer Giacomo Rossini, who spent three days in 1823 experiencing the sensual delights of the king's personal pleasure dome. George's band even played the overture to

Rossini's own opera *The Thieving Magpie* in the composer's honour, and Rossini responded by singing two arias from it, one in falsetto and accompanying himself on the piano. By all accounts the two men – equally vulgar in their own way – got on famously, and the composer's relaxed and informal manner with the king outraged other guests who described him as a 'fat sallow squab of a man'.[5] Rossini later met the king several times in London where they sung duets together.

This was not the royal music of earlier eras. Although the musicians were of the finest quality, no music of note or innovation was produced for the band. The pieces played were mostly arrangements (by the bandmaster) of symphonies from the prince's favourite composers: Beethoven, Haydn, Mozart and Handel. This was music purely for personal enjoyment, a world away from the sacred works of musicians like William Byrd and Henry Purcell, or the magnificence of Handel's coronation anthems. It was as if the monarchy's growing irrelevance was being played out through its music: it was an institution that was growing decadent, mismanaged and with little visible point or purpose. In France, the revolutionaries had cut off the king's head, and abolished the monarchy; in America, Britain's former colonial subjects had established a kingless republic; while here in Britain, there were riots, conspiracies and clamorous calls for reform.

George kept his band with him for the rest of his life. When he finally became king in 1820, they played at his grand coronation, and were later moved permanently to Windsor, within easy reach of London and the king. As his father had found solace in Handel, so George IV found solace in the music of his band, taking them with him on weekend excursions to the Royal Lodge in Windsor Great Park (when they were stationed in the conservatory) and fishing expeditions (where they would be moored in a boat near the royal barge). George was only on the throne for a decade: his self-indulgences soon got the better of him, and his health and mobility quickly declined until his death in 1830 (*The Times* reported: 'never was there an individual less regretted by his fellow creatures than this deceased King'[6]). George's successor, his elder brother William, did not continue the tradition of the band. The musicians were paid off and ordered to return their handsome uniforms.

Frugality was highly characteristic of the new king, crowned William IV on 8 September 1831. He could not have been more different from his brother. A former naval officer, thrifty and pragmatic, who despised pomp and ceremony, William swiftly scaled down George IV's extravagant establishment: apart from winding down the band, he also reduced the number of royal yachts and gave away George's extensive animal collection.[7] He refused to move into the grandly refurbished Buckingham Palace, claiming that the modest royal residence Clarence House was perfectly adequate. He didn't even want to have a coronation, calling it 'useless and ill-timed expense'. Horrified Tory protests persuaded him that this was a necessary formality, but William nevertheless insisted on doing it on the cheap. Costing less than a fifth of George IV's magnificent coronation, it was nicknamed the 'Half-Crownation', and was in all respects a distinctly unimpressive affair. The musical programme was dramatically cut, and included only one new commission, 'O Lord, Grant the King a Long Life' by royal composer Thomas

Attwood. Others were recycled from previous coronations – including Handel's 'Zadok the Priest' – and some texts were omitted altogether. No special organ was built for the occasion; the Abbey's own organ was used instead.

Even Attwood's anthem feels like a musical compromise. Attwood was a musician who always felt himself under the spell of greater talents. As a young man he had studied with Mozart, who said of him: 'He partakes more of my style than any scholar I ever had, and I predict, that he will prove a sound musician.'[8] A sound and respected musician he certainly was: he was employed at various royal posts throughout his career, including music teacher to Caroline, Princess of Wales (George IV's wife), as well as composer at the Chapel Royal from 1797. But his work was always deeply affected by his admiration of Mozart and his experience as the great man's pupil; his music, though recognizably English, never quite developed a unique voice. 'O Lord, Grant the King a Long Life', for example, utilises a central theme based around the melody of 'Rule, Britannia!', a direct reference to William's long naval career, in which he had fought with Lord Nelson against Napoleon. Despite the grand setting – for choir and full orchestra – this 'Homage' anthem (performed directly after the crowning) is in marked contrast to the homage anthems of the past, which were traditionally an opportunity to celebrate the king's divine right. Attwood's anthem makes no mention of such sacred duty, instead relying on a hollow reference to the aged king's personal career by the means of an already popular patriotic air. The music is shorn of its sacred purpose – falling back on a tune that was already becoming hackneyed – and can be seen as symptomatic of the wider problem with the early nine-teenth-century monarchy. William's economical approach would be no more powerful than George IV's era of decadence.

⁂

Reform of the monarchy was essential and upon William's death in 1837 (he reigned for only seven years) this daunting task seemed likely to fall to a teenage girl. Queen Victoria was 18 years old when she came to the throne. The only legitimate child of George III's fourth son, Edward, Duke of Kent, young Victoria was brought up at Kensington Palace, where she received an education typical of a noblewoman in early nineteenth-century England. She studied contemporary moralist teachings and languages alongside history, geography and poetry – neglecting the more 'male' subjects such as classics and mathematics – but, above all, 'feminine accomplish-ments', of which music played a central part. She was taught to play the piano as well as receiving lessons in the art of singing and dancing, taking particular delight in the latter (throughout her reign she would throw sumptuous balls). Her lessons were punctuated by frequent visits to the theatre, where she acquired a lifelong passion for Italian opera.

Once she became queen, it seemed likely that Victoria would continue the hedonistic but hollow passions of her uncle George IV, regarding music as a tool for dancing and for pleasure only. She was the first monarch to make Buckingham Palace her permanent London residence – where a huge, ornate ballroom was built at her personal instigation – and when, in 1839, she hosted a series of concerts here, every single item on the programme was an extract from an Italian opera, mostly by Rossini and Donizetti. She even caused consternation by refusing to support English music, actually turning down requests to become patron of the Society of British Musicians and the English Opera House.[9] But Victoria's education and her musical tastes reflected the inherent conservatism of early nineteenth-century England. Britain was reaching the height of its industrial powers, in an age that regarded material success and utilitarian thinking far more highly than artistic achievement. Beyond the music-making of the domestic parlour, music was regarded as, at best, a meaningless luxury, and at worst an inherently immoral activity tainted by association with the music hall, a den of working-class drunkenness and vice. It was given a low priority in the Anglican Church, choirs and choral resources were depleted and church and cathedral music in general was at a low ebb. Music was viewed by the nobility and the growing middle classes as merely decorative, mostly foreign, and regarded with deep suspicion.

Yet the roles of both monarchy and British music would be transformed during Victoria's reign. Above all, that was down to the man Victoria married, Francis Albert Augustus Charles Emmanuel Saxe-Coburg. Albert, Victoria's cousin and the son of the duke of the small German principality of Saxe-Coburg, was brought to England as a prospective match for the queen on 10 October 1839. Victoria fell in love immediately, recording in her diary: 'It was with some emotion that I beheld Albert – who is *beautiful*.'[10] The pair married barely a year later, and the love that Victoria felt on her initial meeting with the prince would remain the dominant emotional force of her life. Albert's education in Germany had given him a thorough grounding in music, and by the time he was 20 he was both an accomplished instrumentalist – on the organ and the piano – and in possession of a fine tenor voice. He was also a composer: by the time of his death in 1861, he had written 40 songs set to German lyrics along with various pieces of church music. As a young man, Albert used his musical talents to woo Victoria. For their engagement, he presented his bride with a set of his own 'Lieder und Romanzen' (Songs and Ballads) containing a handwritten dedication, 'To my dear Victoria from her faithful Albert'. This was not just a romantic gift, but also a *Romantic* one – the music is clearly in the tradition of German Romantic 'lieder'[11] – the intimate, drawing-room style of singing that had become popular on the Continent during the late eighteenth and early nineteenth centuries. 'Say, sleepest thou, Love?' is just one example of Albert's lieder: a heart-on-sleeve, deeply sensuous song for baritone and piano depicting a prince sere-nading his sleeping love outside her window. Victoria could hardly fail to have been moved by it.

This song, like the rest of the collection, is a valuable insight into Victoria and Albert's early courtship, demonstrating the unex-pectedly erotic and intimate relationship the royal couple enjoyed. At Osborne House, the couple's summer residence on the Isle of Wight, they worked at adjacent desks because they couldn't bear to be apart, and they enjoyed music together in the same way, sitting side by side at the piano to perform duets. At Buckingham Palace, Victoria's extraordinary gold piano still sits in the magnificent White Drawing Room today. It is sumptuously gilded and decorated with dancing cherubs, animals, birds and foliage, and it contains a nostalgic nod to the queen's musical childhood, incorporating the lid of a much older harpsichord that she had played as a girl.[12] The gold piano was purchased by the palace in 1856 – it cost roughly 175 guineas: about a quarter of a million pounds in today's money – and it was here that Victoria and Albert would sit and play out their love for one another in music, in such duets as Mendelssohn's pretty little 'Spring Song', which the composer arranged especially for the couple. Albert was a more accomplished pianist than his wife, so he would have played the more complex arpeggio-ridden second part. No doubt they also tried out some of Albert's own compositions. His musical taste shaped Victoria's throughout their courtship.

Albert's own compositions are by no means great pieces of music. Nor was Albert himself under any illusions about his compositional skill. On the contrary, he once said:

> *Persons in our position of life can never be distinguished artists. It takes the study of a whole life to become that, and we have too many other duties to perform to give the time necessary to any one particular branch of art. Our business is not so much to create, as to learn to appreciate and understand the work of others, and we can never do this until we have realised the difficulties to be overcome.*[13]

But Albert's empathy with the art of music would help to change the tastes of a musically disaffected British nation. His reforms started at home, where he reorganised the queen's private band (which had dwindled to a few wind players under George III) into a full orchestra that would give concerts at Buckingham Palace and Windsor Castle. Now, instead of light opera classics, the programmes were extended to include Beethoven, Mozart, Haydn and Schubert; at Albert's instigation, the queen even became a patron of the struggling English Opera House. Albert's personal enthusiasm and royal patronage of the opera helped to revive its fortunes, and encouraged middle-class audiences to regard theatrical performances with less suspicion and more respect. But perhaps the most significant move of all was Albert's reaching out to a fellow German, who, like Handel before him, was fast becoming a composer the British would regard as their own.

Felix Mendelssohn had a great fondness for the culture, landscape and literature of Britain. The composer visited the country ten times, and stayed frequently at Buckingham Palace, which he called 'the only really nice comfortable house in England'.[14] Mendelssohn was from a respectable, middle-class family of German bankers; he was charming and good-looking with polite manners and a very good grasp of English. He was the perfect face not only for a new, respectable English music, but for Albert's new vision of monarchy: a 'moral monarchy' that would appeal to the emerging middle classes. On one visit, Mendelssohn performed an extract from the chorus of his St Paul oratorio on the organ at Buckingham Palace, while Prince Albert accompanied him by pulling out the organ stops.[15] On another, he accompanied the queen singing his own lieder, as well as some by his sister Fanny, who was also a talented composer. When Victoria sang, or Albert played the organ, or the royal couple played their piano duets, they were the image of domestic respectability, just like the middle-class families performing in their parlours across the country (many of whom could now afford a piano and a house big enough to fit it in). Victoria and Albert's domestic music-making humanised the monarchy. This royal music was a far cry from that of the remote and ridiculous George IV with his lavish Pavilion and private band: this was music that made the queen and her consort accessible, ordinary and likeable. Mendelssohn's intimate association with the royals – which was widely reported in the newspapers – was mutually beneficial, in fact, helping the composer to boost his reputation as Britain's best-loved living musician.

Mendelssohn's popularity was not just due to the quality of his music, nor his royal patronage, but also to his spiritual story. Though born into a prominent Jewish family, he had converted to Christianity and was a devout Protestant. His background was in tune with the times, since a major religious revival was stirring in Britain. The Church of England had fallen to a new low earlier in the century. Its buildings were crumbling, and Anglican church services had become not only devoid of ceremony and ritual, but were often badly organised, understaffed and sparsely attended. On Easter Sunday 1800, only six communicants attended the morning celebration in St Paul's Cathedral.[16] Music was also a victim of the low standards: choirs were poorly trained and poorly maintained, and many had closed down altogether. At St Paul's, the choir became renowned for such hapless incidents as the organist playing one chant while the choir sang another, or a performance of Handel's 'Hallelujah' chorus with only two of the men present.[17] But now a movement was afoot to improve things, and huge new investment in church and chapel construction began. In the 1830s alone, the Church of England received a hefty £1.5 million in state-funded aid for its building programme.[18] Over the first few decades of the nineteenth century, a series of reforms were introduced to improve standards of worship. Choral services were introduced to parish churches, trained choirs were reinstated at the great cathedrals such as Westminster, and those that already existed were improved and expanded. At St Paul's, the choir increased to 40 boys and 18 men; they adopted the new fashion for wearing cassocks and surplices and sitting in the chancel; and fuller programmes of choral services and weekly rehearsals were instated. Standards of music rapidly rose, and with it, a sudden growth in demand for choral music, for hymns and liturgical settings, and for sacred music in general.

Mendelssohn wrote many works specifically for Anglican worship – such as his most popular anthem 'Hear My Prayer' for soprano solo, chorus and organ, containing the celebrated solo 'O for the Wings of a Dove'. He was also responsible for one of our most famous carols, 'Hark! the Herald Angels Sing'. But towering above the rest of his sacred output are his oratorios, *St Paul* (1836) and *Elijah* (1846), more or less the only oratorios by a nineteenth-century composer to achieve lasting popularity on a similar scale to Handel's. Prince Albert took Victoria to see *Elijah* when it was first performed in London in 1847. He was so overcome by the performance that he wrote a dedication in Mendelssohn's libretto:

> *To the noble artist who, surrounded by the Baal-worship of false art, through genius and study has been able, like a second Elijah,*

to remain true to the service of true art; who has freed our ear from the chaos of mindless jingling of tones, to accustom it once more to the pure sounds of truly reflected emotion and regular harmony; to the Great Master, who, in a steady stream of ideas, unrolls before us the whole panorama of the elements from the gentlest rustlings to the mightiest storms; in grateful recollection, Albert.

Elijah is based on the great oratorio models of Handel and Bach – Mendelssohn's interest in the latter was largely responsible for kick-starting the Bach revival – and is a masterful and intensely dramatic work which was an instant success with the public. Audiences appreciated its simple and sincere depiction of Christianity and the melodious, accessible romantic style that was Mendelssohn's trademark. *Elijah* would go on to be performed at enormous choral festivals around the country, such as the Birmingham Triennial Festival. Such festivals were at the heart of musical culture during this period, where gargantuan choirs, orchestras and crowds of spectators gathered in the nave to hear the increasingly popular sacred choral works. Victorian music was beginning to acquire a new respectability as well as a capacity for grandeur and ceremony that it had been lacking for decades. And Mendelssohn, articulating the sense of Britain's spiritual destiny, seemed the perfect candidate to take Britain's royal music into the new century.

Unfortunately, the composer did not live long enough to achieve such an ambition. Mendelssohn died in 1847, after a series of strokes, aged just 38. When he died, there was an outpouring of national mourning in Britain, and Mendelssohn – like Handel before him –

became an almost legendary figure in the public mind. But, during his short yet active life, Mendelssohn had confirmed Prince Albert's belief that culture could act as a civilising force and an evangelising one, a force that Albert was keen to employ in his new vision of monarchy. Mendelssohn and his music had proved to Albert the importance and power of public ceremony. Victoria despised ceremony; she was shy and hated public appearances. But after a decade of marriage – broken down by the stress and strain of repeated pregnancies and postnatal depression – she was bending more and more to Albert's will. It was observed how wife and husband would hold political meetings together, and always speak in terms of 'we': they were 'one person, and as he likes business, it is obvious that while she has the title he is really discharging the functions of the Sovereign. He is King to all intents and purposes.'[19]

Albert became increasingly engaged with cultural affairs on a national scale, and the pinnacle of his achievement was the extraordinary Great Exhibition in 1851. This event, held in Joseph Paxton's 1848-foot-long Crystal Palace of iron and glass, was an exhibition of international manufacturing achievement, including over 100,000 exhibits from 13,937 exhibitors. It was seen by six million people – equivalent to a third of Britain's entire population – and was opened with great ceremony by the queen herself. It was Albert's vision and almost entirely his work. The Crystal Palace itself, originally built in Hyde Park, was taken down after the event and re-erected in Sydenham, south London, where it would be the venue for a series of popular public concerts and provide the home for London's first permanent orchestra. In addition, the exhibition turned a tidy profit, which Albert wished to use to acquire a series of permanent properties in South Kensington, in order to further the general aims of the Exhibition and thus 'extend the influence of Science and Art upon Productive Industry'.[20] These buildings would include, Albert envisaged, a music school and a grand concert hall as well as a series of museums: a new cultural hub for the nation with music at its heart.

But Albert did not see his vision come to fruition. After decades of tireless work on the Great Exhibition and many other projects – including the Gothic redesign of the Palace of Westminster – he succumbed to typhoid and died in 1861. Victoria was distraught, and Albert's death prompted a sustained period of private mourning that was responsible for the queen's lasting popular image as the 'Widow of Windsor'. She refused to come to London or make public appearances. Her sole preoccupation now was to memorialise Albert: the Blue Room at Windsor, where he died, was kept as a shrine, as well as his rooms at Osborne House, where his shaving water continued to be put out daily. But the most prominent shrine of all was the Albert Memorial, first unveiled in Hyde Park in 1876. It features a distinctive frieze that celebrates the Valhalla of cultural achievement for the high Victorians, depicting individual composers, architects, poets, painters and sculptors from history. The British are hardly under-represented, but the British composers are all from the sixteenth, seventeenth and eighteenth centuries – the likes of Tallis, Gibbons, Purcell and Arne – with just one nineteenth-century musical figure, the justly forgotten Sir Henry Rowley Bishop. Forgotten that is, apart from his wonderfully schmaltzy ballad tune, set to the even more schmaltzy words of 'Home Sweet Home'.

It was a curious irony that Albert, a man who had campaigned so tirelessly for the improvement of British arts and sciences, was German. But, then, music itself was regarded in Victorian England as largely a German preserve. Now, however, with Albert dead and Victoria withdrawing into mourning – and Bishop the best composer Britain could come up with – was there any hope of British music being reborn?

AN ENGLISH MUSICAL RENAISSANCE

On 29 March 1871, after four years of work, Queen Victoria attended the official opening of the Royal Albert Hall in South Kensington. She was so overcome with emotion at the occasion that she could not speak, and her son the Prince of Wales had to announce on her behalf 'The Queen declares this Hall is now open'. The national anthem was performed, and large quantities of Rimmel's scent were wafted into the auditorium via the ventilation system to create a sweet-smelling atmosphere[21] befitting this magnificent new building. The Hall, a state-of-the-art work of Victorian architecture, boasted a modern heating and cooling system, a hydraulic lift, 11,000 gas burners that could all be lit within ten seconds and the largest organ in the world. It was the culmination of Albert's grand plan for the Kensington site, which was dubbed derisively 'Albertopolis' by his critics. But 'Albertopolis' – which today includes not only the Albert Hall but also the Victoria and Albert, Science, and Natural History museums – would prove an enduring cultural landmark,

and the Royal Albert Hall in particular would provide the backdrop to some of the greatest moments in British music during the next two centuries.

At the Albert Hall's opening concert on 1 May 1871 there was music from France (by Charles Gounod) and Germany (by Ferdinand Hiller) but the work selected to represent the best of British was a cantata by Arthur Sullivan, *On Shore and Sea*. Sullivan, then just 28 years old, was fast becoming the nation's leading composer. Like Mendelssohn before him, his easy social graces, respectable background and capacity to produce melodious, accessible music made him an ideal Victorian musical figure. In addition, his love of material pleasures – his frequent attendance of dinner parties and exclusive clubs, as well as his passion for gambling – made him identifiable with male-dominated, industrial Victorian society. The nation had not had a truly successful native musical son for over a century, but now times and tastes were changing.

Sullivan's royal connections dated back to his childhood: following in a centuries-old tradition of English composers, his musical career had begun, at the age of 11, as a chorister at the Chapel Royal. The Chapel Royal had survived throughout the eighteenth century and into the nineteenth, albeit in a dilapidated state: from 1817, the fearsome Master of the Children, William Hawes, had ruled with a rod of steel. 'Mistakes in the rendering of the services,' as a fellow student later reported, 'were generally corrected by the Master, William Hawes, aided by a charming little riding whip, which he applied to their backs with benevolent impartiality.'[22] Luckily for the young Sullivan, the legendary choirmaster Thomas Helmore replaced Hawes in 1846, and brought about great improvements in the training and singing at the Chapel Royal – as well as the general wellbeing of the boys. Sullivan joined the choir on 12 April 1854, and so was among the adolescent charges benefiting from Helmore's new Chapel Royal regime. He was clearly a precocious child: the following year, his own anthem 'Sing Unto the Lord and Bless his Name' was performed. His daily choir duties included morning and evening services at St James's Palace, sometimes in the presence of the queen herself.

But it had been over a century since the Chapel Royal had been at the heart of musical culture in Britain, and – unlike his forebears, many of whom had gone on to find employment as composers or Gentlemen of the Chapel Royal – the mature Sullivan utilised his royal connections in more indirect ways. As Victoria retreated into widowhood, the most prominent members of the monarchy were her children, particularly her two sons – Albert Edward, Prince of Wales, and Alfred, Duke of Edinburgh – both of whom happened to be musically inclined. The ambitious Sullivan befriended the princes. Alfred was not only the president of the Royal Albert Hall Orchestra Society (which Sullivan conducted) but also a member of the orchestra and the leader of the violins. He took a great shine to Sullivan, and often invited him to his residence at Clarence House, where the composer would entertain the guests. In 1863, Sullivan also wrote music for Prince Albert's wedding to Princess Alexandra of Denmark, which included the jaunty 'Princess of Wales's March', for military band, later published as a piano solo with a dedication 'by special permission' to the Prince of Wales.

Sullivan's contribution to Prince Albert's wedding was, like George IV's band, royal music without any profound sacred or ceremonial meaning, intended purely for private entertainment. Sullivan was highly skilled at writing this kind of music, and indeed the lighthearted, unchallenging style would become his hallmark when he began to collaborate with W. S. Gilbert in the 1870s to write hugely successful light operas such as *HMS Pinafore*, *The Pirates of Penzance* and *The Mikado*. The transition to light opera was the death of Sullivan's reputation as a serious art music composer, but the financial rewards of the light operetta allowed him to maintain the 'fast' lifestyle he enjoyed. As a former teacher of Sullivan's in Germany put it: 'You Englishmen, who come here and show such promise, become utterly spoiled when you get back to commercial England.'[23]

Yet Sullivan was undoubtedly regarded highly in 1871, and his status was inextricably linked to his intimate associations with royalty. Perhaps the most ringing endorsement of his abilities came five years later in 1876, when he was asked to be the first principal of the National Training School for Music. First proposed by Prince Albert in 1854, the National Training School was envisaged as the heart of a new infrastructure to select and train British musicians, with a national scholarship scheme that offered free musical training to those who were good enough. Music 'conservatories' were still relatively new at this time; until the Royal Academy of Music was founded in 1822, London – like almost all European cities – had no specific institution for the professional training of musicians, and even the Academy had proved to be ineffective.[24] Albert's radical idea died with him, but in the 1870s the Royal Society revived the scheme, and the National Training School was set up in a building flanking the Albert Hall in Kensington.

Sullivan didn't last long as principal – being too preoccupied by his increasingly successful collaborations with Gilbert – and the National Training School itself was plagued by financial difficulties. But Albert's vision endured, taken up by his three sons, Alfred, Duke of Edinburgh, Albert, Prince of Wales, and Prince Leopold, Duke of Albany, as well as Prince Christian, Victoria's son-in-law. All lamented the lack of a coherent national music: at a fundraising event in 1881, the Duke of Albany gave an impassioned speech urging the public to fund the future of English music. He berated the prevalence of foreign music and musicians in Britain and called for a new English music that could quash this foreign dominance. His brothers went on to echo him in similar speeches: 'Why is it that England has no music recognised as national?' the Prince of Wales asked in 1882. 'Because there is no centre of music to which English musicians may resort with confidence.' He proposed a college that would be 'the recognised centre and head of the musical world' and that would serve as a unifying force for all the subjects he would one day lead – 'by inspiring among our fellow national-subjects in every part of the Empire these emotions of patriotism which music is calculated to evoke'.[25]

The National Training School was refounded as the Royal College of Music in 1882 and opened in 1883: Queen Victoria was the royal patron, and the Prince of Wales, the future King Edward VII, was appointed its president. A statue of Prince Albert was erected by public subscription, and placed above Prince Consort

Road in Kensington; dressed in Tudor garments, Albert seems to embody the ideology of this new musical renaissance. It was a storming success: the college began with 42 paying students; by the end of the first year it had increased to 100, and by the end of the first decade there were 310 students, of whom 61 were scholars.[26] A combination of royal endorsement and directorship in the hands of the brilliant George Grove – previously a civil engineer and builder of lighthouses, now writer on music and author of the landmark *Grove Dictionary of Music and Musicians* – helped the College attract the most brilliant musicians of its day.

The two brightest of these talents were Hubert Parry and Charles Villiers Stanford. Like Sullivan, both were respectable

The Royal College of Music, founded in 1876, was central to Prince Albert's vision of a new intellectual and cultural hub in South Kensington. The college formed the heart of the new movement, which transformed nineteenth-century English music, known as the English Musical Renaissance.

English gentlemen; Parry was educated at Eton College and Oxford University, while Stanford had grown up in Ireland and had come to England to study music at Cambridge. Stanford was a driven, ambitious musician who became Professor of Music at his *alma mater* at the age of only 35, where he had done much to augment the status of the university's music degree. At RCM – as a professor of composition and conductor of the orchestra – he influenced a generation of English musicians, numbering among his pupils Gustav Holst and Ralph Vaughan Williams. As a composer, Stanford also did much to elevate the status of English church music, and his musical output features some of the most distinctive sacred music in the repertory, including his stunning and highly original *Service in B♭* with its distinctive, colourful organ part and bewitching, constantly surprising choral melodies. This service has gone on to become a favourite of choral institutions around the country.

Parry is also best known for his large-scale choral music. Despite his Anglican upbringing, the composer wrote surprisingly little liturgical music, but many of his concert works were performed in church settings: for example, his 'Blest Pair of Sirens' for choir and orchestra, as well as his Magnificat, written for Victoria's Diamond Jubilee in 1897. By then he was practically the nation's unofficial composer laureate, providing works for many royal occasions – most famously, his anthem 'I Was Glad', written for the coronation of Edward VII in 1902. In 1895 he would succeed George Grove as the director of the Royal College of Music, and he campaigned tirelessly for the promotion of native music and musicians, as well as contributing to the canon of great new English music himself.

The Royal College of Music was born from a self-conscious attempt, begun by Prince Albert 30 years before, to create a renaissance in British music. The last institution to produce so many talented composers was the Chapel Royal in its heyday. And although the Royal College of Music wasn't an overtly religious institution, and its connections with royalty after its foundation were limited, the composers it produced were inextricably linked with both God and country.

∽

Parry and Stanford's extraordinary choral music was a symptom of the revival in church services and choral societies across the nation in the later nineteenth century. Yet Queen Victoria herself remained resolutely Low Church, feeling most at home in the plain, modest environs of the Presbyterian Church of Scotland. She was also, for decades, reclusive, stunned into lengthy grieving for her late husband, and unreceptive to the new religion and the new music that came with it.

In 1882, the new music came to her instead. It arrived in the form of Walter Parratt, a musician newly employed as organist of St George's Chapel, Windsor. Parratt would play a central role in the English musical renaissance, although his name is remembered less than that of Stanford or Parry, perhaps because he was at best a mediocre composer. But he was an organist of legendary status – by the age of ten he had mastered all of J. S. Bach's 48 Preludes and Fugues, and could play every one from memory[27] – and the year after he joined St George's Chapel he would also be appointed

Professor of Organ at the Royal College of Music. Here he would have influence, like Parry and Stanford, over a whole new generation of musicians, raising both the standard of organ playing and the status of the organist. He was a magnetic personality, with an infectious sense of humour and an exceptional memory, demonstrated not only by his ability to learn long pieces of music by heart, but also by his skill at the chessboard. Indeed, it was through chess – and a shared love of music – that a friendship formed between Parratt and Victoria's youngest son, Prince Leopold.

At St George's Chapel, Parratt brought the new religious–musical revival right to the heart of the royal household. On his arrival, the chapel was in desperate need of reform: the choir was in a decrepit state, the organ was in disrepair and the musical programme on offer was uninspiring to say the least. Chapel records showed that Mendelssohn's famous anthem 'Hear My Prayer' – that beautiful cliché of Victorian piety – had been sung no fewer that 18 times in one year, and there was no fund to finance or, indeed, much interest or impetus, to perform contemporary music. Under Parratt, the organ – whose bellows had been eaten by rats – was rebuilt, and new standards were set for both the choir's performing abilities and the repertoire of music. Many sacred works by contemporary English composers received their first airing. Parratt also reintroduced significant royal composers of the past, such as Tallis and Purcell, who had been neglected for centuries, and secured forever their place in the English canon.

This mini musical renaissance within the St George's Chapel walls did not go unnoticed by the queen. She attended the chapel regularly and struck up a close personal friendship with Parratt. Victoria even encouraged her daughters to write sacred pieces as part of their musical studies – and their compositions would sometimes be performed by the Chapel Royal choir. One former chorister recalled, 'We often sang chants, kyries and hymn tunes which they had composed, and you may be sure that we took special pains with these, in order that the Princess in question might get her full quota of praise from the Royal mother. Princess Christian[28] and Princess Beatrice would always come and thank us when we had sung one of their compositions.'[29] Victoria would always make inquiries about any new composer if their work was premiered there, and she had her own favourite singers whom she would often request to appear with the choir at service. Among the singers she held in high regard was Clara Butt, a legendary contralto with such a powerful voice that it was once remarked that the Albert Hall must have been built in anticipation of her ascendancy.[30] The queen's real favourite, however, was Emma Albani, a Canadian singer, who later became a friend of Victoria's and was invited to Windsor on many occasions. In 1901, she would perform at Victoria's funeral in response to a written request left by the queen herself. Parratt would also often play with the queen alone, and on one occasion when the queen sang along to his accompaniment, she performed a song written by her late husband, Albert.[31]

It was Albert, of course, who had awakened the passion for music within his wife. Victoria never really came to terms with his death, but in later life, and under the influence of Parratt, her love of music, like her faith, became a private solace and comfort to her, as well as a poignant reminder of her beloved husband. Parratt's son, Geoffrey, recalled later how, towards the end of the queen's life, Walter was often called to play to her alone on the private organ. 'These were occasions of which he rarely spoke,' Geoffrey said, 'as he was conscious of their significance and sadness.'[32] Victoria was evidently grateful to Parratt for giving her this musical gift, and for organising an aubade – or morning concert – on the terrace of Windsor castle for her eightieth birthday, so much so that she presented him with one of her own in return: a richly jewelled conducting baton, with his monogram set in enamel and diamonds.[33]

By now there could be no doubt of the high respect afforded to musicians in Victorian society: indeed, Queen Victoria was the first monarch to knight a composer. Henry Bishop had been the first in 1842, followed by Arthur Sullivan in 1883, John Stainer in 1888 and Hubert Parry in 1889. In 1892 Parratt himself had been knighted, and the following year he was made Master of the Queen's Music, bringing him into even closer connection with the court. The queen's own private passion for the art could not be in doubt. But now, with the nineteenth century drawing to a close – and reformers like Parratt, Stanford and Parry now in powerful positions of influence – public royal ceremony and music would be drawn into ever-closer contact, as they had been in centuries past.

JUBILANT STRAINS

After nearly seven decades of imperial rule in France, the Prussians finally crushed the French armies and took Emperor Napoleon III prisoner in 1870. France was declared a republic, and republican fever across the Channel quickly spread to Britain; *The Republican* newspaper was founded and more than 50 republican clubs were established in cities from Aberdeen to Plymouth. The suggested antidote to this increasing republicanism was a new doctrine of nationalism and a greater role for public royal ceremony.

One of the first instances of the new policy came in May 1872, and it was the vision of the Liberal Prime Minister, William Gladstone, an astute politician with the firm belief that religion was central to politics, and that the monarchy was the best embodiment of that relationship. Albert Edward, the Prince of Wales, had been gravely ill with typhoid fever, the same illness that killed his father Prince Albert just ten years earlier. The event marked a notable change in the popular mood, eliciting great national sympathy for the afflicted family – and the Prince's sudden and unexpected recovery became in turn a cause for national celebration. For Gladstone, it was too good an opportunity for royal aggrandising to miss. A great Day of National Thanksgiving for the prince's recovery was held, along with an elaborate ceremony at St Paul's Cathedral, used for a national service for the first time since the eighteenth century. Arthur Sullivan composed an enormous Te Deum – the traditional sacred form of royal rejoicing, employed since medieval times – which was premiered at Crystal Palace by a choir of two thousand to a gargantuan audience of 26,000. The work, the *Festival Te Deum*, was dedicated to Victoria herself. 'I am to say,' wrote Sir Thomas Biddulph from Windsor on her behalf, 'that the Queen rarely accords this privilege to anyone, and is only induced to do so on the occasion in question in consequence of the case, and the performance taking place under the immediate patronage of the Royal Family.'[34] By accepting the dedication, Victoria was further acknowledging, albeit reluctantly, her new, more public role. She did not attend the Crystal Palace performance – cancelling only a few weeks before – and had to be browbeaten by Gladstone and his associates into attending the St Paul's service.

This marks the beginning of a renaissance in royal ceremony, and Sullivan's work rivals the greatest ceremonial music in the royal repertory. It is scored for chorus and full orchestra, plus a military band, which was fast becoming a staple of British patriotic music. The founding of the Royal Military School of Music, Kneller Hall, in 1857 had quickly improved national standards of performance, and after 1872 all bandmasters had to obtain a Kneller Hall qualification.[35] Kneller Hall-trained musicians would provide the soundtrack to the greatest royal occasions of the following decades, from coronations to jubilees to royal weddings. Sullivan's Te Deum exploits the patriotic sound of the military band to the fullest effect, complete with brass fanfares and drum rolls, while also paying homage to significant national religious works, including the hymn 'St Anne (O God, Our Help in Ages Past)' and a distinctive Gregorian psalm tone. Full of elaborate counterpoint and appealing, uplifting melodies – Sullivan's trademark – the work was a complete success, and the composer was 'uproariously cheered' when he took his bows at the end of the Crystal Palace performance. The *Musical Times* reviewed the *Festival Te Deum* with great enthusiasm: 'With much of the breadth of Handel, some of the grace of Mozart and an orchestral colouring almost unique in its masterly handling, this Te Deum ought to service as a gratifying promise that English Music is blossoming into a Spring to be succeeded by a Summer, such as this land has not experienced since the death of Purcell.'[36] Today, Sullivan's Te Deum is largely forgotten, but it helped give the monarchy a new sacred significance – as the greatest royal music has always done – and set a precedent for the 're-sacralising' of royal music over the next century.

The Thanksgiving Day in 1872 was only the beginning. There followed a series of increasingly grandiose acts designed to engineer the monarchy back into the national consciousness. In 1877, Victoria was officially named Empress of India, making her the figurehead of Britain's greatest national project and thereby creating in monarchy almost a substitute for nationalism itself. In 1887, Victoria celebrated her Golden Jubilee with another public Thanksgiving service, this time at Westminster Abbey, where the choir sang the Te Deum composed by the queen's late husband. But grandest of all was Victoria's Diamond Jubilee in 1897, which celebrated not just the queen but the entire British Empire, irrevocably yoking Victoria's image to the many nations over which she presided. The presence of foreign monarchs was vetoed, and pride of place was given to the prime ministers of the newly self-governing white colonies, as well as a gathering of imperial troops from across the globe, representing all its diverse and many-coloured peoples.

'The celebration of Queen Victoria's sixty years' reign has called forth an unprecedented outburst of jubilant strains,' proclaimed the *Musical Times*, 'and millions of Her Majesty's loyal subjects, young and old, have raised their voices in notes of joy and gladness.'[37] Churches and cathedrals around the country joined together on 20 June to sing the newly commissioned Jubilee hymn, 'O King of Kings', by Arthur Sullivan. He was an appropriate choice to pen a Jubilee hymn, having already contributed to that canon with 'Onward, Christian Soldiers' in 1871. 'O King of Kings' has rarely been heard since – perhaps because of the somewhat dry and uninspiring melody Sullivan wrote for it – but the words, written by the Bishop of Wakefield, are more interesting, directly aligning Victoria's long reign to the will of God:

> *For every heart made glad by Thee,*
> *With thankful praise is swelling;*
> *And every tongue with joy set free,*
> *Its happy theme is telling.*

Thou hast been mindful of Thine own,
And lo! we come confessing –
'Tis Thou hast dower'd our queenly throne
With sixty years of blessing.

There was also a strongly imperial theme to one verse (later omitted):

Oh, Royal heart, with wide embrace
For all her children yearning
Oh, happy realm, such mother grace
With loyal love returning.
Where England's flag flies wide unfurled
All tyrant wrongs repelling …

The queen herself would have heard (and possibly sung) the hymn on that day, too, as part of the Thanksgiving service she attended at St George's Chapel. As usual, Walter Parratt presided, playing the organ – and the programme also included the Prince Consort's Te Deum – but by listening to Sullivan's hymn as her subjects sang it around the country, the queen was partaking in a powerful symbolic demonstration through music that unified ruler and ruled. 'O King of Kings' also imparts the queen a sacred mandate with the words 'Tis Thou hast dower'd our queenly throne/With sixty years of blessing'. The controversial subject of divine right had barely been mentioned since the days of the Glorious Revolution: here it is accepted without question and joyfully sung by the British people with one voice.

The unifying and sanctifying power of royal music would be a constant theme throughout the Diamond Jubilee celebrations, the pinnacle of which came, on 22 June, with the service at St Paul's Cathedral. It was the setting for what the *Morning Post* called 'the central ceremonial act' of 'the high festival of the United British Empire for thanksgiving and rejoicing over the Longest and Happiest Reign in History'. Victoria set out from Buckingham Palace for St Paul's in a state carriage pulled by eight cream-coloured horses, accompanied by 17 coaches full of guests. It was a procession on a scale not seen for centuries, and hundreds of thousands of people lined the streets to witness it. The 78-year-old Victoria was, however, lame and overweight – much like Queen Anne nearly two centuries before her – and when she reached St Paul's she felt unable to climb the front steps. Instead the service of thanksgiving was held outside while Victoria remained in her carriage and listened. The performers included 500 singers, as well as the bands of the Royal Artillery and Kneller Hall, and the choir featured some of the greatest musicians of the era – Sullivan, Parratt and Parry among them. A composer named George Martin, now faded into obscurity, conducted his *Jubilee Te Deum*, scored for military band, with the bell of St Paul's Cathedral itself (tuned to an F) incorporated cleverly into the composition; the assembled crowds also sang 'The Old Hundredth' hymn tune to the words of 'All People that On Earth Do Dwell'. The carriages were supposed to move off as the last words of the psalm were being sung, but instead they remained motionless and a terrible silence ensued. The archbishop of Canterbury saved the day by calling for three cheers – the choir and crowds spontaneously broke into 'God Save the Queen', and Victoria was able to ride off in triumph. The cheers could be heard as far away as Trafalgar Square.[38]

One of Victoria's cousins was horrified that the queen was being seen to 'thank God in the street',[39] but, then, the whole event was without precedent. Jubilees were not primarily understood as royal – the word was originally a biblical term – and though George III's 50 years on the throne had been marked in 1809 and was termed a 'jubilee' it had not been celebrated with pageantry. The concept of a 'Diamond Jubilee' did not exist before Victoria's reign, but in 1897 the scale of the public rejoicing for this wholly invented ceremony was worthy of Henry V's victorious return from Agincourt five centuries before. It had a carefully calculated dual power: simultaneously placing Victoria on a pedestal and making her accessible and down-to-earth, showing her 'in the street' among her people. She was at once ordinary and not ordinary at all, and it made her subjects love her all the more.

If she had had her way it wouldn't have happened at all. But in the end, the spirit of the occasion seems to have won Victoria around. Afterwards, she wrote in her diary:

No one ever, I believe, has met with such an ovation as was given to me, passing through those six miles of streets, including Constitution Hill. The crowds were quite indescribable and their enthusiasm truly marvellous and deeply touching. The cheering was quite deafening and every face seemed to be filled with joy.[40]

The Diamond Jubilee solidified Victoria's reputation as the most popular and respected monarch that had ever lived, completely eclipsing her fusty old image as the Widow of Windsor and replacing it with one of a strong, stoical woman who epitomised Britannia. Today, Queen Victoria is a more integral part of our national consciousness than any other monarch from the past two centuries, and a major reason for this is the impressive, well-ordered ceremony that characterised the last years of her reign. That ceremony had the power to dramatically change and challenge national perceptions of the queen, and to shape the reputation of future monarchs. The modern monarchy would become inextricably and uncompromisingly ceremonial.

Grand events like the St Paul's service were only one of the ways in which Victoria's Diamond Jubilee was celebrated musically. Amid the outpouring of Jubilee-themed music by composers across the country, Arthur Sullivan wrote a Jubilee ballet called *Victoria and Merrie England*. The ballet itself has no plot as such, presenting instead a series of tableaux depicting typically English scenes – from Elizabethan May Day festivities to Christmas dinner during the reign of Charles II to the coronation of Victoria herself – but the music is fresh, tuneful and appealing, and the ballet was a huge commercial success. It ran for six months, during which members of the royal family, including the Prince of Wales, attended on 19 separate occasions.[41] And, indeed, the cheerful neo-medievalism of many of the scenes must have appealed to the Prince of Wales, who, in contrast to his mother, would reveal a fondness for reviving old-fashioned pageantry once he became king.

❦

Walter Parratt's son described the moment when Victoria's death was announced at Windsor, on 22 January 1901: 'The bell ... tolled the number of the Queen's years – eighty-one. Then, as was his wont every day, my father went down to the piano in the drawing room, but instead of playing something straight away, he sat still in the semi-darkness and I wondered what he would choose. Eventually he chose the first movement of the Moonlight Sonata, which he played with great feeling, and quietly closed the piano.'[42] While the queen herself had found personal, private solace in music, her son, the new King Edward VII, was not so naturally musical. He was certainly not passionate about serious music – preferring 'the lightest kind'[43] – and he wasn't even particularly interested in that. What he really loved was pageantry. Edward relished the pomp and circumstance of being king, even reviving the official State Opening of Parliament, which he attended only three weeks after Victoria's death, wearing a scarlet tunic and crimson, gold and ermine robes. Naturally, he was also determined to have a thoroughly spectacular coronation.

Victoria's own coronation had been chaotic and badly organised. Infamously, the aged Lord Rollo had tripped and rolled down some steps, while the archbishop of Canterbury had managed to get the coronation ring – designed for Victoria's little finger – stuck on the wrong digit. Edward was determined that his coronation should run more smoothly. Moreover, the length of time since the last coronation meant that very few people alive then would have witnessed the 1837 event, although the general public, newly accustomed to the fashion for pageantry after the recent Jubilee celebrations, were beginning to expect a certain amount of choreographed magnificence from royal events. The 1902 coronation was regarded as an opportunity for a total reinvention, and so, under the direction of Viscount Esher – one of the main architects of Victoria's Diamond Jubilee and a passionate advocate of ceremonial monarchy – a new coronation package was put together, reinventing old traditions and inventing new ones, self-consciously promoting the coronation as an event of not only national, but also imperial and even sacred significance. Edward VII himself had no great religious feeling, but he liked the trappings of High-Church Anglicanism: when asked for his views on the coronation by Viscount Esher, he replied that the clergy should wear 'their best clothes', without any knowledge of what the cope or vestment was or what it signified.

The music had similar ambitions, and the responsibility for its organisation was in the capable hands of the organist of the Abbey and Royal College of Music professor, Frederick Bridge. The time was ripe for a meeting of grand ceremony and music on a national scale. There was now a developing tradition of native music that the country could be proud of, along with well-equipped, well-trained choirs, orchestras and musicians who had the ability to perform it. In line with the overarching vision for the coronation, Bridge proposed a programme that would embrace five centuries of English church music, featuring composers such as Tallis, Gibbons and Purcell. This was a deliberate statement of pride in English musical heritage, drawing on its power to anoint the monarch culturally – and it was a model that every subsequent coronation would follow. Bridge also included modern musicians, such as Arthur Sullivan – who had died in November 1900, only two months before Victoria herself – and Charles Villiers Stanford. But perhaps the highlight was a newly commissioned anthem by Hubert Parry: a setting of the opening words of the service 'I Was Glad When They Said Unto Me' to be used during the king's procession into the Abbey.

The result was one of the most impressive pieces of ceremonial music ever written, and one that followed the fusion of new and old, of sacred and ceremonial, to utter perfection. In its stately majesty, it rivals Handel's 'Zadok the Priest', and, like 'Zadok', it incorporates the movements of the actual procession into the music. While 'Zadok' employs a long, dramatic opening, Parry's anthem begins with a regal orchestral introduction followed by a spine-tingling choral entry, greeting the monarch as he or she enters the Abbey by declaiming 'I was glad' as if in one voice, but in joyful harmony. The mood is celebratory yet dignified; tension builds as the overlapping, imitating parts declaim 'Our feet shall stand at thy gates' – designed to be sung as the monarch processes down the aisle – reaching a glorious climax where the two choirs join to sing 'Jerusalem is builded as a city'. The most unusual part of the anthem – often omitted in performances today – is the inclusion of the *vivats*, shouted by the scholars of Westminster halfway through the performance. The deliberate revival of these joyful Latin exclamations, not heard since James II's coronation in 1685, was an attempt to add historical legitimacy to the service. Parry clearly understood the need for grandeur: it is a magnificent setting for large choir, orchestra, organ and fanfare trumpets. The music is designed, not so much to accompany ceremony, as to function as ceremony itself.

It must have been deeply frustrating for Parry and the organisers – as well as King Edward himself – that the coronation did not go quite as planned. It was intended to take place on 26 June 1902, and a full rehearsal was held two days before. Parry was present at the rehearsal where his own anthem was being performed, and his diary vividly describes the scene:

> Went through the Cloisters and into the S[outh] Transept and came into the Chancel just as the Bishop of London stepped onto the dais where the carved thrones are, and, addressing mainly the performers on the organ screen and the choir, for the rest of the Abbey was almost empty, announced the necessity of the King's undergoing an operation and the Coronation being postponed – and he ended with an appeal to all to join [directly] in a Litany. He then went up to the altar and began. The Choir joined in with a most superb tone, and produced an effect I have never experienced before. So solemn and pathetic. A few kneeling figures on the floor of the Chancel. The sun light streaming in on the ancient recumbent figures on the tombs, the thousands of empty seats! I came away soon after 2 back to College – passing through merry crowds who did not know the news![44]

King Edward was suffering from acute appendicitis and was obliged to undergo an emergency operation. He recovered quickly, and the coronation was deferred until 9 August: but it was, perhaps inevitably, a shadow of its former glory. Edward was not even strong enough to wear the traditional St Edward's crown; and Parry's anthem

– though performed in full force by 430 singers, large orchestra, organ and no fewer than ten fanfare trumpets from Kneller Hall – was something of a shambles. The music was being conducted by Frederick Bridge, who crumpled under the pressure of the grand occasion: mistaking a peer for the king himself, he signalled to the Westminster boys to begin their *vivats* too early, before Edward had even entered the building. Parry reports peevishly in his diary: 'Bridge made a sad mistake in the processional music and seemed to lose his head. Finished the whole anthem before the King came in at all, and had to repeat all the latter part when he did.'[45]

But the coronation had, at least, prompted the composition of another iconic work of royal music, one that would not only capture an intensely patriotic mood, but also something of the relief felt at the signing of the Treaty of Vereeniging in May 1902, to mark the end of the Boer War. It was in the distinctly military atmosphere of the bloody Boer War that Edward Elgar felt inspired to write the *Pomp and Circumstance* marches early in the new year of 1901. These were no light, military marches like those written by Sullivan for Prince Albert's royal wedding but substantial symphonic works written within the traditional quick march form. Elgar described how he wanted to write a serious symphonic march that could actually be marched to, saying '… all marches on the symphonic scale are so slow that people can't march to them. I have some of the soldier instinct in me'.[46] Elgar was not a soldier, but he certainly empathised with the man in the street, having been brought up in humble surroundings as the son of a piano tuner in rural Worcestershire. He was also – to add to his marked feeling as a social outsider

– a devout Catholic. He was not the obvious choice for a national musical icon, but his fame and popularity had grown steadily, and he had begun to move in royal circles. He even composed an 'Imperial March' for Victoria's Jubilee and a cantata, *Caractacus*, for which Victoria herself had accepted the dedication. Elgar's acceptance by royalty reflected a democratisation in society's attitudes towards its composers. Background and education didn't matter any longer: just raw talent, which Elgar had in abundance. He was the perfect choice for Edward: a humble, ordinary man who had a knack for writing works of great ceremonial splendour.

When, in 1901, Elgar composed the first two of his six *Pomp and Circumstance* marches, he knew he was on to something. For the first march, he sketched a Trio melody to follow the main march theme, and he said at the time that it was 'a tune that comes once in a lifetime'. How right he was. The march was premiered in Liverpool and London later that year, and became an enormous success. An apocryphal tale (begun by Elgar himself) purports that it was the king who suggested that the composer add words to the Trio, but it was more likely to have been Clara Butt.[47] In the autumn of 1901, the opportunity arose to do so, when Elgar was commissioned to write a work by the Covent Garden Grand Opera Syndicate for a Royal Gala on the eve of King Edward's coronation. The result was the 'Coronation Ode', a setting for orchestra, chorus and four soloists, and the finale of that ode set the melody of the first Trio section to words by the poet A. C. Benson. It became known as 'Land of Hope and Glory'. Rarely heard in its entirety today, at the time Elgar's 'Coronation Ode' was hugely popular, and it is not hard to see why. It is a sort of miniature oratorio, in length if not in forces, set for choir, solo-ists, and a huge orchestra, and the mood veers wildly – alternately bombastic, sentimental, bellicose, expansive. Such qualities are not very popular today, but they are the essence of Edwardian England – and the new king who gave his name to the age.

The 'Ode' did not receive its intended send-off, due to Edward VII's sudden illness and the postponement of the coronation; instead, it was premiered at the Sheffield Festival later in the year. It is a curi-ous work, by turns operatic, symphonic, sacred and rabble-rousing; but its strongly militaristic and imperial flavour suited the times, and also explains why it is so rarely performed today. 'Land of Hope and Glory', however, took on a life of its own. So attached was Elgar to this grand tune that he arranged it as a self-standing song for solo voice, with different words; the music publishers Boosey saw the commer-cial potential, but demanded that the lyrics be made less specific to one occasion. The original words refer directly to the coronation:

> Land of Hope and Glory,
> Fortress of the Free,
> How may we extol thee,
> Praise thee, honour thee?
> Hark! a mighty nation
> maketh glad reply;
> Lo, our lips are thankful;
> lo, our hearts are high!
> Hearts in hope uplifted,
> loyal lips that sing;

Strong in Faith and Freedom,

we have crowned our King!

But A. C. Benson penned an alternative version:

Land of Hope and Glory,

Mother of the Free

How shall we extol thee,

who are born of thee?

Wider still and wider

shall thy bounds be set;

God who made thee mighty,

make thee mightier yet.

Elgar's 'Land of Hope and Glory', written first in 1902 as part of a Coronation ode for Edward VII. The tune has been more or less adopted as our unofficial national anthem, sung annually – amid much flag waving – at the Last Night of the Proms celebrations in the Albert Hall.

The new song, with the new words, was premiered by Dame Clara Butt at the Royal Albert Hall on Saturday 21 June 1902. It caught the mood of national self-confidence at a time when the British Empire was at its zenith. This simple, heart-rending tune and its stirring words describing fervent love of country have – as Elgar himself came close to predicting – entered the national consciousness, to be sung at sports events and, annually, at the Last Night of the Proms at the Royal Albert Hall. 'Land of Hope and Glory' made Elgar the nation's troubadour, a position confirmed when he was knighted in 1904.

THE HOUSE
OF WINDSOR

Edward VII died on 6 May 1910, and was succeeded by his second son, George. George's relationship with his father differed from those of previous generations of Hanoverians: George loved and admired Edward and was determined to develop and preserve his father's legacy. Despite his intense shyness and abstemious nature, George took part in the ceremonies that had meant so much to his father through a sense of duty – from the State Opening of Parliament ('the most terrible ordeal I have ever gone through', he confided in his diary) to his splendid coronation on 22 June 1911. This coronation was an event his father would have been proud of, the culmination of everything the monarchy had learned about large-scale public events in the previous decades: music and monarchy came together as one in the smoothest-running coronation for centuries. 'This great State function was carried through with due dignity, splendour and solemnity,' reported the *Musical Times*. 'The imposing ceremony was one that kindled the imagination of all who were privileged to be present, and it was calculated to stir the pride of every patriotic Briton.'[48] Works performed included Stanford's specially composed *Gloria in B flat* for orchestra (the composer was now in his sixties) and a new work by Elgar, 'O Hearken Thou', for chorus and orchestra. Elgar's piece set verses from Psalm 5: 'O hearken thou to the voice of my calling, my King and my God; for unto thee will I make my prayer. My voice shalt thou hear betimes, O Lord: early in the morning will I direct my prayer unto thee and will look up.' This is Elgar at his intense, romantic best, a far cry from his more ceremonial 'pomp and circumstance' music. But the private devotion that the text describes was highly appropriate for George V, who was intensely religious, and this music was in fact performed while George took communion as part of the coronation service. Several of the more religious aspects of the service that had been removed for the 1902 coronation were reinstated and lengthened, including the coronation sermon.

Everything, in fact, was bigger and better than in 1902. Parry's 'I Was Glad' was re-performed, but in an orchestrally expanded version with a new instrumental introduction, purportedly 'more arresting and emphatic than was the original one'.[49] Parry also wrote a huge Te Deum – perhaps the musical highlight of the service – a sumptuous setting for full choir and large orchestra including six trumpets. Woven through the music are snippets of the hymn tune 'St Anne (O God, Our Help in Ages Past)' and 'The Old Hundredth (All People That On Earth Do Dwell)', providing welcome 'anchor points' for the listener. George's son (the future Edward VIII) described the coronation thus: 'In that gorgeous, glittering assemblage, watching the stately measures of the prelates and the Great Officers of State in their robes of scarlet trimmed with ermine and gold, listening to the fanfares of trumpets, the rich tones of the organ and the voices of the choir, I became aware as never before of the true majesty and solemnity of kingship.'[50]

For King George it must have been enough pageantry to last a lifetime. But, dedicated to furthering the cause of monarchy as he was, he travelled to India shortly afterwards to undergo another crowning ceremony, receiving homage from his Indian subjects at the spectacular Delhi Durbar in 1911. This event was probably the most spectacular ceremony in the history of the British Empire, intended to celebrate the glory of the monarchy and the loyalty of its Indian subjects to the imperial cause – and the festivities involved an enormous procession including a line of Indian princes riding on jewelled elephants. The Delhi Durbar was highly publicised as the only royal tour by a King-Emperor of India (the durbar itself was followed by a shooting expedition in Nepal and a visit to Calcutta) and it was marked in music by Elgar's *Crown of India* suite, a lavish masque production involving mime and pantomime. The suite was performed at the London Coliseum in 1912 and its plot sketches out, and attempts to justify, Britain's controversial plan to move India's capital city from Calcutta to Delhi, while also promoting the virtues and legitimacy of imperial policy. The work is pure propaganda, and its themes of imperialism sit uneasily with modern listeners. The *Crown of India* is little known and rarely performed today. It is disputed among historians how much Elgar valued the work, and whether it was personal political conviction or financial motivation that compelled him to write it. But the music was certainly popular at the time, revived on several occasions, including the Three Choirs Festival (conducted by Elgar himself) and the British Empire exhibition in 1924; it was also broadcast 102 times on the 'wireless' between 1923 and 1934. Thanks to the Delhi Durbar ceremony, George V had portrayed himself as the figurehead of empire on a national stage.

For George, however, this was ceremony as hair shirt, undertaken not through inclination but as a solemn duty. It would be this devotion to duty that would transform the monarchy once again, as it faced the challenge of ever more rapid political, social and cultural change in the twentieth century.

∞

Just after the outbreak of the First World War in 1914, a book entitled *Das Land ohne Musik* was published in Germany, written by a man named Oscar Schmitz. It was a smug cultural criticism of Britain from the standpoint of the most powerful musical nation in the world – and its title, which translates as 'The Land Without Music', fast became a thorn in the side of British musicians, applied vaguely, liberally – and often wrongly – to the state of British music's past and present. But the book signified the biggest cultural shift in British music for 200 years: the disillusionment with German cultural ideals that had shaped the English arts, and in particular English music, for the past two centuries.

As stories of Germans committing atrocities on Englishmen filtered back to the home front (the first air raid in Britain took place on Christmas Eve 1914), there was a patriotic movement that sought to reject German culture wholesale. For almost a decade, from 1913 to 1922, no German or Austrian composers gained a hearing at the annual Proms concerts.[51] For composers like Parry and Stanford – brought up to worship German greats like Bach, Brahms and Wagner, and whose music was deeply indebted to nineteenth-century German Romanticism – the change was heart-breaking. Parry in particular found the war difficult to come to terms with; he was a fervent Wagnerite and had previously studied in Germany, and many of his works written around this time betray his acute disillusionment with the war. His poignant motets *Songs of Farewell* express the desire to leave behind a world that is destroying itself through nationalistic obsessions. 'My soul, there is a country far beyond the stars, there above noise and danger, sweet peace sits crowned in smiles', one begins. But the best-known work of Parry's from this time was written in 1916, at the suggestion of Robert Bridges, then Poet Laureate and an old friend of Parry's from their schooldays together at Eton. Bridges asked Parry to write a tune for the gathering of an organisation called 'Fight for Right', a patriotic movement set up in 1915 to garner support for the war effort. Its aims were not simply jingoistic: it strove to promote a more universal humanity, and 'justice' rather than 'victory' was its watchword. Parry was far from a supporter of the movement – but he accepted the commission in any case and set a simple melody to the lyrics Bridges suggested: William Blake's poem, 'Jerusalem'. The song was performed at a rally 18 days later, and it became immediately and enormously popular: at one of several all-British concerts in March 1918, the programme ended with Parry's hymn, anticipating what would become almost a national ritual. It was also taken up by the women's movement (to this day, the hymn is the official anthem of the Women's Institute) and performed on numerous occasions throughout the war and after. Today it is as ubiquitous as the national anthem, sung in school assemblies and sporting occasions, as well as at the Last Night of the Proms, where it is taken far more seriously than 'Land of Hope and Glory'. The words express a pride and love of country, but also a deeper, darker sadness and nostalgia for what has been lost – they celebrate Jerusalem, but also mourn it:

> *And did those feet in ancient time*
> *Walk upon England's mountains green?*
> *And was the holy Lamb of God*
> *On England's pleasant pastures seen?*
>
> *And did the Countenance Divine*
> *Shine forth upon our clouded hills?*
> *And was Jerusalem builded here*
> *Among these dark Satanic Mills?*

George V himself heard the song and declared his wish that it should be sung as a popular anthem.[52] And no wonder: at the time 'Jerusalem' was written the monarchy was doing its best to be as English as possible. Anti-German feeling was at its height and the monarchy, with its German roots and a conspicuously German surname – Saxe Coburg-Gotha – was increasingly vulnerable. In 1917, George and his advisers decided to take drastic action. They drew a line under centuries of German dynastic history, culture and family connections by renaming the royal family the House of Windsor. George's German relatives were stripped of their British honours and titles, and those that remained given new British-sounding names.

The ways in which the monarchy projected itself to the nation was about to change fundamentally. The BBC was founded in 1922, and with it the conscious effort to create a national 'canon' of British music. Elgar became synonymous with the new medium, his music an ever-present feature of BBC output during the 1920s and 1930s. In all there were 5110 broadcast performances of Elgar's music during the composer's lifetime, and Elgar himself was broadcast 28 times conducting his own music, beginning with the opening of the Empire Exhibition at Wembley in 1924.[53] The BBC became a unifying cultural force, bringing the nation together for national events that celebrated religion, politics, empire and the monarchy. The royal family were keen to harness the BBC's democratising power, and the result was an alliance between king and corporation almost as close as that between the Crown and the Church of England. From 1932, the sovereign would give an annual Christmas broadcast to homes across the Empire; in sending the king's own voice directly into the drawing rooms of his subjects, the monarchy was reaching out as it had never been able to before.

In 1935, the BBC broadcast the first ever Empire Day Royal Command Concert from the Royal Albert Hall. Sir Walford Davies, then Master of the King's Music, wrote in the *Radio Times*: 'His Majesty, having in mind the values of the pursuit of music throughout the country and Empire at all times, but especially now when the healthy use of increased and even enforced leisure is becoming a world problems, has desire that this Command Concert should be devised to bring together picked "musical troops" from the whole of the British Isle, to typify and help to encourage national music-making in as comprehensive and representative a way as possible.'[54] Its purpose was to trace the long and rich history of British music – much of it royal in origin – from the Agincourt Carol right up to contemporary works like Holst's 'Jupiter', made famous by its setting as 'I Vow to Thee, My Country' for George V's Silver Jubilee only a few weeks earlier. George himself, now almost 70, attended the concert along with his wife, Queen Mary, although the monarchy was not directly involved in the patronage or production of the music. But by the 1930s, music that worshipped the nation implicitly worshipped royalty. Monarchy was no longer simply an alliance to religion: it had become, in essence, a religion itself.

Only six months later, George V died at Sandringham. Once heralds had proclaimed the death of kings: now it was the BBC. John Reith, the first director-general of the corporation, read the final bulletin in person: 'Death came peacefully to the king at 11.55pm'. George's successor was Edward VIII, who would reign for only 12 months, abdicating in December 1936 in order to marry the twice-divorced Wallis Simpson. His younger brother, Albert George, became king as George VI, and his coronation took place in May 1937: the very same date that had been intended for Edward VIII's. After the abdication crisis – a scandal that had shaken the monarchy to its core, and which threatened to undermine its morality and cosy domestic reputation – the coronation was an invaluable opportunity to reassure the British nation by stressing continuity and tradition.

There were many familiar elements to the musical programme – from 'Zadok the Priest' and works by Purcell and Gibbons to the more recent familiarity of Parry's 'I Was Glad' and Elgar's *Pomp and Circumstance* March.

The highlight among the new commissions was Vaughan Williams's Te Deum. Vaughan Williams represented a new generation of British musicians, a product of Prince Albert's cultural renaissance and former student (and now professor) of the Royal College of Music. He was also a key figure in the twentieth-century revival of indigenous British music, in particular the traditional hymns and folk tunes which provided the basis and inspiration for many of his best-known works. Such music was ideal for a monarchy desperate to emphasise its own long-standing tradition, and the Te Deum lived up to these aims, combining fragments of traditional folk songs with martial-sounding fanfares and a march-like main theme. One also detects an air of cynicism in the work, particularly in the weaving in of rebellious folk tunes such as 'It's of a Rich Young Farmer'; Vaughan Williams was a socialist and had a general disdain for the Establishment, even refusing a knighthood. To his dismay, he was himself becoming an Establishment figure and his music would be co-opted not just by royalty but by the entire patriotic movement during the Second World War.

The message of the coronation was all the more important because it would reach more people than any coronation in history: George VI's coronation procession was the first ever to be broadcast on television (although cameras were not used inside the Abbey until 1953). Eight miles of cable weighing several tons was laid around central London, providing the link for live coverage of the procession. The BBC, by now the principal patron of new British music, had commissioned William Walton to write a march, the *Crown Imperial*, originally intended for Edward VIII's coronation; after Edward's abdication, it was used for George VI's coronation. Conducted by Adrian Boult, the BBC's director of music, it would have been familiar to many in the audience – it had been recorded at Abbey Road Studios in April 1937, and broadcast to the nation via the BBC the following month. The *Crown Imperial* – which Walton was concerned about writing, since he believed no one would be able to follow Elgar's *Pomp and Circumstance* marches – is, alongside *Belshazzar's Feast*, Walton's most well-known work, and rivals Elgar for its pomp and vivacity, its bewitching melodies, lively rhythms and stately grandeur. There is also something distinctly filmic about Walton's music: the pace at which it moves, and the colour and textures of the orchestration make it an appropriate soundtrack for the monarchy's move to the small screen. This was the advent of monarchy as modern celebrity, where the intimacy of the royal presence on screen gives the illusion of familiarity and a sense of ownership. Walton claimed he took the title of the march from a passage in Shakespeare's *Henry V*:[55]

> *I am a king that find thee, and I know*
> *'Tis not the balm, the scepter and the ball*
> *The sword, the mace, the crown imperial*
> *The intertissued robe of gold and pearl*
> *The farced title running 'fore the King,*

The throne he sits on, nor the tide of pomp
That beats upon the high shore of this world –
No, not all these, thrice gorgeous ceremony
Not all these, laid in bed majestical
Can sleep so soundly as the wretched slave.

Shakespeare is actually berating the hollowness and falseness of royal ceremony in the speech – kings, Henry says, don't sleep as soundly or healthily as the hard-working peasant after a day's hard labour – but the modern monarchy's 'tide of pomp' was fast becoming its defining characteristic. Walton loved the passage and said it contained 'a whole list of titles for coronation marches'; indeed, he would write the 'Orb and Sceptre' for Queen Elizabeth II's coronation in 1953, and said he had reserved 'The Bed Majestical' for King Charles III.[56]

The coronation also featured a rendition of the national anthem. Frederick Bridge, organist at Westminster Abbey, noted how the anthem had not been performed at Queen Victoria's Golden Jubilee, which he found 'a curious thing … There seemed for many years to be a shyness, if I may use the term, in singing the National Anthem in Church … of late years, especially since this terrible war, this diffidence seems to have happily disappeared, and at the time of writing I am playing the National Anthem daily at the close of the afternoon service.'[57] In 1937, in fact, the order of service published for the coronation finally included a full arrangement of the national anthem, cementing forever its place in the service: this arrangement was transposed down to G major, putting it in a key 'which brings the tune within the compass of every voice'.[58] For those watching on television or listening on the wireless – in every part of Great Britain and across the Empire – as well as those in the assembled congregation, the national anthem had become a touchstone, giving opportunity for all 'to sing with heart and voice, GOD SAVE THE KING'.[59]

King George VI sustained the popularity of the monarchy throughout the tumult of the Second World War, where it even survived a daring daytime air raid of cluster bombs on the palace, narrowly missing the king. He was a popular figurehead – competing, somewhat jealously, with the other wartime icon, Winston Churchill – and when he died in 1952, aged only 57, he left an inheritance that was surprisingly unscathed by war and its aftermath. He also left a daughter who was determined to keep it that way.

Elizabeth II may not be so known for a love of music as some of her forebears, but she reigns with a sense of duty, informed by her own Anglican faith as well as her robust common sense, and music has, throughout her reign, reinforced the power of her calling and the status of the monarchy. Her coronation, on 2 June 1953, typified this, following the patterns established by coronations in 1902 and 1911, and a programme of royal 'classics' from past and present centuries that would cement the 'canon' of royal music in the mind of the public. By 1953 that public had gone global: for the first time, the actual crowning of the monarch was televised and watched by millions across the world. Mingling with self-consciously historical works by Byrd, Gibbons, Tallis, Purcell and Handel – from Purcell's trumpet tune to a minuet from Handel's *Music for the Royal Fireworks*

– the global audience were also introduced to music by the new British musical establishment: Elgar, Vaughan Williams, Walton and Arnold Bax (who was the Master of the King's Music). These great names proved once and for all that Britain was far from 'The Land Without Music'. But even the most contemporary of compositions were in thrall to history: in particular, perhaps the most iconic work of the coronation, Vaughan Williams's grand ceremonial arrangement of 'The Old Hundredth' hymn. This ancient tune dates back to the sixteenth century, and has remained enduringly popular up to the present day. A congregational hymn tune for the coronation was a completely new idea in 1953, and it was Vaughan Williams's unique contribution to include one: he 'was extremely proud of introducing this democratic musical reform into the service'.[60] Beginning with a flourish of fanfare trumpets and magnificent organ, Vaughan Williams's arrangement was written for choir (who sing the middle verses in beautiful harmony, the third also accompanied by a stately solo trumpet), but also gives an opportunity for the entire congregation to sing as one voice at the beginning and end of the work. It is a piece that sums up the story of music and monarchy during the glorious years of royal reinvention. It is the present taking up the past, embellishing it, but using its authority to re-establish the idea of a sacred monarchy. And, thanks to television, it was seen and heard by millions.

The music of 1953 is filled with references to the last great Elizabeth who sat on the throne, the implication being that the new Elizabeth might emulate her. Benjamin Britten, England's greatest mid-twentieth-century composer was commissioned to write an opera called *Gloriana* – first performed at Covent Garden during the coronation celebrations – which centres on the relationship between Elizabeth I and the Earl of Essex. A coronation anthology of new English songs was also published that year, called *A Garland For the Queen* but self-consciously referencing the collection of songs published for Elizabeth I named *The Triumphs of Oriana*. Ten well-known British composers were commissioned by the Arts Council of Great Britain for the modern version – including Arnold Bax, Vaughan Williams, Herbert Howells and Gerald Finzi – and all produced song settings drawing on pastoral, outdoor imagery, such as in Tippett's setting 'Dance Clarion Air' (Shine, stones on the shore,/swept in music by the ocean/Shine, till all this island is a crown). Unlike Elizabeth I, however, the new queen had nothing to do with the collection, and was not a direct patron of music. Elizabeth II was utterly unseduced by the romance of her own historical position or the notion of the 'New Elizabethan Age'. 'Frankly,' she said in her second Christmas broadcast, 'I do not myself feel at all like my great Tudor forebear, who was blessed with neither husband nor children, who ruled as a despot and was never able to leave her native shores.'

During Elizabeth's long reign, music has continued to play an essential role in the public ceremonies of the monarchy – above all, the great occasions of births, marriages, deaths and jubilees. At the Queen Mother's funeral in 2002, William Croft's burial sentences were performed. In 2011, Prince William and Kate Middleton chose a healthy dose of Hubert Parry: 'I Was Glad', the hymn 'Jerusalem' and the anthem 'Blest Pair of Sirens' – decisions that were no doubt influenced by the groom's father, Prince Charles. Queen Elizabeth's eldest son is the only member of the family to have shown a marked interest in serious art music – as a boy he played the cello, and in 2011 made a documentary film exploring his passion for Parry's music. When and if Charles himself inherits the throne, perhaps the nation will once more see a monarch engage on a personal level with music.

In the era of Elizabeth II, the gulf between popular and 'serious' music widened, with the kinds of songs heard in churches and concert halls appealing to an ever-smaller percentage of people. Mass culture was a much more powerful force than in the heyday of the Chapel Royal, and a different kind of music was popular now. Pursuing the same logic as they had in the past, pop became the music with which the monarchy would now associate itself. The Prince's Trust, the young people's charity set up by the Prince of Wales in 1976, has held rock concerts to raise money and garner popular approval; in 1986, the big-draw names included Paul McCartney and Tina Turner, and in 1996 Bob Dylan and Eric Clapton performed for the charity in Hyde Park. The Queen's Jubilee Concert in 2012 – attended by queen herself, now 86, and wearing earplugs – did not feature the music of the highly respected current Master of the King's Music, Peter Maxwell-Davies. Instead, it featured pop 'royalty' like Elton John and Kylie Minogue, and a rendition of the national anthem led by former Take That singer Gary Barlow. Today, this is the music of monarchy as much as the great and ancient British classics. Classical music is commissioned on occasion – from Maxwell-Davies's annual Christmas carols to

Paul Mealor's motet for William and Kate's wedding – but it is increasingly rare, since it is neither popular with the masses, nor, for the most part, particularly critically acclaimed.

But what's most striking about the 60 years which have passed since 1953 is not the new royal music which has been created – but how much has passed away. Most of the great actors in the coronation ceremony – the peerage, the armed forces, the Church of England – are now pale shadows of themselves.

Above all, we have lost the chief inspiration for the music of monarchy. Not, of course, the Queen, who happily is still with us. The difference is that today she is respected, rather than revered. The idea, alive and well in 1953, that monarchy has a sacred role and power, is gone – I think beyond repair.

Now the sacred monarchy survives only in its music.

But there, at least, it remains eternally, magnificently alive.

ENDNOTES

PART ONE

1. It cannot be proved definitely that Henry V was indeed Roy Henry, although it is highly likely: for more information, see Margaret Bent, 'Roy Henry', in Grove Music Online. Oxford Music Onine, http://www.oxfordmusiconline.com
2. For more information, see Richard Taruskin, *Oxford History of Western Music*, vol. 1, p423
3. For more information, see Robert Nosow, *Ritual Meanings in the Fifteenth-century Motet* (Cambridge University Press, 2012), p. 37.
4. Peter Holman, *Four and Twenty Fiddlers* (Clarendon Press, 1993), p. 37.
5. Edwin B. Warren, *Life and Works of Robert Fayrfax 1464–1521* (American Institute of Musicology, 1969), p. 25.
6. Jervis Wegg, *Richard Pace: A Tudor Diplomatist* (Barnes and Noble, 1971), p. 128.
7. David Greer and Fiona Kisby, 'Cornysh', in Grove Music Online. Oxford Music Online (accessed 11 October 2012).
8. Roger Bray, 'Music and Musicians in Tudor England', in Bray (ed.), *The Sixteenth Century*, p. 39.
9. Philip Thorby [Liner Notes], *The Field of Cloth of Gold*, Musica Antiqua of London (Amon Ra Records, released 1991), CD.
10. Holman, *Four and Twenty Fiddlers*, (Clarendon Press, 1993) p. 70
11. An early string instrument and forerunner to the violin.
12. For more information, see Eric Ives, *The Life and Death of Anne Boleyn* (Wiley-Blackwell, 2005).
13. Nicholas Temperley, *The Music of the English Parish Church*, Vol. 1 (Cambridge University Press, 1983), p. 12.
14. Le Huray, *Music and the Reformation in England*, (Barrie and Jenkins, 1967) p. 8.
15. Ibid., p. 9.
16. Ibid., p. 13.
17. Morehen, 'English Church Music', in Bray (ed.), *The Sixteenth Century*, (Wiley–Blockwell, 1995) p. 94.
18. Several notes sung to one syllable of text.
19. Skidmore, *Edward VI*, p. 277.
20. Morehen, 'English Church Music', in Bray (ed.), *The Sixteenth Century*, pp. 94–5.
21. Nick Sandon [Liner Notes], *Tallis: The Complete Works*, Vol. 3, *Chapelle du Roi* (Signum Classics, released 1997), CD.

22   Temperley, *The Music of the English Parish Church*, p. 27.
23   John Cassell, *Illustrated History of England*, Vol. 2 (W. Kent and Co., 1858), p. 370.
24   Hyder E. Rollins (ed.), *Old English Ballads, 1553–1625*, chiefly from MSS (Cambridge University Press, 1920), p. 19.
25   Queen Mary's nickname was Marigold.
26   This ballad is printed in Rollins (ed.), *Old English Ballads*, p. 19.
27   A small keyboard instrument, often also called 'virginals' – although the two instruments are slightly different.
28   David Scott, 'Elizabeth I, Queen of England', in Grove Music Online. Oxford Music Online (accessed 12 October 2012).
29   Le Huray, *Music and the Reformation in England*, p. 31.
30   Scott, 'Elizabeth I, Queen of England', in Grove Music Online. Oxford Music Online (accessed 12 October 2012).
31   Joseph Kerman, 'Byrd, William', in Grove Music Online. Oxford Music Online (accessed 12 October 2012).
32   Margaret Bent, 'La Contenance Angloise', in David Fraser (ed.), *Fairest Isle: BBC Radio 3 Book of British Music* (BBC Books, 1995), p. 14.
33   Doe and Allinson, 'Tallis, Thomas', in Grove Music Online. Oxford Music Online (accessed 12 October 2012).
34   Ibid.
35   For more information, see Kenneth Fincham and Nicholas Tyacke, *Altars Restored: The Changing Face of English Religious Worship, 1547– c. 1700* (Oxford University Press, 2007).
36   Nicholas Temperley, et al., 'London (i)', in Grove Music Online. Oxford Music Online (accessed 12 October 2012).
37   John Milsom, 'The Triumphes of Oriana', in Fraser (ed.), *Fairest Isle*, (BBC Books, 1995) p. 29.
38   Ibid., p. 26.
39   Holman, *Four and Twenty Fiddlers*, p. 111.
40   Ibid., p. 118.
41   Quoted in Sarah Gristwood, *Elizabeth and Leicester* (Bantam, 2008), p. 239.
42   Alan Kendall, *Robert Dudley, Earl of Leicester* (Cassell, 1960), p. 155.
43   David Brown and Ian Harwood, 'Johnson, Edward (i)', in Grove Music Online. Oxford Music Online (accessed 12 October 2012).
44   This is an anecdotal story related in David Scott, 'Elizabeth I, Queen of England', in Grove Music Online. Oxford Music Online (accessed 12 October 2012). But it has been disputed: see Holman, *Four and Twenty Fiddlers*, p. 122.

PART TWO

1   Peter Holman, *Four and Twenty Fiddlers*, p. 173.
2   Quoted in Ian Spink, 'Preface and Acknowledgements', in Ian Spink (ed.), *The Blackwell History of Music in Britain: The Seventeenth Century* (Wiley-Blackwell, 1991), p. ix.
3   Quoted in Matthias Range, *Music and Ceremonial at British Coronations* (Cambridge University Press, 2012), p. 34.
4   Ibid.
5   Anthony Boden, *Thomas Tomkins: The Last Elizabethan* (Ashgate, 2005), p. 95.
6   Ibid., p. 87.

7   Peter Holman, 'Court in Country', in David Fraser (ed.), *Fairest Isle: BBC Radio 3 Book of British Music* (BBC Books, 1995), p. 32.

8   Quoted in John Harper and Peter Le Huray, 'Gibbons, Orlando', in Grove Music Online. Oxford Music Online.

9   The name of this group changed over time: it later became known as 'Lutes and Voices', but was known as 'The Consort' during James's reign. For more information, see Holman, *Four and Twenty Fiddlers*.

10   Peter Holman and Paul O'Dette, 'Dowland, John', in Grove Music Online. Oxford Music Online (accessed 15 October 2012).

11   John Milsom [Liner Notes], *1605: Treason and Dischord – William Byrd and the Gunpowder Plot: The King's Singers* (Signum Classics, released 2005), CD.

12   James M. Sutton, 'Henry Frederick, prince of Wales (1594–1612)', *Oxford Dictionary of National Biography* (Oxford University Press, 2004; online edn, January 2008) http://www.oxforddnb.com.ezproxy.londonlibrary.co.uk/view/article/12961, accessed 9 October 2012.

13   Boden, *Thomas Tomkins: The Last Elizabethan*, (Ashgate Publishing, 2005) p. 98.

14   Quoted in James M. Sutton, 'Henry Frederick, prince of Wales (1594–1612)', *Oxford Dictionary of National Biography*, online edition, accessed 9 October 2012.

15   Jerry Brotton, *The Sale of the Late King's Goods* (Pan Macmillan, 2007), p. 3.

16   Quoted in Holman, *Four and Twenty Fiddlers*, p. 213.

17   Quoted in Christopher D. S. Field et al., 'Fantasia', in Grove Music Online. Oxford Music Online (accessed 9 October 2012).

18   For more information, see Holman, *Four and Twenty Fiddlers*, chapter 9

19   Quoted in Thomasin Lamay (ed.), in *Musical Voices of Early Modern Women* (Ashgate, 2005), p. 416.

20   Quoted in Susi Jeans and O. W. Neighbour, 'Bull, John', in Grove Music Online. Oxford Music Online (accessed 17 January 2013).

21   A galliard is a lively, triple-metre dance popular at court during the sixteenth and early seventeenth centuries.

22   Boden, *Thomas Tomkins: The Last Elizabethan*, p. 123.

23   John S. Bumpus, *A History of English Cathedral Music: Part 1 1900* (Kessinger, 2004), p. 80.

24   Quoted in Boden, *Thomas Tomkins: The Last Elizabethan*, p. 124.

25   Matthias Range, *Music and Ceremonial at British Coronations*, (Cambridge University Press, 2012) p. 38.

26   Laudian polemicist Peter Heylyn is quoted in Anthony Milton, 'That Sacred Oratory: Religion and the Chapel Royal During the Personal Rule of Charles I', in Andrew Ashbee (ed.), *William Lawes (1602–1645): Essays on his Life, Times and Work* (Ashgate, 1998), p. 71.

27   Range, *Music and Ceremonial at British Coronations*, p. 59.

28   Ibid., pp. 38–9.

29   See ibid., Chapter 2, for more details.

30   Quoted in Charles Carlton, *Charles I: The Personal Monarch* (Routledge, 1995), p. 197.

31   Quoted in Boden, *Thomas Tomkins: The Last Elizabethan*, p. 133.

32   Graham Parry, *Glory Laud and Honour: The Arts of the Anglican Counter- Reformation* (Boydell Press, 2008), p. 162.

33   Ibid., p. 166.

34 Ibid., p. 1.

35 'The Correspondence of John Cosin', quoted in ibid., p.1.

36 Carlton, *Charles I: The Personal Monarch*, (Routledge, 1983) p.128.

37 Ian Spink, 'Music and Society', in Spink (ed.), *The Blackwell History of Music in Britain: The Seventeenth Century*, p. 59.

38 Quoted in Carlton, *Charles I: The Personal Monarch*, p. 150.

39 Ibid., p. 149.

40 Murray Lefkowitz, 'The Longleat Papers of Bulstrode Whitelocke; New Light on Shirley's "Triumph of Peace"', *Journal of the American Musicological Society*, Vol. 18, No. 1 (Spring, 1965), p. 45.

41 Lewis Winstock, *Songs and Music of the Redcoats: A History of the War Music of the British Army 1642–1902* (Leo Cooper, 1970), p. 17.

42 Charles Carlton, *Charles I: Going to the Wars: The Experience of the British Civil Wars 1638–1651* (Routledge, 1994), p. 23.

43 Randle Holme, in Isaac Herbert Jeaves (ed.), *The academy of armory, or, A storehouse of armory and blazon…* (Roxburghe Club, 1905), pp. 153–4.

44 William Chappell and George Macfarren, *Popular Music of the Olden Time* (Cramer, Beale and Chappell, 1859), Vol. II, p. 414.

45 Quoted in Layton Ring, 'The Death of William Lawes', in Ashbee (ed.), *William Lawes (1602–1645)*, p. 161.

46 David Pinto, 'Lawes, William', in Grove Music Online. Oxford Music Online (accessed 11 October 2012).

47 Temperley, *The Music of the English Parish Church*, p. 12.

48 Quoted in Boden, *Thomas Tomkins: The Last Elizabethan*, p. 172.

49 Ian Spink, 'Music and Society', in Spink (ed.), *The Blackwell History of Music in Britain: The Seventeenth Century*, p. 30.

50 Percy Scholes, *The Puritans and Music in England and New England* (Oxford University Press, 1934), p. 144.

51 Quoted in Holman, 'Court in Country', in Fraser (ed.), *Fairest Isle*, p. 38.

52 Andrew Ashbee, 'Jenkins, John', in Grove Music Online. Oxford Music Online (accessed 11 October 2012).

53 A small bass viol popular in England during the seventeenth century.

54 For more information, see Frank Traficante (ed.), *John Jenkins: The Lyra Viol Consorts*, Vols 67–8 (AR Editions, 1992), p. xi.

55 Chappell and Macfarren, *Popular Music of the Olden Time*, Vol. II, (Kesinger Publishing Co, 2004) p. 434.

56 Bruce Wood, *Purcell: An Extraordinary Life* (Oxford University Press, 2009), p. 5.

57 Range, *Music and Ceremonial at British Coronations*, p. 25.

58 Holman, *Four and Twenty Fiddlers*, p. 400.

59 Wood, *Purcell: An Extraordinary Life*, p. 6.

60 Peter Dennison and Bruce Wood, 'Cooke, Henry', in Grove Music Online. Oxford Music Online (accessed 11 October 2012).

61 Andrew Ashbee (ed.), *Records of English Court Music*, I (Snodland, 1986), p. 19.

62 Quoted in Robert Latham and William Matthews (eds), *The Diary of Samuel Pepys Companion* (HarperCollins, 1995), p. 264.

63 Jonathan Keates, *Purcell: A Biography* (Chatto & Windus, 1995), p. 30.

64 Bruce Wood, 'Blow, John', in Grove Music Online. Oxford Music Online (accessed 11 October 2012).

65 Peter Dennison and Bruce Wood, 'Cooke, Henry', in Grove Music Online. Oxford Music Online (accessed 12 October 2012).

66 Bruce Wood, 'Humfrey, Pelham', in Grove Music Online. Oxford Music Online (accessed 11 October 2012).

67 Spink, 'Music and Society', in Spink (ed.), *The Blackwell History of Music in Britain: The Seventeenth Century*, p. 60.

68 Ian Woodfield and Lucy Robinson, 'Viol', in Grove Music Online. Oxford Music Online (accessed 11 October 2012).

69 Quoted in Holman, *Four and Twenty Fiddlers*, p. 289.

70 Ibid., p. 312.

71 Daniel Heartz and Patricia Rader, 'Branle', in Grove Music Online. Oxford Music Online.

72 Spink, 'Music and Society', in Spink (ed.), *The Blackwell History of Music in Britain: The Seventeenth Century*, p. 55.

73 A plucked string instrument, a member of the lute family with a distinctively long neck.

74 Holman, *Four and Twenty Fiddlers*, p. 306.

75 Peter Holman [Liner Notes], *Four and Twenty Fiddlers: Music for the Court Restoration Band, The Parley of Instruments* (Hyperion, released 1993), CD.

76 Chappell and Macfarren, *Popular Music of the Olden Time*, Vol. II, p. 523.

77 Spink, 'Music and Society', in Spink (ed.), *The Blackwell History of Music in Britain: The Seventeenth Century*, p. 55.

78 Ibid.

79 Holman, *Four and Twenty Fiddlers*, p. 401.

80 Quoted in Range, *Music and Ceremonial*, p. 75.

81 Jean Lionnet, 'Fede, Innocenzo', in Grove Music Online. Oxford Music Online (accessed 11 October 2012).

82 Spink, 'Music and Society', in Spink (ed.), *The Blackwell History of Music in Britain: The Seventeenth Century*, p. 56.

83 Keates, *Purcell: A Biography*, p. 144.

84 Wood, *Purcell: An Extraordinary Life*, p. 113.

85 Ibid., p. 115.

86 Numerous different versions of this text survive: this is a short extract of the text generally understood to have been the original version, sung during the last year of James's reign. In some later versions, the credit of being 'an ass' is transferred to King James himself. For more details and the full number of verses see Chappell and Macfarren, *Popular Music of the Olden Time*, Vol. II, p. 568.

87 Quoted in Winstock, *Songs and Music of the Redcoats*, p. 24.

88 Chappell and Macfarren, *Popular Music of the Olden Time*, Vol. II, p. 570.

89 Range, *Music and Ceremonial in British Coronations*, p. 105.

90 Ibid., p. 95.

91 Holman, *Four and Twenty Fiddlers*, p. 431.

92 Spink, 'Music and Society', in Spink (ed.), *The Blackwell History of Music in Britain: The Seventeenth Century*, p. 63.

93 Holman, *Four and Twenty Fiddlers*, pp. 432–3.

94 Ibid., p. 414.

95 Quoted in Spink, 'Music and Society', in Spink (ed.), *The Blackwell History of Music in Britain: The Seventeenth Century*, p. 56.

96 Robert Thompson, 'Purcell, Henry (1659–1695)', *Oxford Dictionary of National Biography*, online edition (accessed 11 October 2012).

97 Peter Holman et al., 'Purcell', in Grove Music Online. Oxford Music Online (accessed 11 October 2012).

98 Wood, *Purcell: An Extraordinary Life*, p. 165.

99 For more information, see Andrew Pinnock, 'Flat trumpet', in Grove Music Online. Oxford Music Online (accessed 11 October 2012).

100 Quoted in Keates, *Purcell: A Biography*, p. 262.

101 Ibid., p. 263.

102 Ibid., p. 276.

103 Quoted in Susan Foreman, *From Palace to Power: An Illustrated History of Whitehall* (Alpha Press, 1995), p. 37.

PART THREE

1 Donald Burrows, *Handel and the English Chapel Royal* (Oxford University Press, 2008), p. 33.

2 Watkins Shaw et al., 'Clarke, Jeremiah (i)', in Grove Music Online. Oxford Music Online.

3 Abel Boyer, *The History of the Reign of Queen Anne Digested into Annals* (A. Roper and F. Coggan, 1708), VI, p. 223.

4 Peter Holman, 'Pride or Prejudice? Music in the Eighteenth Century', in David Fraser (ed.), *Fairest Isle*, BBC Radio 3 Book of British Music (BBC Books, 1995), p. 48.

5 Richard Platt, 'Theatre Music I', in H. Diack Johnstone and Roger Fiske (eds), *The Blackwell History of Music in Britain: The Eighteenth Century* (Wiley-Blackwell, 1991), p. 110.

6 Jonathan Keates, *Handel: The Man and His Music* (Pimlico, 2009), p. 59.

7 Burrows, *Handel and the English Chapel Royal*, (Open University, 1981) p. 82.

8 Watkins Shaw and Graydon Beeks, 'Croft, William', in Grove Music Online. Oxford Music Online (accessed 15 November 2012).

9 William Croft received only £73 per annum, according to Burrows, *Handel and the English Chapel Royal*, p. 254.

10 Christopher Hogwood, *Handel* (Thames & Hudson, 2007), p. 69.

11 Anthony Hicks, 'Handel, George Frideric', in Grove Music Online. Oxford Music Online (accessed 15 November 2012).

12 For more information, see Burrows, *Handel and the English Chapel Royal*, p. 180.

13 Ragnhild Hatton, *George I* (Yale University Press, 2001), p. 132.

14 John Van der Kiste, *King George II and Queen Caroline* (Sutton Publishing, 1997), p. 58.

15 This is uncertain. For more details, see Burrows, *Handel and the English Chapel Royal*, p. 172.

16 Hogwood, *Handel*, p. 72.

17 Roger Fiske, 'Music and Society', Diack Johnstone and Fiske (eds), *The Blackwell History of Music in Britain: The Eighteenth Century*, p. 16.

18 For more information, see Colin Timms, *Polymath of the Baroque: Agostino Steffani and His Music* (Oxford University Press, 2003).

19 Jeremy Black, *The Hanoverians: The History of a Dynasty* (Hambledon Continuum, 2006), p. 80.

20 Not to be confused with the musical conservatoire, which is entirely unrelated to the operatic venture and was not founded until 1822.

21 Hogwood, *Handel*, p. 80.

22 Donald Burrows, *Handel* (Oxford University Press, 1994), p. 132.

23 Quoted in Victor Schoelcher, *The Life of Handel* (London, 1857), pp. 369–70.

24 Quoted in Burrows, *Handel*, p. 107.

25 Johann Adam Hiller, *Treatise on Vocal Performance and Ornamentation* (Cambridge University Press, 2006), p. 180.

26 Julie Anne Sadie, *Companion to Baroque Music* (Oxford University Press, 1998), p. 288.

27 For more information, see Burrows, *Handel*, pp. 121–2.

28 Charles Burney, *A General History of Music: From the Earliest Ages to the Present* (Nabu Press, 2010) IV, p. 307.

29 For more information, see Donald Burrows and Robert D. Hume, 'George I, the Haymarket Opera Company and Handel's "Water Music"', *Early Music* (Aug, 1991), Vol. 19, No. 3.

30 Winton Dean, 'Senesino', in Grove Music Online. Oxford Music Online (accessed 15 November 2012).

31 Quoted in Range, *Music and Ceremonial at British Coronations*, p. 132.

32 Hogwood, *Handel*, p. 87.

33 For more details on the performance, see Burrows, *Handel and the English Chapel Royal*, pp. 272–9.

34 Range, *Music and Ceremonial at British Coronations*, p. 133

35 Van der Kiste, *King George II and Queen Caroline*, p. 97.

36 For more information, see Peter Holmon, 'Handel's Lutenist, the Baroque *Mandolino* in England, and John Francis Weber', a paper given at the Fifteenth Biennial Conference on Baroque Music, Southampton, July 2012.

37 Nicholas Temperley et al., 'London (i)', in Grove Music Online. Oxford Music Online (accessed 15 November 2012).

38 Quoted in Thomas McGeary, Handel, *Prince Frederick and the Nobility Reconsidered* (Göttinger Händel-Beiträge, 2004), VII, p. 160.

39 Quoted in Hogwood, *Handel*, p. 121.

40 Matthew Kilburn, 'Frederick Lewis, prince of Wales (1707–1751)', *Oxford Dictionary of National Biography* (Oxford University Press, 2004); online edn, May 2009. (http://www.oxforddnb.com.ezproxy.londonlibrary.co.uk/view/article/10140, accessed 15 November 2012).

41 Van der Kiste, *King George II and Queen Caroline*, p. 125.

42 Quoted in Burrows, *Handel and the English Chapel Royal*, p. 364.

43 Quoted in Hubert Langley, *Doctor Arne* (University of Michigan Press, 1938), p. 8.

44 Patrick Piggott, *The Innocent Diversion: A Study of Music in the Life and Writings of Jane Austen* (D. Cleverdon, 1979), p. 150.

45 For more details, see Michael Burden, *Garrick, Arne and the "Masque of Alfred": Case Study in National, Theatrical and Musical Politic* (Edwin Mellen Press, 1994).

46 Murray Pittock, *Poetry and Jacobite Politics in Eighteenth-Century Britain and Ireland* (Cambridge University Press, 1994), p. 83.

47 Quoted in William Cummings, *Dr Arne and Rule, Britannia* (Novello, 1912), pp. 35–6.

48 'God Save the Queen', *The Oxford Dictionary of Music*, revised 2nd edn, Oxford Music Online (accessed 15 November 2012).

49 Quoted in Christopher Hogwood, *Handel: Water Music and Music for the Royal Fireworks* (Cambridge University Press, 2005), p. 73.

50 Ibid., p. 88.

51 Hogwood, *Handel*, p. 149.

52 Schoelcher, *The Life of Handel*, p. 220.

53 Quoted in Hogwood, *Handel: Water Music and Music for the Royal Fireworks*, pp. 83–4.

54 Ibid., p. 95.

55 Hogwood, *Handel*, p. 98.

56 Howard Smither, *A History of the Oratorio* (University of North Carolina Press, 1977), II, p. 295.

57 Quoted in Nick Harding, *Hanover and the British Empire: 1700–1837* (Boydell Press, 2007), p. 183.

58 Linda Colley, *Britons: Forging the Nation, 1707–1837* (Yale University Press, 2005), p. 204.

59 Quoted in Jeremy Black, *George III: America's Last King* (Yale University Press, 2006), p. 156.

60 Range, *Music and Ceremonial at British Coronations*, p. 167.

61 Constance Hill, *Fanny Burney at the Court of Queen Charlotte* (University of California Press, 1912), p. 47.

62 Christopher Wright, *George III* (British Library, 2005), pp. 100–101.

63 Keates, *Handel: The Man and his Music*, (Gollancz, 1985) p. 22.

64 Anthony Hicks, 'Handel, George Frideric', in Grove Music Online. Oxford Music Online (accessed 15 November 2012).

65 Donald Burrows, *Handel: Messiah* (Cambridge University Press, 1991), p. vii.

66 *Morning Herald and Daily Advertiser*, Thursday 27 May 1784.

67 Ibid.

68 Hogwood, *Handel*, p. 256.

69 Colley, *Britons*, p. 209.

70 For more information, see Paul Rice, *Music and the French Revolution* (Cambridge Scholars, 2010).

PART FOUR

1 Christopher Hibbert, 'George IV (1762–1830)', *Oxford Dictionary of National Biography* (http://www.oxforddnb.com.ezproxy.londonlibrary.co.uk/view/article/10541, accessed 27 December 2012).

2 Christopher Hogwood, *Haydn's Visits to England* (The Folio Society, 1980), p. 43.

3 Quoted in Adam Carse, 'The Prince Regent's Band', in *Music and Letters*, Vol. 27, No. 3 (July 1946), p. 147.

4 Hibbert, 'George IV (1762–1830)', *Oxford Dictionary of National Biography* (http://www.oxforddnb.com).

5 Jessica Rutherford, *A Prince's Passion: The Life of the Royal Pavilion* (Royal Pavilion, Libraries and Museums, 2003), p. 66.

6 Quoted in Jeremy Black, *The Hanoverians: The History of a Dynasty* (Hambledon Continuum, 2006), p. 153.

7 Hibbert, 'George IV (1762–1830)', *Oxford Dictionary of National Biography*.

8   Nicholas Temperley, 'Attwood, Thomas', in Grove Music Online. Oxford Music Online (accessed 27 December 2012).

9   Nicholas Temperley, 'The Prince Consort, Champion of Music', in *Musical Times*, Vol. 102, No. 1426 (December 1961), p. 763.

10   H. C. G. Matthew and K. D. Reynolds, 'Victoria (1819–1901)', in *Oxford Dictionary of National Biography*, http://www.oxforddnb.com.ezproxy.londonlibrary. co.uk/view/article/36652 (accessed 27 December 2012).

11   Literally 'songs' in German.

12   The harpsichord was by now no longer fashionable, the piano – with its wider expressive and dynamic range – having steadily grown in popularity during the eighteenth century. The distinct tonal difference between the two instruments is due to the way the sound is produced: a harpsichord's strings are plucked, whereas a piano's are struck with hammers.

13   Theodore Martin, *The Life of the Prince Consort* (London, 1875), Vol. 4, p. 15.

14   Wilfrid Blunt, *On Wings of Song: A Biography of Felix Mendelssohn* (Hamish Hamilton, 1974), p. 224.

15   The idiomatic expression 'pulling out the stops' originates with the organ – the 'stops' are positioned above the keyboard, and are pulled out by the organist to determine which organ pipes are employed.

16   Nicholas Temperley, 'Cathedral Music', in Ian Spink and Nicholas Temperley (eds), *The Blackwell History of Music in Britain: The Romantic Age, 1800–1914* (Blackwell, 1988), p. 171.

17   Timothy Storey, 'Music 1800–2002', in Derek Keene, Arthur Burns and Andrew Saint (eds), *St Paul's: The Cathedral Church of London 1604–2004* (Yale, 2004), p. 404.

18   Robert Stradling and Meirion Hughes, *The English Musical Renaissance: 1860–1940* (Manchester University Press, 2001), p. 12.

19   Stanley Weintraub, 'Albert [Prince Albert of Saxe-Coburg and Gotha] (1819–1861)', in *Oxford Dictionary of National Biography*.

20   Quoted in Stradling and Hughes, *The English Musical Renaissance*, p. 19.

21   Arthur Jacobs, *Arthur Sullivan: A Victorian Musician* (Oxford University Press, 1984), p. 65.

22   Quoted in ibid., p. 9.

23   Stephen Banfield, 'The Artist and Society', in *The Blackwell History of Music in Britain: The Romantic Age, 1800–1914*, p. 18.

24   In 1866, it was found that only 22 per cent of professional players had studied at the RAM. See David Wright, 'The South Kensington Music Schools and the Development of the British Conservatoire in the Late Nineteenth Century', in *Journal of the Royal Musical Association*, Vol. 130, No. 2 (2005), p. 238.

25   Quoted in Stradling and Hughes, *The English Musical Renaissance*, p. 30.

26   Donald Tovey and Geoffrey Parratt, *Walter Parratt: Master of the Music* (Oxford University Press, 1941), p. 74.

27   Frederick Hudson and Rosemary Williamson, 'Parratt, Sir Walter', Grove Music Online. Oxford Music Online (accessed 27 December 2012).

28   Princess Helena, Queen Victoria's third daughter and fifth child, who was known as Princess Christian after her marriage to Prince Christian of Schleswig-Holstein.

29   Russell Thorndike, *Children of the Garter: Being the memoirs of a Windsor Castle Choirboy during the last years of Queen Victoria* (Rich & Cowan, 1937), p. 93

30 J. A. Fuller Maitland et al., 'Butt, Dame Clara', in Grove Music Online. Oxford Music Online (accessed 27 December, 2012).

31 'Sir Walter Parratt, M. V. O., Master of the King's Musick', *The Musical Times and Singing Class Circular*, Vol. 43, No. 713 (1 July1902), p. 450.

32 Tovey and Parratt, *Walter Parratt: Master of the Music*, p. 98.

33 'Sir Walter Parratt, M. V. O., Master of the King's Musick', *The Musical Times and Singing Class Circular*, p. 450.

34 Quoted in Jacobs, *Arthur Sullivan: A Victorian Musician*, p. 75.

35 Jeffrey Richards, *Imperialism and Music: Britain 1876–1953* (Manchester University Press, 2001), p. 413.

36 Quoted in ibid., p. 23.

37 Ibid, p. 137.

38 Ibid., p. 138.

39 Greg King, *Twilight of Splendor: The Court of Queen Victoria During Her Diamond Jubilee* (Wiley, 2007), p. 21.

40 Ibid., p. 263.

41 Richards, *Imperialism and Music*, p. 31.

42 Tovey and Parratt, *Walter Parratt: Master of the Music*, (Manchester University Press, 2002) p. 98.

43 Ibid., p. 101.

44 Jeremy Dibble and C. Hubert, *H. Parry: His Life and Music* (Clarendon Press, 1992), p. 385.

45 Ibid., p. 387.

46 Jerrold Northrop Moore, *Edward Elgar: A Creative Life* (Clarendon Press, 1987), p. 339.

47 Robert Anderson, *Elgar* (Dent, 1993), p. 53.

48 Richards, *Imperialism and Music*, p. 110.

49 Ibid., p. 109.

50 Quoted in Range, *Music and Ceremonial*, p. 16.

51 Stradling and Hughes, *The English Musical Renaissance*, p. 118.

52 James Carroll, *Jerusalem, Jerusalem: How the Ancient City Ignited Our Modern World* (Houghton Mifflin Harcourt, 2011), p. 236.

53 Richards, *Imperialism and Music*, p. 77.

54 Ibid., p. 171.

55 Michael Kennedy, *Portrait of Walton* (Clarendon Press, 1992), p. 93.

56 Ibid., p. 94.

57 Quoted in Range, *Music and Ceremonial*, p. 236

58 Ibid., p. 255.

59 Quote in ibid., p. 255.

60 Quoted in ibid., p. 248.

INDEX

Note: Page numbers in bold refer to illustrations and photographs

ACKNOWLEDGEMENTS

Katie Greening would like to thank the following people:

This book would not have been possible without the advice, support and expertise of the following: the team at Oxford Film and Television, in particular Peter Sweasey, Nicolas Kent, Chris Walker, Annie Lee and Sue Jones; Dr David Skinner, Professor Peter Holman, Professor Jeremy Dibble and Dr Matthias Range; Albert DePetrillo and Joe Cottington at BBC Books; my agent Karolina Sutton and the team at Curtis Brown; the staff at the British Library who provided both countless books and countless cups of tea. Finally, to my family and friends (you know who you are): thanks for everything.

PICTURE CREDITS

BBC Books would like to thank the following individuals and organisations for providing photographs and for permission to reproduce copyright material. While every effort has been made to trace and acknowledge copyright holders, we would like to apologise should there be any errors or omissions.

The British Library Board 58, 83; National Portrait Gallery, London 82; Mary Evans Picture Library 128, 275; The Bridgeman Art Library 140, 218, 242, 243, 250, 312; WireImage/Getty Images 334.

Plate section 1: Alamy 6 (top), 7 (top), 8 (bottom); The Bridgeman Art Library 1 (bottom), 3 (top), 5 (bottom), 6 (bottom right), 8 (top); The British Library Board 1 (top), 2 (top, bottom left), 7 (bottom) 8 (middle); The Trustees of Lambeth Palace Library 6 (bottom left); Mary Evans Picture Library 5 (top); Oxford Film and Television/Chris Openshaw/The 18th Earl of Pembroke & Montgomery and Trustees of Wilton House Trust, Wilton House, Wilton, Sailsbury, Wiltshire, UK 4 (top); Oxford Film and Television/Chris Openshaw 4 (bottom); Royal Collection Trust/ © Her Majesty Queen Elizabeth II 2012 3-4 (bottom); Used by permission of the Royal College of Music, London 5 (centre).

Plate section 2: Alamy 8 (top); The Bridgeman Art Library 1 (bottom), 3 (top and bottom), 4 (top left), 5 (top and bottom), 6 (top left and right), 7 (top); The British Library Board 4 (bottom); Woodlands Books Ltd 8 (bottom); Corbis 1 (top), 6 (bottom); Painted Hall at the Old Royal Naval College © thedpc.com 2 (top); Mary Evans Picture Library 4 (centre); Royal Collection Trust/ © Her Majesty Queen Elizabeth II 2012 7 (bottom); Victoria and Albert Museum, London 2 (bottom).